W9-DHS-411

INSIGHT GUIDES

Created and Directed by Hans Höfer

PHILADELPHIA

Edited and updated by John Gattuso
Managing Editor: Martha Ellen Zenfell

Editorial Director: Brian Bell

Houghton Mifflin

APA PUBLICATIONS

"Last week I went to Philadelphia," W.C. Fields once joked, "but it was closed." Fields made a career out of knocking his hometown, portraying it as a dark and dour bastion of Quaker sobriety. But other Philadelphians know better. For years, they've listened to new arrivals describe how delighted they are by Philadelphia's charming neighborhoods, easy-going pace and deep sense of history.

A city with these attributes lends itself especially well to the approach taken by the 190-title award-winning *Insight Guides* series, created in 1970 by **Hans Höfer**, founder of Apa Publications. Each book encourages readers to celebrate the essence of a place rather than try to tailor it to their expectations and is edited in the belief that, without insight into a people's character and culture, travel can narrow the mind rather than broaden it.

Höfer

To set the record straight, Apa Publications enlisted the talents of **John Gattuso**, who lived and worked in a 100-year-old row house near South Philly's Italian Market. Gattuso's work with *Insight Guides* reflect a wide range of interests, and a roaming heart. A degree in anthropology made him the perfect choice to be the project editor and principal writer on several of Apa's cultural titles including *Insight Guide: Native America*, *Insight Guide: The Wild West*, and two *Insight Guides* to America's national parks. Although Gattuso has now moved from the Philly area, he regularly returns to keep this book up to date.

Gattuso approached the project with enthusiasm from the start. "As far as I'm concerned," he says, "Philadelphia is one of the best-kept secrets on the

Gattuso

East Coast. It's a rarity – a city built on a human scale, urban without being overwhelming, with a real sense of community holding its neighborhoods together." He penned four chapters on the area's history before turning his attention to a variety of city topics and traditions, including everything from Main Line matriarchs to soft pretzels with mustard. When it came time to assemble a team of writers and photographers, Gattuso searched for people who could combine detailed knowledge of Philadelphia with the sort of engaging and lucid journalistic style that is the hallmark of the series.

Edward A. Jardim started his long career in the newspaper business as a copy boy at the *Philadelphia Inquirer*, before taking an editorial post with the *New York Daily News*. It was from a window at the *Inquirer* building that Jardim first witnessed the outlandish antics of the Philadelphia Mummers, the subject of his essay "Mummermania". "I had heard people talk about 'that crazy parade down in Philly,' but I had never actually seen it. After studying up on the subject, I had a real itch to be down on Broad Street next New Year's Day." Jardim also takes a wry and revealing look at the city's most beloved historical figures, William Penn and Benjamin Franklin. In addition to his writing duties, Jardim provided invaluable editorial assistance, lending his sharp eye and seasoned sensibility to the development of the text.

Another early recruit was **Lou Harry**, a staff writer at *Philadelphia Magazine*. Born and raised in Wildwood, New Jersey and formerly a contributing editor at *Atlantic City Magazine*, Harry was eminently qualified to cover the New Jersey Shore. He also shares his expertise in the arts, giving a frank

Jardim

Harry

assessment of Philadelphia's cultural scene. "It seems to me the main problem for Philadelphia arts is Philadelphia audiences," he says. "The arts are here; the question is whether the audience will show up. Of course, that's good news for visitors, who shouldn't have any trouble finding tickets for the best offerings."

Few people could write about Lancaster County's Amish people with the same knowledge and authority as **Donald B. Kraybill**, professor of sociology at Elizabethtown College and director of the Young Center for the Study of Anabaptist and Pietist Groups. He is also the author of *The Riddle of Amish Culture* and *The Puzzles of Amish Life*, and editor of *The Amish and the State*.

Kraybill

Dave Nelson, a lawyer by trade, writes widely on his three passions: running, church history and streetcars. Nelson, who earned his street smarts as a bus driver and cabbie in his native Chicago, now does most of his touring in running shoes or trolley cars, both of which he used to explore University City, the subject of his "Places" essay.

Nelson

Most of this book's stunning images are the work of three talented men. A native Philadelphian, **Joseph Nettis** has been photographing his hometown for more than 40 years. Assignments have taken him as far afield as Russia, Japan, Israel and Spain, but he still does much of his wandering in town. "I've become Philadelphia's Boswell," he says – "a kind of historian with a camera" who has "a professional responsibility to keep up with the changes that have swept through the city."

Another photographer, **Robert Llewellyn**, has had nearly 25 books

Nettis

published, including two that are concerned with Philadelphia topics. Based in Virginia, Llewellyn was surprised at how "un-urban" Philadelphia is. "It's cozy without being congested. It reminds me of a European city, with classic low-rise architecture, lovely cafés, outdoor markets, a variety of historic and high-tech buildings, and a lively mix of cultures," he says. His advice to amateur shooters: "The late afternoon and early morning light is fantastic for picking up the textures of the architecture. And there are a lot of fascinating details, so be prepared to get close with your camera."

Llewellyn

Lensman **Ken Yanoviak** came to Philadelphia in 1980 to study documentary film at Temple University and has since contributed to a number of locally based publications. "I like to get up early and tour the neighborhoods on my bicycle," says Yanoviak. "It's like going fishing – looking for just the right images." Yanoviak got to know the Quaker City from the street up. "I spent two years pounding the pavement for a local newspaper photographing and interviewing ordinary people. One thing Philadelphia has going for it is diversity. There's a great mix of all sorts of people and places."

Yanoviak

Special thanks should be given to **Susan Oyama** who is based at the Library Company of Philadelphia, as well as **Shirley Mays** at Independence National Historical Park and **Lindsay Eckford** for assistance in locating the proper images. Thanks also to **Professor Charles E. Welch**, **Palma Lucas** and **Rose DeWolf** for providing information on the Mummers. In Apa's London editorial office, **Carole Mansur** proofread and indexed the manuscript.

CONTENTS

History

Looking Closely
by John Gattuso 21

Beginnings: The Holy Experiment
by John Gattuso 25

Birth of a Nation
by John Gattuso 33

Industrial Might and Civil War
by John Gattuso 39

Modern Metropolis
by John Gattuso 47

The Philly Sound
by Lou Harry 50

Features

I'd Rather be in Philadelphia
by John Gattuso 63

Proper Philadelphia
by John Gattuso 69

Culture in the City
by Lou Harry 76

The Barnes Method
by Lou Harry 81

Mummermania
by Edward A. Jardim 83

The Amish
by Donald B. Kraybill 87

Places

Introduction
by John Gattuso 101

Old City
by John Gattuso 105

Benjamin Franklin
by Edward A. Jardim 117

Society Hill and Penn's Landing
by John Gattuso 121

South Street and Queen Village
by Lou Harry 131

Washington Square West
by John Gattuso 139

CONTENTS

Rittenhouse
by John Gattuso 147

Pretzel Logic
by John Gattuso 153

City Hall and Downtown
by John Gattuso 157

William Penn
by Edward A. Jardim 163

**Museum District and
Fairmount Park**
by John Gattuso 167

University City
by Dave Nelson 177

South Philly
by John Gattuso 187

*The Great South Philly
Cheesesteak War*
by John Gattuso 191

Three Urban Villages
by John Gattuso 195

North Philadelphia
by John Gattuso
and Edward A. Jardim 201

Pennsylvania Dutch Country
by Lou Harry 209

Valley Forge
by John Gattuso 215

Bucks County
by John Gattuso 219

By the Sea
by Lou Harry 227

Maps

Center City 102
Queen Village 133
Fairmount Park 171
University City 178
Urban Villages 196
Pennsylvania
Dutch Country 210

TRAVEL TIPS

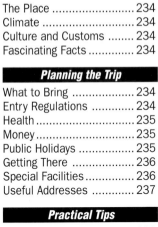

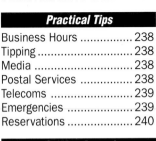

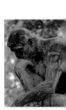

Getting Acquainted
The Place 234
Climate 234
Culture and Customs 234
Fascinating Facts 234

Planning the Trip
What to Bring 234
Entry Regulations 234
Health 235
Money 235
Public Holidays 235
Getting There 236
Special Facilities 236
Useful Addresses 237

Practical Tips
Business Hours 238
Tipping 238
Media 238
Postal Services 238
Telecoms 239
Emergencies 239
Reservations 240

Getting Around
On Arrival 240
Public Transportation 240
Private Transportation 241

Where to Stay
Hotels 242
Bed & Breakfast/Inns 244
Seaside Lodgings 245
Youth Hostels 247
Campgrounds 247

Eating Out
What to Eat 247
Where to Eat 247

Attractions
Culture 253
Historic Sites 257
Festivals 258

Shopping
Shopping Areas 261
What to Buy 262

Sports and Leisure
Participant Sports 263
Spectator Sports 264
Outdoor Activities 264

Further Reading
General 265
Other Insight Guides 265

Art/Photo Credits 266
Index 267

LOOKING CLOSELY

Few American cities are tied as closely as Philadelphia to the very roots of American identity. Benjamin Franklin, the Declaration of Independence, the Liberty Bell, the Founding Fathers – these are more than historic figures, they're players in a national mythology, the signs and symbols with which Americans identify themselves.

From the very beginning, Philadelphia was a city of ideas. William Penn envisioned a City of Brotherly Love, a place of refuge where people of all faiths could worship freely under a tolerant Frame of Government. Less than 100 years later, Thomas Jefferson, writing in a rented parlor on 7th Street, penned the words that severed the colonies from Britain, declaring that "all men are created equal." Eleven years later, the Founding Fathers assembled at Independence Hall to draft a new Constitution designed to "secure the Blessing of Liberty to ourselves and our Posterity," a piece of work that John Adams called the "greatest single effort of national deliberation that the world has ever seen."

Philadelphia is also a city of firsts – the country's first capital, first fire company, first hospital, first subscription library and first insurance company, not to mention less earthshaking but no less beloved inventions like the Philly cheesesteak, soft pretzels with mustard, and the Twist.

And yet, despite its illustrious beginnings, Philadelphia has had longstanding problems with its public image. Some people say the "city of firsts" is second-rate. And most of the critics are Philadelphians themselves. In fact, the city once tried to promote itself with the slogan: "Philadelphia isn't as bad as Philadelphians say it is."

Oddly, it's often outsiders who administer the much-needed slap in the face that brings Philadelphians to their senses. It's not unusual to hear new arrivals rave about the city – its charming 18th-century homes and churches, lovely neighborhoods, spirited ethnic communities, civilized attitude, manageable size, fine cultural institutions, great shopping and good restaurants.

If you've overlooked Philadelphia in the past, take a closer look. It's the town where the nation began, a city with American soul.

Preceding pages: Swann Memorial Fountain; City Hall; Independence Hall; Fairmount Park; an aerial view of Society Hill; the Philadelphia Exchange; a revealing look at the Museum of Art; pirouettes in Elfreth's Alley. **Left,** Rittenhouse Square.

It was a hell of a piece of real estate. And William Penn got it for a song. Charles II named it Pennsylvania in honor of Penn's father, Admiral Sir William Penn, a naval commander and loyal courtier. "Penn's Woods" was an enormous tract of land, a vast empire of rich river valleys, rolling mountains and trackless forests stretching from Chesapeake Bay to Lake Erie, and spreading west of the Delaware River as far as the setting sun.

Penn was granted the charter in 1681 in payment of a debt of £16,000 owed by Charles II to his father. An aristocrat by birth and Quaker by conversion, Penn saw the colony as a "holy experiment," an opportunity to replant and reshape English society – and turn a profit in the bargain. Quakers were having a rough go in England. More than 10,000 were thrown into jail for nonconformity. Penn himself had been locked up in the Tower of London for his espousal of radical theology. ("My prison shall be my grave before I will budge a jot," the young firebrand wrote.)

Quaker acres: The New World seemed the Quakers' only hope, and Charles II, struggling to hold on to the crown, was glad to see them go. Land-rich, cash-poor and eager to be rid of agitators, the beleaguered monarch signed Penn's charter, requiring only two beaver pelts a year and "the fifth part of all gold and silver ore found." With a stroke of the royal quill, William Penn – a 39-year-old Quaker, author of theological manifestos, colonial administrator and visionary – became the sole proprietor of a virgin territory rivaling the size of England itself.

Penn immediately began planning his capital city. He named it Philadelphia, the City of Brotherly Love, imagining a "greene countrie towne" of homes, gardens and orchards that, unlike the crowded cities of England, "will never be burnt and will always be whole-

some." The street plan he designed for the city remains essentially unchanged: a two-mile-long gridiron stretching between the Schuylkill and Delaware rivers, a large central park (now City Hall Plaza), and four town squares equidistant from the center.

It was to be a city of refuge, a great New World sanctuary where the persecuted masses of Europe – Quakers, Mennonites, Amish, Moravians and Pietists – and all "men of universal spirit" could worship freely and

live under a rational and benevolent system of government. "Ye shall be governed by laws of your own making," Penn told his colonists, "and live [as] a free, and if you will, a sober and industrious people." In his famous Frame of Government, he provided that "No person shall be molested or prejudiced for his or her conscientious persuasion or practice. Nor shall he or she at any time be compelled to frequent or maintain any religious worship contrary to his or her mind... If any person shall abuse or deride any other for his or her different persuasion or practice in matters of religion, such person shall be

Preceding pages: detail from early map of America, *circa* 1507. **Left**, an early settler. **Right**, Lenape Native American family, 1702.

looked upon as a disturber of the peace and be punished accordingly."

By the time Penn arrived in 1682, house lots were already being laid out by his surveyor, Thomas Holme. Tracts of 5,000 acres were offered for sale in the countryside, with an 80-acre bonus in the Liberty Lands just north of the city. The land was so rich, so obviously fertile, it must have been an easy sell. Penn had little need to exaggerate when he wrote to a friend in England, "The soil is good, air serene and sweet from the cedar, pine and sassafras, with wild myrtle of great fragrance. I have had better venison, bigger, more tender, as fat as in England. Turkeys of

fished and farmed along the Delaware River and its many tributaries. Compared to his countrymen in Virginia and New England, Penn dealt fairly with the Native Americans, requiring that they be well-paid for land occupied by white settlers. Although he already held title, he insisted on buying the land for Pennsbury, his 8,000-acre estate situated outside the city. Artists have romanticized Penn's supposed meeting with Lenape chief Tammany at Shackamaxon Creek, though whether such a meeting occurred is uncertain. In any case, Philadelphia was the only colonial town without a fortress or barricade, in large part because William Penn

the wood I had of forty and fifty pounds weight. Fish in abundance, especially shad and rock. Oysters are monstrous for bigness. In the woods are divers fruits, wild, and flowers that for color, largeness, and beauty excel…" To harried Quakers and other religious dissenters, and to poor villagers and city-dwellers across Europe, Penn's colony must have seemed a land of milk and honey.

Prior to Penn: But then, people had been enjoying the fruits of this land long before Penn arrived. There were the Indians, of course, a branch of the Algonquin family known as the Lenni-Lenape who hunted,

expected to live peaceably with the Lenape Native Americans.

Unfortunately, fair-dealing with natives was not a Penn family trait. William Penn's son Thomas cheated the Lenape out of prime land in the so-called Walking Purchase of 1737. The Lenape agreed to sell land along the Delaware "as far as a man can go in a day and a half" – so the crafty younger Penn hired trained runners to do the pacing. They covered significantly more territory than the Lenape wanted to part with. Later, in 1763, a group of frontier vigilantes known as the Paxton Boys attacked a colony of Christianized Indians near Lancaster, killing and scalping seven of them, and then lynched 14 others who were hiding in the Lancaster jail. Afterwards, the Paxtons marched to Philadelphia intending to capture the Assembly and demand more protection on the frontier. Fortunately, a delegation led by Benjamin Franklin, who denounced the gang as "white savages," managed to turn the marauders away before they entered the city – although not before promising to pay a bounty on every scalp the Paxton Boys took in their battles against "hostile" tribes.

The site Penn chose for Philadelphia saw early European settlers, too. Both the Dutch still stands. Under the benign rule of a lusty 400-pound governor known (affectionately, it is presumed) as Printz the Tub, the Swedes carved out a life of rude comforts and relative prosperity. Numbering only about 2,000 souls, the Swedish settlements were no match for the well-armed Dutch, who, in 1655, informed the Swedes that they were guests in New Holland and were expected to pay for the privilege. The Dutch, in turn, got their comeuppance about nine years later when the British took over New Amsterdam, renamed it New York, and claimed the entire Atlantic Coast from the Carolinas to New England. The Delaware Valley came under

and British had made several failed attempts to set down roots in the Delaware Valley ever since Henry Hudson sailed into the waterway in 1609 in search of the Northwest Passage. ("One of the finest, and best, and pleasantest rivers in the world," Hudson wrote of the Delaware.) While the British and Dutch bickered over who owned the valley, a small colony of Swedes set up house near present-day Wilmington and spread north along the river to the future site of Philadelphia, where the Swedes' Gloria Dei Church, built in 1700,

Above, Philadelphia's busy waterfront in 1730.

Dutch control again briefly in 1673, but a quick deal at the negotiating table put it back in British hands.

The early years were rough going for Penn's first batch of settlers, many of whom lived in caves hollowed out of the river bank. Penn had stayed only two years during his first visit to the colony, but when he made his final visit in 1699 (this time for only 20 months), Philadelphia was already a thriving town of wharves and warehouses, merchants and craftsmen. There were three churches, fine brick homes, well over 20 taverns, and traffic of some 800 ships per year. The population stood at about 2,000, representing a polyglot mix of English, Welsh, Irish, Germans, Swedes, Finns, Dutch, African slaves, and the occasional group of Indians visiting town to trade. The countryside was also being settled. In 1683, Daniel Pastorius founded Germantown with a group of 13 Mennonite families, and villages in Bucks and Chester counties sprang up just as quickly as land could be cleared. To the west, far-off Lancaster would become America's first inland city. Ironically, Pennsylvania's reputation for tolerance had attracted so many sects – among them Mennonites, Pietists, Presbyterians and Anglicans – that by 1700 the

Anglicans, Quakers against Presbyterians, and Quakers against Quakers. Smugglers found Philadelphia a convenient refuge from England's hated Navigation Acts, and riots of various sorts erupted with some regularity, culminating in the "Bloody Election" of 1742. Nor was Penn's town the haven of virtue and wholesomeness he envisioned. Town folk persisted in using the streets as a garbage dump. Hogs, dogs and livestock ran wild in the streets. Pickpockets and other petty criminals gave Philadelphia a reputation for lawlessness. The prospect of governing the town seemed so daunting that more than one elected official chose to pay a fine

Quakers constituted a minority of about 40 percent, although they were still dominant in political affairs.

Row houses: As with all utopias, the City of Brotherly Love fell somewhat short of the vision that inspired it. Rather than filling the street grid from river to river, the town tended to hug the wharves, sprawling north and south along the Delaware. In place of a "greene countrie towne," speculators built shoulder-to-shoulder row houses, leaving little room for gardens and orchards. At times, brotherly love was in short supply as well. Political rivalries set Quakers against

rather than serve time in city government.

But if Philadelphia was a little rough around the edges, there were still opportunities enough to attract a number of extraordinary individuals. Merchants like Samuel Carpenter, Isaac Norris and Jonathan Dickenson amassed fortunes in the triangle trade between Britain, the West Indies and the colonies, bringing the city its most reliable source of income. James Logan came to Philadelphia as William Penn's secretary and made himself rich on real estate and the fur trade. A man of extraordinary intellect, he assembled one of the largest libraries in America, helping to make Philadelphia a center of learning and culture. Others came too – Rittenhouse, Syng, Wistar, Powel, Cadwalader, Morris – whose children and grandchildren were destined to become prominent figures in the city.

But no one would leave a greater stamp on Philadelphia than a printer from Boston who had run off as a teenager. If William Penn was the city's architect, Ben Franklin was her carpenter, hammering together ideas and institutions that would serve Philadelphia for generations. Franklin left his mark on almost every aspect of the growing town. He established America's first hospital, first fire

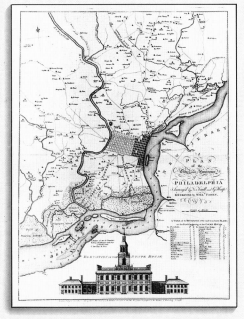

insurance company, first circulating library and first fire company. He vastly expanded the colonial postal service, whipped the city's defenses into shape, helped found the College of Philadelphia (forerunner of the University of Pennsylvania) and the American Philosophical Society. He composed, edited and published the enormously influential *Pennsylvania Gazette* and *Poor Richard's Almanack*, turning homespun aphorisms into a national creed. By the late 1750s, he was a

Left, viewing the port from Kensington. **Above**, William Penn's plan of the city.

celebrated figure in Europe, where he represented colonial interests and delighted high society in London. A man of insatiable curiosity and probing intellect, Franklin numbered among his achievements as an inventor the Franklin stove, bifocals, glass armonica and the lightning rod. His experiments with electricity – culminating in the famous kite-flying episode – won international acclaim and deepened Philadelphia's reputation as a citadel of knowledge.

Cultural center: Franklin's growing renown in Europe was a reflection of Philadelphia's rising status. By the mid-1700s, William Penn's little Quaker village was fast becoming one of the largest cities in the British empire. It was home to many of America's most illustrious families, a leader in commerce and trade, a center of culture on the edge of an untamed continent, and the undeclared capital of the American colonies.

Penn's holy experiment evolved in unimagined ways, yielding neither the spiritual nor material riches he expected. Frustrated with British politics and mired in debt, Penn grew disillusioned. "O Pennsylvania, what hast thou cost me!" he wrote in a letter to James Logan. "Above thirty thousand pounds more than I ever got from it, two hazardous and most fatiguing voyages, my straits and slavery here, and my son's soul almost."

And yet, Penn laid the groundwork for the greatest political movement of the century. He advanced ideas that would help give birth to a nation and set the stage for a new era in the history of government. In 1750, in celebration of the 50th anniversary of Pennsylvania's Charter of Privileges, a bell was ordered from England.

It was hung in the Pennsylvania State House (now Independence Hall), the majestic Georgian structure built to house colonial government. The bell cracked the first time it was rung; it was recast once, and then again, before cracking a final time. No one, not even Benjamin Franklin, a man whose gaze was habitually fixed on the future, could have suspected the full significance of this "liberty bell." Nor could he imagine the revolutionary implications of the inscription on its crown: "Proclaim Liberty thro' all the Land to all the Inhabitants thereof."

The colonies never really panned out for Britain. There was an empire to administer, wars to fight, domestic unrest to subdue. It was a period of benign neglect for America, a time of discovery and growth. While the royals were looking the other way, America came of age.

By the early 1760s, George III decided that it was time to put an end to all that. With the French contained in North America and the Seven Years' War winding down in Europe, he turned his attention to his increasingly restless subjects in America. And, as always, the job at hand was to squeeze as much money out of them as possible.

Stamp Act: George III launched the effort in 1763 with a battery of laws that prohibited colonial currency and cracked down on trade between the northern colonies and the West Indies. Before the colonials could mount an effective protest, Parliament also passed the Stamp Act (1765), requiring colonists to pay taxes on legal documents, newspapers and other paper products.

To outraged Americans, the new restrictions were worse than the old Navigation Acts and smacked of the same arbitrary use of power. Newspapers decried the Stamp Act and mobs took to the streets, terrorizing tax collectors and attacking the homes of government officials. In England on a diplomatic mission, Benjamin Franklin reluctantly assented to the Stamp Act and – much to his later regret – even recommended a few friends for the post of Pennsylvania tax man. When news reached Philadelphia of Franklin's complicity, rioters went to his house and threatened his ordinarily mild-mannered wife, Deborah, who met the mob with sharp words and loaded muskets. Franklin got the message. He immediately denounced the Stamp Act and lobbied Parliament for repeal, reminding English merchants that there were

Preceding pages: signing the Declaration of Independence. **Left,** revolutionary musket. **Right,** Benjamin Franklin organized the first fire company in America.

no imported goods that the colonists couldn't "do without or make themselves."

While Franklin was making his case in London, Philadelphians joined other colonists in a boycott of British goods. By March 1766, the boycott had caused so much damage to British commerce that the king relented and lifted the tax. But George III wasn't a man who took defeat lightly. In 1767 his Chancellor of the Exchequer, Charles Townshend, levied a tax on a variety

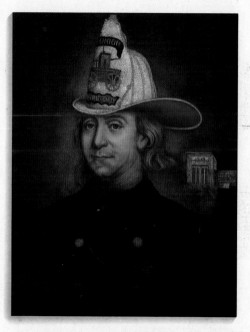

of imported items, including paper, lead, glass and tea. Although the reaction in Philadelphia was less radical than in Boston or New York, the Philadelphia press denounced the Townshend Acts in scathing terms and prodded the city's merchants into a sweeping nonimportation agreement. Writing anonymously, the influential lawyer John Dickinson issued his widely read *Letters from a Farmer in Pennsylvania*, attacking the legality of the Townshend Acts, calling for unity among the colonies, and positing the subversive notion that taxation without representation constituted a form of tyranny.

A second colonial boycott forced the repeal of the Townshend Acts in 1770, but London wasn't ready to surrender just yet. As a symbol of the "supremacy of Parliament," a tax on tea remained. The tea tax won no friends in Philadelphia, and when the first loads arrived in Delaware Bay, tea merchants were warned to refuse the shipment lest they be visited by the local "Committee for Tarring and Feathering." News of the Boston Tea Party had reached Philadelphia, and, wishing to avoid a similar episode, the tea ships sped back to England.

The tea fiasco was more than the king could tolerate. Parliament imposed a series

Englanders is no more. I am not a Virginian, but an American."

Independence: The situation worsened almost immediately after the delegates left Philadelphia. In Boston, a tense standoff between redcoats and patriots turned bloody. On April 19, 1775, the "shot heard round the world" was fired at Concord, Massachusetts. The die was cast; the Revolution was set in motion. "These are the times that try men's souls," Thomas Paine, an adopted Philadelphian, wrote in his pamphlet *The Crisis*, helping to whip up support for the revolutionary cause. "The summer soldier and sunshine patriot will, in this crisis, shrink

of "Intolerable Acts," closing the port of Boston and dissolving the Massachusetts Assembly. Patriots in Philadelphia called for a colonial conference, and in September 1774 the First Continental Congress convened at Carpenters' Hall. The delegates defined their cause in a "Declaration of Rights" and drew up a broad nonimportation agreement against British goods. But more importantly, the First Continental Congress successfully unified the colonies in a common cause. As Virginia delegate Patrick Henry declared: "The distinction between Virginians, Pennsylvanians, New Yorkers, and New

from the service of their country, but he that stands it now deserves the love and thanks of man and woman."

The Second Continental Congress convened at the Pennsylvania State House and chose George Washington as commander of "all continental forces," such as they were. On May 15, 1776, John Adams introduced a resolution urging the colonies to reorganize as states. On June 7, Richard Henry Lee called for a resolution on independence. A committee including Thomas Jefferson, Benjamin Franklin and John Adams was appointed to draft the document, but it was

Jefferson who wrote the first draft, with Franklin and Adams making only a few changes (including the deletion of Jefferson's condemnation of slavery).

Inspired by Enlightenment thought, Jefferson invoked the natural rights of all men to justify American independence. "We hold these Truths to be self-evident, that all Men are created equal, that they are endowed by their Creator with certain inalienable Rights, that among these are Life, Liberty, and the Pursuit of Happiness..." With these words, the young Virginian transformed what had been, in essence, a tax revolt into a manifesto of human rights that would influence people and governments around the world. Unanimously adopted on July 4, 1776, the Declaration of Independence severed America from the mother country in a single, decisive stroke.

It was, the delegates knew, an act of treason punishable by death. "There must be no pulling different ways: we must all hang together," John Hancock urged his fellow delegates at the signing. To which Benjamin Franklin is said to have replied: "Gentlemen, we must indeed all hang together or we shall most assuredly hang separately."

When the Declaration was read outside the State House on July 8, the bells of the city clanged in celebration, although, contrary to tradition, the Liberty Bell, hanging in the building's unsteady bell tower, probably remained silent "lest... the steeple should fall down." Nor is it likely that Betsy Ross, the legendary designer of the Stars and Stripes, was asked by General Washington to supply the infant nation with its first flag, although she was a well-known seamstress.

Washington's punishing defeat at New York City put an abrupt end to Philadelphia's celebration. As wounded soldiers poured into town and the dead were buried *en masse* in Washington Square, the redcoats marched south through New Jersey toward Philadelphia. On Christmas Day in 1776, Washington and his forces made their famous midnight crossing of the Delaware River and struck enemy camps at Trenton and then again at Princeton. When the Brit-

ish finally moved against Philadelphia several months later, Washington intercepted them at Brandywine Creek, but his "ragged, lousy, naked regiments" – most of them ill-equipped and with little or no training – were soundly routed. With the sounds of battle rumbling in the distance, Philadelphia patriots prepared to evacuate. Congress fled west to Lancaster and then to York. Printing presses were carted into the countryside, and the Liberty Bell was removed from the State House and hidden in a church cellar in Allentown. Philadelphia streets, an observer wrote, were a scene of "horses galloping, women running, children crying, delegates

flying, and altogether the greatest consternation, fright and terror that can be imagined."

About three weeks later, a rebel division led by "Mad Anthony" Wayne was virtually wiped out in the Paoli Massacre, just outside the city. Several days later, the redcoats marched into Philadelphia unopposed, greeted by cheering loyalists. The Americans were forced to retreat. While the British enjoyed the comforts of Philadelphia's finest homes and taverns, Washington's freezing and hungry troops suffered at Valley Forge. Oddly, General Howe and his compatriots never followed up on their victory in

Left, the Stamp Act repeal. **Right**, the Boston Massacre spurred the colonies toward war.

Philadelphia, preferring instead to indulge themselves in the pleasures of the city. The British pulled out of Philadelphia the following spring and returned to New York, giving Washington time to train his men and Congress the chance to solicit much-needed foreign aid. Benedict Arnold served for a time as the military commander of Philadelphia, only to betray the patriots at West Point.

The bloodshed continued for another four years after the occupation, raging along the entire East Coast, before Cornwallis got bottled up by a French fleet and finally capitulated at Yorktown. The war was over and independence won, but Philadelphia, and the

western lands; and in Europe, John Adams and Thomas Jefferson complained about inconsistent foreign policy. According to Washington, the fledgling United States was "fast verging to anarchy and confusion."

Taking its cue from James Madison's Annapolis Convention, Congress called for a national conference to amend the Articles of Confederation. The delegates to the Constitutional Convention, as it later came to be known, convened in May 1787 at the Pennsylvania State House, where many had signed the Declaration of Independence only 11 years earlier. Among their first official acts were the election of George Washington as

rest of the nation, faced an uncertain future.

"A more perfect Union": By 1787, it was clear that the decentralized system of government established under the Articles of Confederation lacked the authority to hold the sprawling nation together. Since the end of the war, Congress had grown so ineffective that some delegates chose not to attend. The states were constantly at each other's throats over boundary disputes, trade and tariffs. Economic disparity between seaports and farming towns precipitated a rebellion in Massachusetts; shots were fired between Pennsylvanians and Virginians over title to

president of the conference and a vow to conduct their affairs in strict secrecy. It was immediately evident that the 55 Constitutional framers would do more than amend the Articles. They would completely restructure the federal government.

The men assembled in Philadelphia couldn't have been more qualified for the job. "An assembly of demi-gods," said Thomas Jefferson, whose diplomatic responsibilities held him in Paris. "If all the delegates named for this Convention at Philadelphia are present," a French diplomat remarked, "we will never have seen, even in Europe, an assembly more respectable for the talents, knowledge, disinterestedness, and patriotism of those who compose it."

In addition to Washington, the most notable were James Madison, the brilliant young Virginian who was chiefly responsible for drafting the document; Alexander Hamilton, the radical New Yorker whose proposals for the new government included a lifetime executive and senate; from Delaware, John Dickinson, author of *Letters from a Farmer in Pennsylvania*; and Benjamin Franklin, who attended every session despite his advanced age and failing health. Although none of the delegates was completely satisfied

executive with limited veto power, and an independent "supreme" judiciary. Considering the range of opinion, the document was crafted with amazing efficiency. A final draft of the Constitution was completed in a scant four months and adopted by the Convention only two days later. And although ratification faced bitter opposition from various quarters, the states ultimately confirmed the Framers' work. During the signing, Ben Franklin commented on the carving of a sun that adorned Washington's chair. "I have," he said, "often and often in the course of the session and the vicissitudes of my hopes and fears as to its issue, looked at that [sun

with the document (three refused to sign, and several resigned), Franklin voiced the prevailing opinion: "I consent to this Constitution because I expect no better, and because I am not sure that it is not the best."

In fact, it was a series of compromises that resulted in many of the Constitution's fundamental provisions: a three-branch system of checks and balances, a bicameral legislature elected by state and population, a four-year

Left, re-enactment of the Battle of Germantown. **Above left**, James Madison, architect of the Constitution; General George Washington.

behind the president without being able to tell whether it was rising or setting. But now at length I have the happiness to know that it is a rising and not a setting sun."

For 10 years Philadelphia served as the nation's capital. Robert Morris, the nation's wealthiest man, gave his Walnut Street home to President Washington as an official residence. Congress occupied the Philadelphia County Court House (now Congress Hall), and the Supreme Court convened at Old City Hall. Philadelphia, birthplace of the nation, was poised to plunge into the new century as America's most powerful city.

INDUSTRIAL MIGHT AND CIVIL WAR

The years following the Constitutional Convention were a golden age in Philadelphia. Although the federal government shifted its base of operations to the District of Columbia in 1800, Philadelphia remained the wealthiest, most sophisticated and most powerful city in the nation. With more than 65,000 residents, it was not only the largest urban center in America, it was the largest English-speaking city outside Great Britain. As headquarters for the Bank of the United States (1791), the Mint (1792) and the Second Bank of the United States (1816), it was the nerve center of American finance. And as one of the busiest ports on the Atlantic Coast and a leader in the trade with China, it was a major player in international commerce.

Culturally, Philadelphia was still the enlightened metropolis of Benjamin Franklin, James Logan and other prominent men of art and science. Among the distinguished institutions established in this period were the Academy of Fine Arts (1805), the Academy of Natural Sciences (1812), the Athenaeum (1814) and the Franklin Institute (1824). As the center of the publishing industry, it attracted major authors.

Writers in residence: Edgar Allan Poe wrote some of his best-known works while living in a run-down brick house on North 7th Street. Years later, Walt Whitman retired to a spot just across the river, in Camden, New Jersey. Philadelphia also boasted some of America's most respected professional people – doctors like Benjamin Rush, Caspar Wistar and Philip Syng, and architects like Benjamin Latrobe, William Strickland and John Notman. Among artists of stature identified with Philadelphia were Charles Willson Peale, Thomas Sully, Thomas Eakins and Gilbert Stuart.

Socially, the city was an island of comfort on the edge of a still wild continent. A "city to be happy in," Nathaniel P. Willis called it, with little of New York's chaotic ambience

or Boston's starched-collar moralism. Visitors remarked on the city's tidy brick houses, stately public buildings, and easygoing sophistication. "How… am I able to communicate a just notion of the intelligence, the refinement, the enterprise of Philadelphians," wrote Scottish author William Chambers, "their agreeable and hospitable society, their pleasant evening-parties, their love of literature, their happy blending of the industrial habits of the north with social usages of the south? All this must be left to conjecture, as well as the Oriental luxury of their dwellings, and the delicate beauty of their ladies." As Gilbert Stuart was fond of saying, Philadelphia was the "Athens of America."

Iron and coal: The early 1800s were also a period of profound transformation. With the development of efficient steam engines in the late 1700s and the discovery of anthracite coal in western Pennsylvania in the early 1800s, Philadelphia was poised on the brink of the Industrial Revolution and prepared to march ahead. By the 1820s, Philadelphia was America's first and largest industrial center, turning out everything from turbines to toilets, pig iron to chandeliers. Factories, mills and foundries sprang up on the outskirts of Old City, spouting thick black smoke over Southwark, Manayunk, Kensington and Nicetown, where the flood of new immigrants provided cheap and plentiful labor.

Although the opening of the Erie Canal diverted shipping to New York, Philadelphia nevertheless became a major hub in an extensive network of turnpikes, canals and railways. Manufactured goods poured from the city, and coal and other raw materials were taken in. Industrialists like William Cramp and Matthias Baldwin amassed fortunes manufacturing ships and locomotives. Haberdasher John B. Stetson made a financial killing on his classic cowboy hat. And countless unnamed laborers turned out products as diverse as textiles, refined sugar, water pipes and cigars.

But while the captains of industry were raking in family fortunes, the people who

Left, after the American Civil War, industry was powerful and steam was king.

actually did the work – most of them immigrants from Ireland and Germany – were struggling to stay alive. Starting in the 1820s, they poured into Philadelphia by the thousands, many of them poor, hungry, illiterate and desperate for work. By 1850, the population of Philadelphia County shot up to 408,000, a third of them foreign-born. Immigrants crowded into cramped apartments, ramshackle shanties and tiny, broken-down "Father, Son and Holy Ghost" (or Trinity) houses with one room, and one family, per floor. Neighborhoods like Southwark and Moyamensing, as well as the hidden alleyways of Old City, were particularly rancid,

Catholics and other foreigners, whom they linked with a trumped-up papist conspiracy. At the height of activity in the early 1840s, a nativist gang burned down two Catholic churches and several homes in Kensington. When a pitched battle broke out a few months later between nativists and Catholics at St Philip de Neri Catholic Church in Southwark, it took the militia four days to stop the fighting, although not before 15 people had been killed and 50 wounded.

Violence was also directed against the black community plus anyone, black or white, who was associated with the small but intense anti-slavery movement. Although never

with frequent outbreaks of cholera and yellow fever, and gangs like the Moyamensing Killers and Blood Tubs marauding the streets. After the cholera epidemic of 1849, the Sanitary Committee reported on the appalling conditions of Philadelphia's slums, "where extremes of filth and misery and loathsome disease met the eye; where horrid heaps of manure from hog and cow pens, putrifying garbage and refuse of every kind… gave off their noxious gases."

As if living conditions weren't bad enough, immigrants also had to face nativist agitators, who focused their bigotry on Irish-

widely accepted, the abolition movement had deep roots in Philadelphia, partly because of the traditional Quaker condemnation of slavery. The American Anti-Slavery Society was founded in Philadelphia in 1833, and Philadelphia was a major way station in the Underground Railroad before the American Civil War. But in the minds of nativists (and, ironically, many immigrants), abolition was associated with miscegenation, racial conflict and national disunity. And more important yet, it threatened Philadelphia businessmen with the loss of lucrative Southern markets. During the worst of the violence, attacks on black people were almost a daily occurrence. Churches were burned, houses looted, blacks killed in the streets. In a series of riots that erupted in 1842, a black church and an abolitionist meeting house were burned to the ground, four people were killed and more than 25 people were seriously injured. "There is probably no city in the known world," an English Quaker sadly noted, "where dislike, amounting to hatred of the coloured population, prevails more than in the city of brotherly love!"

Civil War: The riots in Philadelphia reflected a broader conflict being played out in cities and villages throughout America. Slav-

Unitarian Church in Philadelphia, abolitionist minister William Henry Furness declared: "The long agony is over!" But the agony of America's bloodiest war had only just begun.

As the birthplace of the nation, Philadelphia immediately joined the effort to keep the nation whole. Philadelphians were among the first volunteers to respond to Lincoln's call for 75,000 men, and its burgeoning industrial might was channeled into war production. But as the war dragged on for month after month and the hope of speedy victory seemed increasingly remote, Philadelphia's enthusiasm turned to discontent. When Robert E. Lee marched Confederate troops

ery was driving the nation apart, and by the late 1850s the issue was rapidly approaching the flash point. In November 1860, Abraham Lincoln was elected president without a single Southern electoral vote. He visited Philadelphia en route to his inauguration, informing the crowd that "there is no need of bloodshed and war… The government will not use force unless force is used upon it." Several weeks later, Fort Sumter was bombarded by Confederate artillery. At the First

into Pennsylvania in the summer of 1863, Philadelphians could hardly be stirred to defend their city. "Many men are pleased with the prospect of invasion," a Philadelphian wrote in his diary. "Nothing would rejoice them more than to see our whole government laid in ashes." General Lee's army collided with Union forces (under the command of Philadelphia's own General George G. Meade) outside the town of Gettysburg. The battle that ensued over the following three days in July was the bloodiest in American history. At one point in the fighting – during Pickett's charge – 7,000 Confederate

Left, anti-Catholic rioters clash with police, 1844. **Above**, Independence Hall, 1876.

soldiers were slaughtered in a heroic but uncoordinated attempt to break the Union lines. In all, the Confederates suffered more than 28,000 casualties, the Federals more than 25,000. Although Lee retreated to Virginia, it was a costly Union victory.

Four months later, Lincoln traveled to Gettysburg for the dedication of a cemetery at the battlefield. His famous address there on November 19, 1863, majestic in cadence and brevity, reaffirmed the Chief Executive's commitment to hold the Union together: "We here highly resolve that these dead shall not have died in vain, that this nation, under God, shall have a new birth of

along the Delaware River, spilled across the Schuylkill River, and reached out to once isolated warrens like Germantown and Manayunk. Immigrants continued to pour into the wretched precincts of Southwark and Moyamensing, although by the late 1880s there tended to be as many Italians, Poles and East European Jews as Irishmen and Germans. Southern blacks moved into the city as well, many occupying the slum areas between Lombard and South streets or crossing the Schuylkill into West Philadelphia. By the turn of the century, Philadelphia had the largest black population of any northern city. The population of the now-consolidated city

freedom – and that government of the people, by the people, for the people, shall not perish from the earth."

The war ended less than two years later. The nation did indeed experience a "new birth of freedom," but Lincoln, cut down by an assassin's bullet, would never see its fruition. Philadelphians jammed the streets to watch the fallen president's casket inch toward Independence Hall where the martyr's body lay in state.

In the post-Civil War years, Philadelphia continued to grow in leaps and bounds. Penn's "greene countrie towne" spread seven miles

(encompassing the whole of Philadelphia County) topped 1.2 million, with nearly 25 percent foreign-born. Even with the construction of thousands of new row houses, the housing stock remained inadequate.

Philadelphia's well-to-do were on the move, too. From the best neighborhoods of Old City, they moved west into sumptuous Victorian mansions around Rittenhouse Square. Later, in the 1880s, the wealthiest of the lot migrated again, this time to suburban estates along the Pennsylvania Railroad's exclusive Main Line. City Hall moved west, too, from cramped quarters at Independence

Square to a Second Empire behemoth (the largest building of its day) at Broad and Market streets. Following the westward trend, the University of Pennsylvania moved into glorious new digs in West Philadelphia in 1871; Fairmount Park expanded on both sides of the Schuylkill River; the Academy of Fine Arts relocated to an ornate hall designed by Frank Furness; and several new colleges, including Drexel, Temple, Swarthmore and Bryn Mawr, advanced the city's reputation as a place of learning.

Throughout the postwar period, industry was king. Ironworks ringed the city. More than 33 percent of America's oil was shipped

Philadelphia prepared to celebrate the nation's centennial with the biggest, boldest, most extravagant party the country had ever seen. The Centennial Exhibition of 1876 attracted exhibitors from hundreds of countries and more than 10 million visitors. Powered by the towering 700-ton steam engine known as the Corliss Machine, the Exhibition put Philadelphia's industrial might on a world stage. It was a glorious moment, marking the final emergence of Philadelphia as a world-class city of enormous wealth and vital energy.

"The Centennial is to ring the death knell of that non-enterprising, fearing-to-dare spirit

from Philadelphia, and coal continued to pour out by rail and sea. Philadelphia textile factories outproduced any in the country. Merchants like John Wanamaker, the Gimbels, and Strawbridge & Clothier gave birth to retail empires. And in its fight to the death with competitors in New York and Baltimore, the Pennsylvania Railroad became the largest corporation in America.

With the aftershock of war fading and the heartbeat of industry pounding in its veins,

Left, Philadelphians were among the first volunteers for war. **Above**, modern re-enactment.

which has so long ruled us," a newspaper reported. But for all its industrial might, Philadelphia never acquired the spitfire image of New York, its neighbor and chief competitor. Despite the meteoric pace of industrialization, Philadelphia was still in many respects the Quaker City – prosperous, progressive, but clad in gray. Once the cradle of radical nation-building ideas, Philadelphia became known as the home of the comfortable social classes. It was the "workshop of the world," but also the "city of homes," set in its habits, and hunkered down into "potbellied" complacency.

The rise of industry in Philadelphia breathed new life into a very old style of government. This was the "Machine Age," and the term referred to politics as surely as it did to industry. It started in 1865 when James McManes – an Irish-born Republican ward leader – was elected trustee of the city's gas works. The first in a long line of political bosses, "King James" ran the gas works like his own personal fiefdom, doling out contracts in return for a percentage and muscling bankers, businessmen and government officials. Not that too many people really minded. In the words of one journalist, Philadelphia was "corrupt and contented." Ballot-stuffing, vote-buying, graft and patronage were tolerated so long as the veil of gentility remained intact.

When the United States entered World War I in 1917, political bickering took a backseat to the war effort. As one of the nation's great industrial centers, Philadelphia – "workshop of the world" – was quickly transformed into the "arsenal of democracy." Almost overnight, mills and factories were retooled for wartime production. The Baldwin Locomotive Works turned out artillery shells, the Ford Motor Company made steel helmets, and the giant Hog Island shipyard, the world's largest, cranked out the better part of a navy. Patriotism ran high in Philadelphia, often to the detriment of the city's large German population. The city pulled its advertising from German-language newspapers, and classes in German were removed from the public-school curriculum. Even Santa Claus was unpopular.

Two events broke the city's newfound spirit of unity. The first was a fallout in Philadelphia's ongoing political warfare. During the vicious Republican primary election of 1917, thugs hired by the Vare brothers – the city's reigning political bosses – severely beat their opponent and killed a

Preceding pages: "rockets' red glare" over Independence Hall. **Left,** Liberty Place soars over City Hall. **Right,** Fairmount Park trolley-bus.

policeman who came to his defense. Reformers howled, thousands of ordinary citizens turned out in protest, and the killer was thrown into jail. Nevertheless, the Vare candidate was swept into office.

Influenza epidemic: An even more devastating blow came in 1918 when the worldwide influenza epidemic swept the city. At its worst the epidemic took hundreds of lives each day. Bodies accumulated so quickly that they were interred in mass graves.

Men returning from the war in Europe found Americans engaged in a very different kind of war: the campaign against John Barleycorn. Young men who had fought for freedom in the trenches of the Argonne – and had tasted old-world life-styles – discovered that they couldn't buy a drink in a Philadelphia saloon. Prohibition backfired in Philadelphia even more than in other cities. The illicit liquor trade turned into a gold mine for organized crime, especially for the *mafiosi* sinking roots in South Philadelphia. By some estimates, more speakeasies were doing business during Prohibition than legitimate taverns previously. A report in *Collier's Magazine* estimated that Philadelphia's 1,185 bars, 13,000 speakeasies and 300 bordellos raked in about $40 million a year, and a substantial piece of the action was being pocketed by politicians and the police department. Gang warfare broke out in the streets as rival bootleggers battled over turf. But it was poisoning, not murder, that took the heaviest toll. The Philadelphia coroner reported 10 to 12 deaths daily as a result of bad whiskey.

The city's response was lackadaisical at best. The police seemed unwilling to intervene. Not surprisingly, a shakedown in the police department netted some 200 cops who

were on the pad. Even after the mayor appointed a Marine Corps general to enforce the ban on liquor, little seemed to change. It was clear to many observers that organized crime had infiltrated City Hall.

Orgy of speculation: Even in conservative Philadelphia, it seemed, the lure of the high life was irresistible. The city may have been going to hell in a hand basket, but Philadelphians hardly seemed glum about the future. Like other Americans, they poured money into speculation, sending the price of real estate and the value of stocks through the roof. It didn't matter that the economy was

standing on a mountain of credit, or that the city was being cheated of millions by the Vare machine. As long as money kept changing hands, the Pennsylvania Railroad kept chugging down the tracks, and smoke kept billowing from factory chimneys, everything seemed bullish.

But when the bottom fell out of the stock market on Black Thursday – October 24, 1929 – the "orgy of speculation" came to a screeching halt. The Great Depression dawned slowly on Philadelphia, but no less painfully than in other cities. When the Mummers paraded down Broad Street on New Year's Day in 1930, there were still few signs of the hardships to come. But when it hit, it sent the city reeling. Income was slashed. Unemployment skyrocketed. People were robbed of their livelihoods, their homes, their dignity. Makeshift Hoovervilles sprang up in parks and alleyways, labor strikes turned violent, and bread lines snaked along sidewalks. By 1933, 50 local banks had failed, and many of the city's most prominent industries were forced to shut down or cut back.

Thanks to obstructionists in Philadelphia's Republican administration, federal relief – in the form of President Franklin D. Roosevelt's New Deal – was slow to reach the city. According to Mayor J. Hampton Moore, laziness and inefficiency were to blame for the city's problems. "There is no starvation in Philadelphia," he proclaimed, refusing to offer a cent in relief.

Then, in 1941, the nation entered World War II, and the city was swept into the war effort. Once again, Philadelphia was transformed into an arsenal of democracy, cranking out weapons, ships, airplanes, uniforms, helmets and other instruments of war. Philadelphia's German and Italian population – its newspapers, social clubs and businesses as well as openly pro-Nazi organizations – were raided by federal agents. In order to meet labor demands, women and blacks were encouraged to work in war industries. By 1944, women accounted for nearly 40 percent of the work force, and the number of black workers had doubled. As before, Quaker pacifists opted for alternative service in hospitals and relief work.

When Japan surrendered in 1945, Philadelphians celebrated as never before. Thousands gathered around City Hall; parties broke out in the streets; fireworks streaked across the sky. But underlying the jubilation were disturbing questions about Philadelphia's future. The city itself was in bad shape. Neighborhoods were run-down, buildings dilapidated. Old City – home to Independence Hall, the Liberty Bell and other historic sites – was literally falling apart. With the exception of the Benjamin Franklin Parkway, Philadelphia had seen almost no new development or rehabilitation.

Industry was slipping, too. Without the Montgomery and Chester counties swelled, the city's population declined. With its tax base eroding and social services on the rise, the city was in a financial stranglehold. By the late 1960s, the administration regularly operated on a deficit. By the late 1980s, the city was on the verge of bankruptcy.

The postwar years weren't all bleak, however. Under the leadership of Richardson Dilworth and Joseph S. Clark, a coalition of activists and blue-blooded liberals pushed for reform in the city's corruption-riddled government. After exposing widespread graft, embezzlement and patronage, the reformers pushed for a new Home Rule Char-

demands of a war to sustain them, Philadelphia's manufacturers were forced to close down, cut back or move out, leaving a glut of wartime laborers – especially Southern blacks – without a livelihood. Many companies left altogether, relocating to the South or West where taxes were lower and non-union labor was plentiful. Automobiles and inexpensive housing lured thousands of predominantly white middle-class families into the suburbs. While the population of neighboring Bucks,

Left, hunger marchers protest, 1936. **Above**, street celebration on V-J Day.

ter curbing government excesses and establishing an independent mayoralty and City Council. The newly installed Democrats also embarked on an ambitious program of redevelopment. The old Chinese Wall – the elevated railway that blocked development north of Market Street – was torn down and the gleaming towers of Penn Center were erected. The delapidated Dock Street Market was relocated to a new distribution center in South Philadelphia, clearing the way for a thorough rehabilitation of the run-down 18th- and 19th-century homes of Society Hill. In Old City, the federal government finally

THE PHILLY SOUND

It was the 1950s. The big record producers hadn't yet caught on to the power of rock 'n' roll and the door was wide open for small record companies to get a tune on the charts. With good publicity, a one-hit wonder could rocket to stardom. It was happening in Memphis, in Chicago and in Philadelphia. But Philly had something the other towns didn't: the TV dance show *American Bandstand*.

The show was born in 1952 when WFIL-TV realized that its lineup of British movies just didn't cut it. Since the station manager had

been talked into buying thousands of dollars-worth of short musical films, the station went along with an idea by radio deejay Bob Horn to do a music show aimed at the kids. On the first show, Horn interviewed jazz virtuoso Dizzy Gillespie, showed clips of singer Peggy Lee, and gave birth to a TV phenomenon.

But the real lifeblood of the show didn't arrive until a month later, when the station began airing promos inviting teenagers to dance in the studio. The success of *American Bandstand* had an influence on another young

Above, former disc jockey Dick Clark created a generation of teen idols.

disc jockey, Dick Clark. The name of his radio show, formerly called *Caravan of Stars*, was changed to *Bandstand* to cash in on the television show's success. When Horn was fired in 1956, Clark was the logical person to take over the job.

On August 5, 1957, with Clark in command, *American Bandstand* hit the national airwaves. Exposure to millions of kids brought with it a huge power to make stars. A prominent spot on the "*American Bandstand* Teenage Top 10" – a list of songs chosen on whim by Clark and his staff – could turn a nobody into an overnight sensation. Small wonder that the US Congress brought Clark up before a special subcommittee to investigate improprieties in the recording business – he was thought to own a percentage of some of the tunes he was promoting on the show.

But the kids kept right on dancing; they didn't care. The *Bandstand* format was simple. Music played, kids danced, performers lip-synced the lyrics of their latest record, and Dick Clark "related" to the kids with a little between-song patter. Through them, the country learned dances like the Twist, the Duck, the Mashed Potato and the Loco-motion. The kids would then rate the tunes: "I like the beat; it's easy to dance to. I give it a 95!" became a popular cliché.

The fact that *Bandstand* was based in Philadelphia was a godsend to local crooners. Fabian, Bobby Rydell and Frankie Avalon grew up within three blocks of each other in South Philly; Chubby Checker was nearby, too. It was the same neighborhood that had produced Mario Lanza, Eddie Fisher, Al Martino and Buddy Greco. The new idols' image was all-American. Outfitted in suits and conservative dresses, the *Bandstand* kids made rock 'n' roll respectable. If the Elvis pelvis worried preachers and parents, Dick Clark made them feel the whole thing was just good clean fun.

But the days of the Philly Sound were numbered. In 1964, *Bandstand* moved to California, emulating the teens who had ditched the Philly Sound in favor of the Beach Boys. Since then, Philly has launched Patti LaBelle, Teddy Pendergrass, the Hooters, Tommy Conwell and rapper The Fresh Prince, among other chart-toppers. And the club scene still has exciting new acts. But the city hasn't really been a musical hot spot since the kids stopped doing the Hully-Gully at WFIL-TV. ■

took action to save Independence Hall. In 1951, the National Park Service acquired Independence Park and quickly set to work restoring historic sites and buildings.

Rise of Rizzo: But perhaps the most significant action taken by the Dilworth-Clark administrations came in 1961. Currying favor with South Philadelphia's large Italian-American community, Dilworth made career cop Frank Rizzo a police inspector. The 1960s were a turbulent time in Philadelphia. A seemingly endless series of demonstrations, strikes and disturbances often paralyzed the city. An old-school cop with a reputation for head-banging, Rizzo confronted them a baton, a power broker too comfortable with boss-style politics.

Rizzo ran for mayor in 1971, promising to restore order in the streets and crack down on radicals. The law-and-order message was exactly what working-class whites and upper-class conservatives wanted to hear. The "Cisco Kid" won handily. But Rizzo's tough talk served only to exacerbate racial, ideological and ethnic rifts. A small but persistent coalition of opposition groups – from municipal unions to homosexuals – exerted constant pressure. As the city prepared for the American Bicenntenial celebration of 1976, Rizzo fended off a recall movement

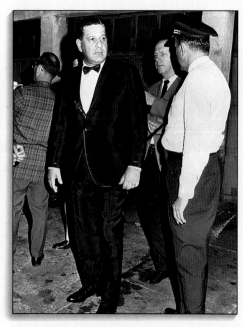

with his usual hard-hitting style. To his supporters in the neighborhoods, his strong-arm tactics were a godsend in a city that was being throttled by crime and crippled by pressure groups.

They cheered when he raided hippie hangouts, cracked down on protesters and "kept a lid on" a near-riot on Columbia Street. To his detractors, Rizzo was heavy-handed and dictatorial, a cop too handy with

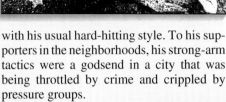

Above left, MOVE follower announces a demonstration; Frank Rizzo with his signature tuxedo and nightstick.

that nearly brought the entire administration down around his ears.

It was in this atmosphere of deep political division that Rizzo directed the first standoff with a radical back-to-nature group called MOVE, whose members – all of whom used the surname Africa – had transformed a West Philadelphia house into an armed compound in preparation for what they believed was an inevitable "confrontation with the system." MOVE had long been a thorn in Rizzo's paw. Obeying the dictates of spiritual leader John Africa, MOVE members staged unruly protests, seeming to invite clashes with police.

At their headquarters in West Philadelphia, MOVE members harassed neighbors, allowed the house to become infested with rats and roaches and overrun with dozens of dogs, and were occasionally seen with firearms. After months of trying to evict the members, police stormed the house on August 8, 1978, and a police officer was killed in the ensuing shoot-out. The house was demolished, several MOVE members were convicted, and, as far as most people were concerned, the MOVE story had come to an end.

In 1980, Rizzo's grip on power came to an end despite efforts to amend restrictions on a third term. Much of the social and political

tensions that drove the city apart remained unresolved, as did the city's shaky financial situation. Mayor William J. Green presided over the city for four undistinguished years. And then, in 1984, W. Wilson Goode, Philadelphia's first African-American mayor, took office on a platform of good clean government and racial healing.

By the time Goode took the oath of office, the contradictory trends that would characterize the 1980s were already affecting the city. While so-called yuppies gentrified Queen Village, Old City, Manayunk and other borderline neighborhoods, city serv-

ices were being overtaxed by an alarming rise in homelessness. While glass-and-granite towers were erected for booming corporations in center city, drug abuse and crime skyrocketed in the neighborhoods. A vicious struggle for power erupted among the *mafiosi* of South Philadelphia. Drug gangs and crack houses invaded the blighted neighborhoods surrounding center city. The murder rate went through the roof.

MOVE came back, too. John Africa and his followers moved into a house on Osage Avenue in West Philadelphia and armed themselves for a second confrontation. Although slow to respond, Mayor Goode was finally pressured to take action on May 13, 1985. But this time the assault on MOVE headquarters went tragically wrong.

Firebomb: Frustrated in their attempt to talk – and then blast – the occupants out of the house, police used a helicopter to drop a bomb on the roof of the building. The bomb set fire to the building, and the fire was allowed to burn right out of control. Eleven MOVE members, including five children, were either killed in the blaze or shot, and 61 houses were destroyed. The devastation, headlined across the country, was horrific. After a controversial eight-month investigation, the MOVE Commission Report excoriated Goode and other key officials, but no one was legally indicted. Surprisingly, Goode defeated Frank Rizzo in the hotly contested election of 1987.

In 1992, former district attorney Edward Rendell took charge of the city and, generally speaking, has done a fine job whipping Philadelphia back into shape, in economic and other terms. Rizzo – a bulldog to the end – made a bid for the seat but succumbed to a heart attack in mid-campaign. As hundreds of mourners waited to pay their last respects outside the Cathedral of Saints Peter and Paul, it seemed that the city had reached the end of an era. Philadelphians had survived the social firestorms of the 1960s and '70s; they had weathered the "greed is good" ethic of the 1980s. Now, in the 1990s, they look uncertainly toward a new century.

Left, NASA photo of Philly. **Right, leading the pack at the University of Pennsylvania.**

City of Brotherly Love? That may be the official nickname, but for all the abuse it gets, Philadelphia might be more aptly titled the City of Hard Knocks.

"A well-lit cemetery," quipped the vitriolic H. L. Mencken. Novelist Owen Wister dismissed the place as a "City of Moderation," and still another writer, Nathaniel Burt, called it a "Salesman's Graveyard."

It's the metropolis everyone loves to hate. "It is a handsome city," Charles Dickens allowed in 1842, "but distractingly regular. After walking about it for an hour or two, I felt that I would have given the world for a crooked street." And another eminent Victorian, Anthony Trollope, disparaged it as a "right-angled parallelogramical city."

No Sin City: Why all the barbs? Well, sure, Philly has a bit of an image problem. In this age of the adman, when cities are hawked to tourists like any other can of beans, a town known as "Quaker City" isn't the sexiest product a copywriter has ever had to sell – "Sin City" it ain't, after all. But then, Philadelphia isn't the kind of town you can easily boil down to a catchy slogan. It's got more character, more complexity, than that.

Consider, too, that Philadelphia is a victim of geography. Sandwiched between New York City and Washington, DC, it's prone to feelings of inferiority. And recalling the city's glory days, when it was both the financial and political capital of the nation, only makes matters worse. Back then, people seemed to take a more upbeat view. "I like this Philadelphia amazingly, and the people in it," reported Mark Twain, a man of many dislikes, in 1853. "The handsomest and most populous city in the United States," said French botanist André Michaux.

Of course, the single greatest purveyor of Philadelphia's inferiority complex was a

Preceding pages: Franklin and friend near the Delaware River; service with a smile; Pennsylvania Dutch Country; four pounds for a dollar at the Italian Market. **Left**, reflections at the University of the Arts.

Philadelphian himself. "I was born in Philadelphia, God rest its soul," quipped W.C. Fields, the tomato-nosed tippler who put his hometown at the butt-end of countless one-liners. Fields's tipsy wisecracking persona represented everything that sober, serious-minded Philadelphia was not – including fun. When asked what he would like inscribed on his tombstone, Fields delivered the famous stinger, "On the whole, I'd rather be in Philadelphia."

Bum rap: So what is it about Philadelphia that inspires such ribbing? Is it really America's sleepy urban backwater, so far behind the times that, as the joke goes, "a postman was shot in the street after being mistaken for a Confederate soldier"? Or has Philly been getting a bum rap all these years?

Well, for starters, Philadelphia really is a Quaker City. Founded in 1681 by William Penn, an aristocratic member of the Religious Society of Friends (as the Quakers are properly known), the city was imprinted from the very beginning with Quaker sensibilities. Penn had his radical side. He believed in religious freedom, equality, representative government – revolutionary ideas that helped spur America toward independence. But as a Quaker he was committed to rather conservative beliefs, too – notions about plainness, humility and order.

Thanks to Penn, much of this Quaker ethic was built right into the city. Unlike Boston or New York, which grew according to their own chaotic logic, Philadelphia was laid out in advance. Penn's plan was a simple street grid – precise, symmetrical, everything at right angles. It was the very picture of classical order, and early visitors often remarked on the town's trim and tidy appearance. A "beautiful city," wrote Frances Trollope in 1832; "nothing can exceed its neatness." Charles Francis Adams thought there was "something solid and comfortable about it, something which shows *permanency*." And in 1818, a Swedish traveler, Baron Axel Klinckowsrom, regarded it as "one of the loveliest cities in the world."

Yes, some back then found the orderliness unnerving. Writer Alexander Mackay, bemoaning the widespread use of brick, likened the place to "a great, flat, overbaked brick-field." Sir Augustus Foster, an English diplomat, thought it "built too much in the shape of a chessboard to be beautiful."

But today those same visitors probably would find this classical city of brick bumped up with more exuberant styles of architecture – the Victorian extravagance of City Hall, for example, and eclectic concoctions like the Pennsylvania Academy of Fine Arts. More recently, center city has given rise to a fresh generation of glass-and-granite sky-

in matters of refinement, culture and – critically important – good breeding. As the novelist Pearl S. Buck, a resident of neighboring Bucks County, put it: "In its own dignified and aristocratic way, Philadelphia claims its pre-eminent position in age, history and culture in the United States."

Naturally, not everyone shared the elite's high opinion of itself. "My impression of the old families of Philadelphia Quakers was that they had all the effeteness of a small aristocracy," philosopher Bertrand Russell remarked acerbically. "Old misers of ninety would sit brooding over their hoard while their children of sixty or seventy waited for

scrapers, heirs to the pioneering modernism of the PSFS Building. And if it's sheer disorder you're looking for, the Italian Market is a study in chaos.

But the Quaker ethic is more than skin-deep. It is sunk into the marrow of the city. And nowhere does one find it in a purer form than among Philadelphia's famous upper crust. The blue bloods have long since abandoned center city for Chestnut Hill and the Main Line (located, quite literally, on the Pennsylvania Railroad's main suburban spur), but Philadelphians have traditionally considered themselves the *crème de la crème*

their death with what patience they could command. Various forms of mental disorder appeared common. Those who must be accounted sane were apt to be very stupid."

The city has also come under fire for being excessively clubby, as if Philadelphia society were a members-only affair with a strict quota on new recruits. "This old city is full of joiners," noted television commentator Charles Kuralt. "There's a club on every corner. Nowhere does the outsider feel as far outside as in Philadelphia."

And yet, for all its supposed exclusivity, few cities have opened their arms as widely to the outcast and unwanted. From the beginning, William Penn envisioned Philadelphia as a city of refuge, a sanctuary for persecuted people of many faiths and nations. And to this day the city is home to immigrant communities from around the world. In fact, immigrants and expatriates have always been among the city's most outstanding citizens. Feeling poorly treated in Boston, young Ben Franklin arrived with little more than a pocketful of bread and a head full of good ideas. A dissolute Edgar Allan Poe rolled into town in 1838 with his 15-year-old wife and did some of his best work in a little house on North 7th Street. When *Leaves of Grass* was denounced as indecent, Walt Whitman found a new publisher in Philadelphia, and a home across the river in Camden, New Jersey.

True, Philadelphia does have a certain sniffishness. Thomas Eakins, perhaps the city's premier artist, was ousted by the Pennsylvania Academy of Fine Arts in 1886 for his insistence on using nude models in the classroom. But if, as the critics charge, Philadelphia is America's cultural "temperate zone," perhaps its very conventionality urges its artists and thinkers toward the exotic and unconventional.

David Lynch, known for his bizarre films, admits to experiencing his "first thrilling thoughts in Philadelphia" as a student at the Pennsylvania Academy of Fine Arts. And it was amid the stark monotony of a typical row-house neighborhood that Man Ray had his first surrealist impulse, as recounted in his autobiography: "The earliest recollection I have of my introduction to paint is at the age of five... One afternoon the house painters had gone, leaving the shutters freshly painted a bright green, standing against the wall to dry... I placed my hands on them and then carefully smeared my face with paint."

Yo, Philly!: And finally, to drive the last nail into the coffin of Philadelphia's alleged snobbishness, it should be recalled that while the cry of "tallyho!" may still be heard at fox hunts, it was Philadelphia (with the help of film star Sylvester Stallone's *Rocky*) that put the colloquial salutation "Yo!" into the pages of the *American Heritage Dictionary*. To wit: "**yo** (yo) *interj. Slang.* Used as a greeting or to attract someone's attention."

Such linguistic curiosities may seem trivial, but they point up the complex, sometimes schizophrenic character of this city. Established on radical ideas, Philadelphia is, at heart, a rather conservative town. Famous for its blue-blooded sensibilities, it is occupied by sprawling blue-collar neighborhoods. Home to innumerable clubs and special organizations, it opens its heart to strangers. Known for its Quaker reserve, it is home to the flamboyant antics of the Mummers. A City of Brotherly Love, it is, like many

American cities, vexed by drugs and violent crime. Perceived to be fixated on past glories, it has a long tradition of enlightened thought and progressive policy-making.

Philadelphians take their knocks, but they usually do it with a smile. They hear visitors say how surprised they are at finding the city so interesting and enjoyable. Like the author Henry James, who visited the city in 1905, travelers discover, often quite unexpectedly, that they "liked poor dear queer flat comfortable Philadelphia almost ridiculously." Some even agree with W. C. Fields. They'd rather be in Philadelphia, too.

Left, Philadelphia's finest take a break. **Right**, playing the field downtown.

In Boston, Mark Twain observed, they tend to ask, "How much do you know?" In New York, "How much is he worth?" And in Philadelphia, "Who were his parents?"

From the early days of Penn's colony through the founding of the great fortunes of the industrial elite and right up to the present, Philadelphia has been a home to America's true aristocracy, a British-style ruling class whose members trace their bloodlines to the city's oldest and wealthiest families – hallowed names like Cadwalader, Biddle, Ingersoll, Drexel, Morris, Chew, Cassatt. Boston has its Brahmins, New York has its Rockefellers, but few American cities can claim an upper class that is founded so strongly on lineage.

Henry James said that Philadelphia was not a place but "a state of consanguinity," and Christopher Morley found it a "surprisingly large town at the confluence of the Biddle and Drexel families... surrounded by cricket teams, fox hunters, beagle packs and the Pennsylvania Railroad."

Society matrons lament that the *nouveau riches* have all but replaced the old families, and the sociologists concur – "the new rich have totally overwhelmed the old rich," Professor E. Digby Baltzell has said. But if the ancient bloodlines are an endangered species, the mystique of Proper Philadelphia lives on, as do the social climbers who lust to buy into the tradition.

The Philadelphia story: The ideal Proper Philadelphian, according to Professor Baltzell, is: "Of English or Welsh descent, his great-great-great-grandfather would have been a prominent Philadelphian in the great age of the new republic... His family would have been listed in the Social Register... he would have gone to either Harvard, Yale or Princeton, where he would have belonged to one of the more exclusive clubs... [he] would enter one of the fashionable and powerful law firms in the city and eventually become a partner... he

would be on the board of directors of several cultural and economic institutions... [and he] would live either in Chestnut Hill or the Main Line..."

A fair enough definition, but the world at large probably relates better to the image of Proper Philadelphia promulgated by popular works of fiction like *The Philadelphia Story*, Philip Barry's play, later made into a memorable film starring Katharine Hepburn and Cary Grant, both terribly dashing and witty if

a bit silly, frolicking on the Main Line with cocktails in hand, acid on the tongue, and society reporters yapping at their heels. It's a charming little story, with lots of razor-sharp repartee and a happily-ever-after finale. However, the message is unmistakably elitist. Tracy Lord, played by Hepburn, dumps her ambitious rags-to-riches fiancé, has an eye-opening dalliance with Everyman Jimmy Stewart, then flies back to the arms of Cary Grant, her slightly alcoholic ne'er-do-well but very upper-crusty ex-husband. The moral of the story, it seems, is that aristocracy triumphs over meritocracy. Well-bred boy

Preceding pages: society wedding. **Left**, Devon Horse Show. **Right**, the Main Line's hunt country.

gets well-bred girl. The class distinctions remain intact.

The plot was reworked as the 1956 musical *High Society* and, if the world had any doubts about Philadelphia's aristocratic leanings, there was the real-life fairy tale of its star, Grace Kelly. The very epitome of Philadelphia refinement, although not a member of a true First Family, she confirmed the city's claim to privileged blood by marrying a genuine prince, Rainier III of Monaco.

Ironically, most of the players in this real-life Philadelphia story are Philadelphians by heredity only, since so many patrician families have abandoned the city for the creature

comforts of the suburbs. Although most of the glorious mansions on Rittenhouse Square have been bulldozed or gutted for retail space, there are still pockets of old money in center city – the stolid town houses on Delancey Place, for example, and super-exclusive social clubs like the Philadelphia Club, Rittenhouse Club, and their not-quite-so-snooty cousin, the Locust Club. But the bulk of old money has long since migrated to the Main Line, a string of posh suburban towns with affected Welsh names like Bryn Mawr, Tredyffrin and Radnor. It's no coincidence that they settled on the city's western flank.

Engineered by the board of directors of the almighty Pennsylvania Railroad, the Main Line is exactly that: the main rail link to the western suburbs. To start the ball rolling, executives of the railroad were expected to desert their fancy city digs and lead the migration to the promised land.

One might expect that Proper Philadelphians, ensconced in the plush precincts of the Main Line, would have long been relegated to the periphery of city life – a sort of social exotica ordinary Philadelphians keep around for sentiment's sake. With few exceptions, the old guard gave up on politics, turning over City Hall to the ward bosses and political street fighters. Blue blood is still present on the boards of various corporate and cultural institutions, but given their marginal presence in the machinery of the city, old Philadelphians play an inordinate role in defining the city's character.

Critics who charge the city with complacency and a lack of ambition might as well be talking about Proper Philadelphians, who see themselves, above all, as non-strivers, securely placed at the tip-top of the pyramid and therefore above the vagaries of social mobility. In part, this is an expression of the elite's own sense of importance, a certainty that they are the cream of Philadelphian, maybe even American, society – a separate people occupying a separate, elevated world.

In *The Perennial Philadelphians*, Nathaniel Burt's exhaustive exposition on the traditions of the upper crust, he refers to this expansive sense of self as Position: "This sense of Position, of being an important member of an important community of other such people of importance, is the firm core about which the Old Philadelphian's psychology is built. It is sense of Position that gives to so many Philadelphians that air of condescension which can be infuriating, or amusing, but which continually tends to peep out from under the good humor and the good manners. It is sense of Position, in fact, that defines them as Old Philadelphians."

There is a story along these lines that tells of a Philadelphia debutante who was introduced to the Queen of England. "And what is your lineage, my dear?" the queen asked. "The Main One," the girl replied without a hint of self-consciousness. (It should be noted that such an overblown sense of self is apparently not shared by their noble counterparts across "the puddle." After a visit to Philadelphia in 1955, Edward VII was left with a rather confused impression of the city's leading citizens. "I met a very large and interesting family named Scrapple," he reported, "and I discovered a rather delicious food they call biddle." As the family is Biddle and the food is scrapple, so much for Position.)

Main Line: Traveling the back roads of the Main Line into the "hunt country" of Chester and Delaware counties, it's easy to see that the old families do, in many ways, live in a niscent of the countryside in Europe, with long, tree-lined driveways leading up to handsome, ornate houses of various styles – a French country manor, a Tudor estate, a Victorian mansion – all borrowing architectural cues from the old-world gentry.

That these suburban folk are "landed gentry" is sheer affectation, of course. Proper Philadelphians never made their living off the land. They merely built their homes in the country and made their money in the city. But then, the importance of appearances is not to be underestimated. Like a fine instrument, young people of good breeding must be properly tuned in order to perform well in

world apart. Although less than an hour from the city, it feels as if you've crossed an invisible boundary into a paradise of country living, a world of gentleman farmers and riding clubs, where lush rolling fields are crisscrossed with hedgerows and fieldstone walls, thick woods are honeycombed with bridle paths, and an occasional clutch of horsemen breaks through the tree line and lopes gracefully across a meadow. It is reminiscent

Left, W.C. Fields: "On the whole, I'd rather be in Philadelphia." **Above**, James Stewart, Cary Grant and Katharine Hepburn in *The Philadelphia Story*.

public. And Main Liners have always seen to it that their offspring are properly groomed to take their place among the elite.

Like all tribes, Proper Philadelphians have ceremonies by which they identify themselves – charity balls, society weddings, polo matches, club memberships and the like. Young ladies of standing are still presented at lavish debutante balls. Young men are expected to join the correct fraternities and to show an interest, if not actually an aptitude, in the right sort of sporting events. And naturally, children of both sexes are schooled at the finest institutions – Chestnut Hill Academy, Yale, Harvard, Bryn Mawr College.

The ultimate event in Proper Philadelphia's social season is the annual Assembly Ball. Established in 1748 by a group of 59 distinguished colonists, the Philadelphia Assembly is a sort of extended family reunion. And membership in the family is strictly limited. To be invited to the Assembly Ball is to be counted among the *crème de la crème* of Philadelphia society. Only descendants of the founders and their spouses are eligible for the honor, and even this is no guarantee. A member's children must be formally approved before attending the Assembly, divorced couples are utterly excluded, and

guests must come from adequate stock and from a city other than Philadelphia. It's arcane, archaic and ever so snobby. And that, it seems, is the point.

And then, of course, there are the horses. Proper Philadelphians are crazy for the beasts. Thoroughbreds, naturally – it's only fitting that the well-born have an affinity for the well-bred. Back in the glory days before the income tax, the gentry kept horseflesh and hounds for fox-hunting. Nowadays, you can still hear a "tallyho!" or two in hunt country, but most equestrians concentrate on the standard English-style events. Competitions are held throughout the year, but the defining event of the season is the Devon Horse Show, one of the largest outdoor horse shows in the country.

But don't expect cowboys and bucking broncos; rodeo this ain't. The standard outfit is breeches, silk cravat, tailored English jacket, leather boots and velvet-covered helmet. If it seems old-fashioned, it's meant to be. Culturally speaking, this is an exercise in continuity, a form of ancestor worship, a symbolic connection with the past. Anthropologists would call it a consolidation ritual, an event in which a social group identifies its members and cements its special bonds. The effect is only heightened by the procession of antique-style carriages, coaches and four-in-hands, attended by a contingent of English-style grooms in jodhpurs, top hats and thigh-high boots.

Tallyho!: The equestrian arts reach their most refined state in an event known as dressage, in which regal horses execute a repertoire of equestrian gymnastics – piaffes, pirouettes, flying changes. It is ballet on the hoof, a profoundly beautiful display of precision and control. And as with all public outings on the Main Line, good breeding and good manners are essential.

There should be no confusing this ancestor worship with stodginess. In fact, in recent years the upper crust has gotten downright racy. The parking lot is crammed with sports cars that carry price tags well into the six digits, and as one blonde beauty put it, "I like horses and I like to party." And the parties are quite a sight. A recent bash featured an Elizabethan theme, with trumpeters heralding guests as they entered, knights decked out in full armor, and a troupe of Renaissance dancers and a court jester romping around the nattily dressed guests.

Sociologists tell us that such ostentation is a sign of how far the elite has fallen. Such is the fate of old Philadelphians. With each generation, their fortunes and families become ever more dispersed, leaving the door open for the New Rich, who, with sometimes unseemly ambition, launch their own lineage of Proper Philadelphians.

Left, elegant living. **Right**, old-world style at the Devon Horse Show.

"Last week I went to Philadelphia," W.C. Fields once wisecracked, "but it was closed."

It's a pretty sour judgment for a city that once upon a time was regarded as the "Athens of America." Times have changed, and the mantle of leadership in the arts long ago shifted to hectic, cosmopolitan New York City. Still, there is a degree of excitement in Philly's art world – it just has to be ferreted out. While a recent study found Philadelphia to have the fewest number of arts events per person among American cities of comparable size, it's not exactly a creative wasteland.

The difficulty is that many of the city's finest arts groups – the American Music Theater Festival and the Opera Company of Philadelphia among them – don't have their own performance spaces and therefore must rent theaters on what is often a show-by-show basis.

Among the most promising developments in recent years is the transformation of Broad Street into a full-fledged Avenue of the Arts stretching both north and south of City Hall. The Arts Bank recently moved into a restored building at Broad and South streets, adding much-needed performance and rehearsal space. The Philadelphia Clef Club of the Performing Arts built a brand-new facility dedicated solely to jazz performance, history and education. The Wilma Theater is planning to move into its new venue in early 1997. And, with any luck, construction of a new concert hall for the Philadelphia Orchestra will begin soon after.

Staging ground: Proximity to New York has been the Philadelphia theater's greatest blessing and sometime curse. Early on, the town that gave birth to the matinee idol Edwin Forrest, as well as a fair chunk of the Barrymore clan, was a launching pad for Broadway shows. But as Broadway fizzled over the last two decades, Philadelphia was left to forge its own theatrical identity.

The city's largest subscription company is the Walnut Street Theater, offering standard, middle-of-the-road fare for a largely suburban crowd. It is worth looking into almost

exclusively for its crowd-pleasing, larger-than-life restagings of Broadway musicals during the holiday season. The Forrest Theater sticks to the tried-and-true formula of big-time Broadway road shows such as *Phantom of the Opera* and *Les Miserables*.

The real excitement in town is in the smaller theaters, most notably the Arden Theatre Company, a young and young-at-heart crew that presents exciting original literary adaptations, chamber musicals, and the classics at

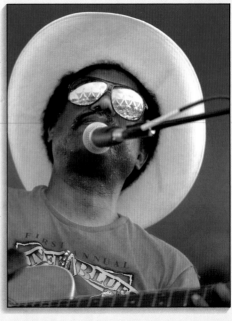

a new site in Old City. Novel Stages, formed at around the same time, suffers from the lack of its own theater facility, but the work is generally fresh and intelligent. With either company you don't find elaborate sets or well-known actors, but you will get a much better sense of Philadelphia theater. And you'll probably have a better time, too.

Exciting work can also be found at the Philadelphia Theater Company, a polished presenter of off-Broadway fare; the Wilma Theater, with the best of cutting-edge drama and black comedy; and the American Music Theater Festival, which each year takes on the herculean task of producing a slate of original musicals.

Freedom Theater, a showcase for black actors, directors and playwrights, recently completed the renovation of a new theater at its North Broad Street complex, offering an effective opportunity for the group's enormous potential to be realized.

Adventurous theatergoers should not miss the Philadelphia Festival Theater for New Plays. Each year the company gives first

strong resident company that received national attention for its recent five-hour adaptation of *Sister Carrie* and its cross-cultural kabuki-style *Achilles*. On the Jersey side, Princeton's McCarter Theater has been treated to a well-deserved artistic facelift thanks to the director, who has brought to the theater American premieres of works by playwrights David Rabe and Edward Albee as well as name-recognition actors like Ed Asner, Linda Hunt and Laura San Giacomo.

stagings to works by national figures like Jules Feiffer and Chaim Potok and to local talent as well. Among the most notable in the latter category have been the plays of Bruce Graham, the company's playwright in residence who has yet to be fully appreciated by the outside world. His latest work, whatever it may be, is the must-see of each season.

A jaunt into the suburbs finds the People's Light and Theater Company in Malvern, a

Preceding pages: Pennsylvania Academy of the Fine Arts. **Left**, Penn's Landing RiverBlues Festival. **Above**, City of Brotherly LOVE.

Kids' stuff: For the younger crowd, there's the outstanding International Festival of Theater for Children, bringing the best in children's entertainment to five stages and their environs in West Philadelphia.

Economic troubles have hit the Philadelphia dance community hard. Despite its consistent excellence, the Pennsylvania Ballet is usually upstaged by its boardroom dramatics. Just a pirouette away from bankruptcy in 1990, the company staged an eleventh-hour fund-raising coup that managed to save its life. Now it is back on its toes and is one of the city's few must-sees. The highly regarded local company, Philadanco, offers an excellent modern alternative.

Philadelphia's music scene has experienced a good deal of action, too. Almost every other classical performance group in town plays in the considerable shadow cast by the Philadelphia Orchestra. Its singular lush sound, shaped by the eminent maestros Leopold Stokowski and Eugene Ormandy, largely accounted for its vaulting to a position as one of the country's great music-making ensembles of this century. In 1991, their successor Riccardo Muti passed the baton of the Philadelphia Orchestra to German-born conductor Wolfgang Sawallisch.

some "moonlighting," found a home at the Walnut Street Theater, where it plays a series of evening concerts. The Philly Pops, led by charismatic Peter Nero (of *Breakfast at Tiffany's* fame), continues to entertain with lighter fare.

Both the Opera Company of Philadelphia and the Pennsylvania Opera Theater have responded to budget cuts by shifting toward opera's greatest hits – attracting newcomers but disappointing serious-minded loyalists. Both companies attract overseas talent, with the Opera Company of Philadelphia singing in the original language (although recently English titles have been added) and the Penn-

What is heard at the Academy of Music is part of the excitement of each new season.

The orchestra can be enjoyed at the Academy or at its summer home at the Mann Music Center in Fairmount Park. Purists sometimes complain about the distracting dog howls, honking horns and airplane roars at the Mann, but the rest of us love these concerts, especially from the vantage-point of the free seats on the lawn, where the music is often accompanied by picnic dinners and the pop of wine corks.

Concerto Soloists, featuring many of the Philadelphia Orchestra's members doing

sylvania Opera Theater performing in English. You'll also find smaller groups for just about every taste. Relache, for example, presents newly commissioned work. Orchestra 2001 offers works by 20th-century composers. They perform at various city venues.

Jazz talent, both local and national, can be sampled at Zanzibar Blue, Ortlieb's Jazzhaus or the new Philadelphia Clef Club of the Performing Arts on South Broad Street. Rockers from the Philadelphia area and elsewhere can be heard at the Chestnut Cabaret and Ambler Cabaret. Up-and-coming local bands tend to play any number of rock clubs. Visitors can find information on a full schedule of folk performances through the Philadelphia Folk Song Society, which offers monthly concerts of its own.

Torch singers and Broadway belters are featured at the American Music Theater Festival's Cabaret series at the Hotel Atop the Bellevue. Over in Atlantic City, New Jersey, a favorite hangout for Philadelphians, the casinos import everything from Broadway revues and lounge acts to big-name singers and comedians.

There are also the annual Philadelphia Folk Festival, the Mellon Jazz Festival and Presidential Jazz Weekend (at a variety of

sampling the masterworks inside. This is a shame, since the museum houses an excellent mix of "greatest hits," including Van Gogh's *Sunflowers*, Picasso's *Three Musicians* and Du Champ's *Nude Descending a Staircase*, as well as period rooms, Pennsylvania Dutch crafts and furnishings, and an impressive collection of Asian and Islamic art. More popular with kids is the museum's cache of armor and armaments.

The imposing size of the Museum of Art can make it easy to overlook the relatively unassuming Rodin Museum, just a short walk down the Benjamin Franklin Parkway. You'll pass *The Thinker* (a favorite photo

locations in and around the city), and the Jambalaya Jam, RiverBlues Festival and Singer-Songwriter Festival (at the Penn's Landing outdoor arena).

Visual arts: Your first stop on any art tour of Philadelphia should, of course, be the Philadelphia Museum of Art, which stands with dignity at the end of the Benjamin Franklin Parkway. On a summer day, it often seems that more people are interested in running Rocky-like up its monumental staircase than

Left, an evening performance at the Academy of Music. **Above**, street corner serenade.

opportunity) and a beautiful garden as you enter the largest collection of Auguste Rodin's work this side of France.

You will find a considerably more intimate setting at the Pennsylvania Academy of the Fine Arts, the first art school and museum in the country. The building itself is a work of art. It was designed by renowned Philadelphia architect Frank Furness in an imaginative, if sometimes dizzying, array of styles. The museum's permanent collection offers a first-rate survey of American art, including Benjamin West's *Penn's Treaty with the Indians* and major works by Horace Pippin,

Winslow Homer, Thomas Eakins and Academy founder Charles Willson Peale. The museum also mounts temporary exhibits, including work by students and faculty.

For more modern sensibilities, there is the Institute of Contemporary Art, housed in industrial-style digs on the University of Pennsylvania campus. Its definition of art includes video, performance and other alternative media. The galleries have featured works by such notables as performance artist Laurie Anderson and the controversial photographer Robert Mapplethorpe. The University Museum is also on campus, with a world-class collection of art and artifacts

ond Saturdays. As this is the case, can Third Thursdays be far behind?

The best of Philadelphia filmmakers, usually graduates of either the University of the Arts or Temple University's radio-television-film program, are part of the bill of fare at the Philadelphia Festival of World Cinema and the International Gay and Lesbian Film Festival, both of which feature the work of film makers from around the world.

For slightly more conventional flicks, the best places are the Ritz 5 and the Ritz at the Bourse, both of which feature foreign and limited-release films. (They sell great popcorn, too.) The Film Forum and the Temple

from traditional cultures throughout the world as well as temporary exhibits.

Realizing that private galleries weren't getting a whole lot of public attention, the enterprising Old City Art Association coordinated simultaneous openings for many of its member galleries. This creative buffet is now called First Fridays, and in addition to seeing the work of local and national artists, the monthly happening has become a rare thing in Philadelphia – a great social scene. First Fridays have been so successful, in fact, that the galleries around Rittenhouse Square have copied the strategy and instituted Sec-

University Cinematheque present a rapidly changing list of oldies but goodies, primarily for true fans who prefer celluloid to videotape.

And finally, two of Philadelphia's most exciting arts spots don't fit into any category. Every self-respecting bohemian in the city has the schedule for the International House and the Painted Bride Arts Center posted prominently on their refrigerators. International music, unusual dance events, performance art and offbeat films are the norm at both of these locations.

Above, Asian exhibit at the Museum of Art.

THE BARNES METHOD

When they talk about "The Method" in Philadelphia, chances are they're not talking about Stanislavsky or Strasberg but about Albert Barnes. He was an eccentric art collector whose Method has made Philadelphia the center of a heated debate in the art world. At issue is whether a private collector has the right to keep a world-class art collection out of the public eye and whether the edicts of a long-dead collector should dictate how people view masterpieces.

Dr Albert Barnes, a native of working-class Kensington and a graduate of the University of Pennsylvania, made his millions by inventing Argyrol, an antiseptic. He never enrolled in an art course but channeled his fortune into a collection of French Impressionists that, at the time, was looked down upon by the critics. He made his bid for respectability in 1923, showing his collection of paintings by Cézanne, Matisse, Picasso and Modigliani at the Pennsylvania Academy of the Fine Arts. The reviews were not good. Outraged, Barnes sequestered his collection in his Main Line mansion, and set up the Barnes Foundation, a nonprofit, tax-exempt educational organization.

The collection of some 800 paintings – including 180 Renoirs, 60 Matisses, 59 Cézannes, 19 Picassos and assorted Seurats, Modiglianis, Rousseaus, El Grecos and Titians – was sizable enough to be a tourist attraction. But Barnes had other plans. Firmly against the use of historical explanation and the comments of both critics and the artists themselves, he concluded that art should be analyzed scientifically. To that end, the paintings in the Barnes collection were hung in deliberate patterns stressing context. They were surrounded by antiques which Barnes felt shared characteristics with the work. To eliminate other unnecessary information, Barnes removed the works' dates and titles. And only students of his Method saw them, at least until 1961.

That was when a lawsuit challenged the right of the Barnes Foundation to be tax-exempt as long as the works were not available to the general public. After that, the Barnes Foundation was a bit more accessible, but still under the strict edicts of Barnes's will. No photo-

Right, Albert Barnes and Salvador Dalí.

graphs were allowed, paintings were not to be loaned out, rehung or reproduced. Appraisers and critics weren't welcome.

The rules began to change again in 1990, when attorney Richard Glanton was named president of the Barnes Foundation. How he came to the position is yet another twist in the institution's bizarre history. Barnes had offered to donate his collection to the University of Pennsylvania if it would teach the Barnes Method, but no such deal could be worked out – even during his lifetime the Method was considered a bit shaky. But Lincoln University, the country's oldest black college, in Chester County, did agree to teach it. Barnes didn't give up the collection, but he permitted the school

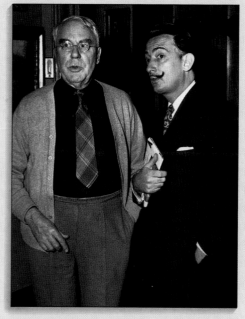

to put five trustees on the Barnes board. Thus Glanton, a Lincoln trustee, took over.

Since then, there have been a whole lot of changes at the foundation despite claims made by loyal students of the Barnes Method that Glanton was trying to destroy the original concept. Much of the collection was sent on an extremely popular world-wide museum tour. A hefty new book on the Barnes collection has been published. And the building itself has been thoroughly renovated. Friends of the Barnes are shocked, art lovers are excited, and legal scholars are pondering the implications. See for yourself. The Barnes Foundation is at 300 North Latch's Lane in Merion. ∎

Only in Philadelphia do they carry on the organized silliness that is the Mummers Parade. They prance, strut, cavort and clown their way up Broad Street on a gaudy long day's journey into night. It happens every New Year's Day, unless Mother Nature decides to kick up her heels – the weather at that time of year can be as outlandish as the paraders' own garish accoutrements.

There's no pre-Lenten excuse here, as with the Mardi Gras revelers in sultry, jazz-happy New Orleans, or the raucously Latin *carnavaleiros* down in samba-surfeited Rio. No, here in the City of Brotherly Love this curious residue of medieval European folklore and North American cakewalk-minstrelsy has somehow outlived Puritan proscription and endured various stresses and strains – the advent of women paraders, a court-ordered prohibition on the use of blackface, intrusive television cameras and the suburban diaspora.

Silly Philly: Since the dawn of another century – the 20th – these Mummers and their descendants have been carrying on this vaguely disreputable affair, and why is anybody's guess. In their dishabille finery, they gather early in the morning at Snyder Avenue in South Philadelphia and begin their trek up Broad Street. When they reach the judges' stand at City Hall, a building whose architectural grotesquerie provides a weird counterpoint to their own procession, they rev up their insistent string banjos and high-pealing glockenspiels, their saxophones and blatant drums, as they arc around the square intoning the Mummers anthem, "Oh! Dem Golden Slippers," and all the old familiar strains, figuratively on their toes as they pursue the prize money that will make their day, at least, financially redemptive. Like their zany umbrellas and brash female impersonations, it's all a bit crazy. And, for true-blue Philadelphians, irresistible.

What is it that keeps these Mummers go-

ing? Well, for one thing, it's no doubt the long pull of tradition, as Palma Lucas suggests. She helps run the Mummers Museum at Washington Avenue and "Two Street" (as old-timers call 2nd Street), in the heart of Mummer land, and she partly ascribes the phenomenon to Philadelphia's historic and geographical situation as a cosmopolitan port of entry whose end product was "an accumulation of various traditions." Swedes, Finns, English, Scots-Irish, Germans, Italians – a mélange that keeps the stew simmering.

An expert on Mummer history (and a parade judge), Professor Charles E. Welch, Jr, points out that the city was a hotbed of vaudeville early in the century, and that burlesque and minstrel shows also were popular, and perhaps this, too, suggests a nexus with Mummermania.

The phenomenon's modern version began on the first day of a new century – January 1, 1901. The city's officialdom yielded to the importunings of some municipal boosters – headed by a theatrical producer and press agent named H. Bart McHugh – and gave shape to what had been a more or less spontaneous eruption of year-end revelry.

Shootin' and struttin': The annual celebrations, and attendant misdemeanors, had largely been spawned by social clubs whose members went around cadging cakes from bakeries and staging balls and street fests. It had gone on throughout much of the 19th century – the first social club of which anything is known, Dr Welch says, was the Chain Gang, founded in the 1840s in the South Philadelphia area that is the central point in Mummers' tradition.

Momus was the Greek god of censure and mockery, hence the etymology for mummery – in medieval French, *momeur*, "one who goes merrymaking in disguise during festivals." In 1806, sober-minded Philadelphians, annoyed by the insidious spectacle of masquerade balls that were deemed suspiciously foreign in origin, pushed a prohibition of them through the Pennsylvania legislature, and the ban stayed on the books until 1859.

Left, Mummer madness, a much-loved New Year's Day tradition in Philadelphia.

The period following the American Civil War seems to have given impetus to new forms of urban social behavior, and Mummer activity increased in those years.

Actually, the roots go even deeper. The practice of shooting firearms dates as far back as the 1630s or so, when Swede and Finnish settlers began the custom – what else was there to do on the frontier? They would discharge their guns and make a hullabaloo in the days and nights just before the new year. It is from this practice that the Mummers organization of today gets its full name: the Philadelphia New Year Shooters and Mummers Association.

English settlers, and Scots-Irish, brought with them their traditions as well – going from house to house begging cakes and ale, performing comic plays and "fantastical" folk drama, frequently in mask. Germans and French added their seasoning to this cosmopolitan Philadelphia stew, as later, in the 20th century, did Italians with their idiosyncratic comic flair.

One other major influence on the Mummers' development was American minstrelsy. The minstrel show, featuring whites in cork-daubed blackface, was a great, if largely invidious, popular form of entertain-

ment for much of the 19th century in the United States, and it was inevitable that it would have a big impact on Mummer madness. In 1964, a time of racial stress in the nation, many in the black community protested the survival of what they deemed an outdated form of stereotype. Mummers resisted, then yielded to a judicial prohibition on blackface, and the custom was abandoned.

What does persist, however, as a black contribution to the Mummer style is the cakewalk, a peculiar type of strutting that has become the most distinctive feature of the parade. The cakewalk ("a strange dance developed from walking steps and figures typically involving a high prance with backward tilt") has left a solid imprint on the Mummer psyche – as solid as the adoption of the 1879 composition by the black songwriter James M. Bland, "Oh! Dem Golden Slippers," as the parade's chief musical standard.

High-tech nonsense: What was once a spontaneous neighborhood frolic engaging the voluntary enthusiasm of mechanics and tradesmen and other ordinary folks, in the late 19th-century style, is today a large-sized production supervised by public officialdom and mindful of the demands of the television age – stations pay hundreds of thousands of dollars for broadcast rights. Some die-hard Mummer fans may carp at this wayward shift in focus, but the additional revenue produces greater financial reward in prizes offered for the best of the parade performers. Awards are made in four basic categories: Comic, Fancy, String Band and Brigade, and prize money is running upwards of $325,000.

As the parade lurches toward a new century, new logistical wrinkles pop up. They are ticked off by observers like Rose DeWolf of the *Philadelphia Daily News:* a shorter route and a longer time-span, shrinking crowds and a more selective preening for the television cameras, exaggerated props and burgeoning production costs.

Plans are afoot to streamline the event, with perhaps a parade "czar" to keep things in check. "It's almost as if it's been a victim of its own success," DeWolf says. "What used to be a nice parade that lasted six hours now lasts 12 hours." Professional choreographers and professional costume designers are employed, she continues, in an extravagant effort "that would put Broadway productions to shame." And the end result is to narrow the focus to high-tech performances at two locations, Washington Avenue and City Hall, thereby giving short shrift to parade-goers along the entire route.

"Let's get back to the old folksy thing," DeWolf pleads. But whatever its misdirection, she doesn't think the Mummers parade will ever go away. "It's something that people here get carried away about. I don't think it will disappear."

That it would ever come to an end seems unlikely just considering the sheer numbers:

Originally, the parade organization encompassed a Fancy Division, consisting of four clubs, and Comic Division, with eight clubs. The advent of the third division, the String Bands, came on New Year's Day in 1902 with the participation of the Trilby String Band – again an outgrowth of a custom wherein ragtag groups of musicians (and near-musicians) cavorted on South Philadelphia streets on the holiday. The newest of the divisions is the Fancy Brigades, offshoots of the Fancy Clubs. Their hallmark is especially lavish costumes and floats and extravagant productions.

In 1975, spurred in part by interest in the

25,000 participants in the four parading Mummer divisions, their investment of between $30,000 and $40,000, and a municipal expenditure of another half-million or so.

A great deal of effort, as well as dollars, is spent in keeping the tradition going. Meetings and rehearsals take place weekly, and many members drive from the suburbs. Production costs run very high, and some Mummers have even reportedly re-mortgaged their homes to cover financial shortfalls.

Left, young Mummer in the 1930s. Above, 25,000 people participate in the Mummers Parade.

American Bicentennial, a push for establishment of a Mummers Museum began, and, assisted by city and state funding, ground for the museum was broken in 1979 at Two Street and Washington Avenue. The building's garish colors and Art Deco-like design match the Mummers' outlandishness, and it is a worthy stop on the tourists' trail.

Whatever its trials and tribulations, the march of the Mummers and Shooters is likely to keep on cakewalking up Broad Street as they respond to the urge each new year to match the nonsense of life with their own touch of high-struttin' absurdity.

THE AMISH

A long line of cars crawls along in frustration, trying to pass slow-moving Amish buggies on a highway in Lancaster County. It's not just a traffic jam; it's a clash between modern and traditional values. The Amish are a people apart; yet, the more they try to separate themselves from the modern world, the more they attract its attention.

Responding to an invitation by William Penn, they settled the fertile countryside west of Philadelphia, and for 300 years they have managed stubbornly to cling to many of the customs and beliefs they brought to the New World. They are the "gentle people" of pacifism and personal humility, baffling the rest of the community by their tenacious hold on the past and seemingly arbitrary code of behavior. They forgo electricity; they farm with horses instead of using tractors; they shun higher education, and they forbid the ownership of cars.

Unlike many fundamentalist groups, however, they do not base their style of life on unquestioned Old Testament edicts. Indeed, they are masters of compromise, cunningly balancing convenience against tradition and making delicate bargains that embrace enough of the modern world to give them prosperity while rejecting those aspects likely to threaten the integrity of their family life.

Origins: Lancaster County's 18,000 Old Order Amish are loosely linked to their other North American cousins scattered across nearly 900 congregations in 22 states and the Canadian province of Ontario. Their religious roots stretch back to the 16th-century Anabaptists who parted ways with the Protestant Reformation in 1525 in Switzerland. Although Europe was their homeland, there are no Amish there today.

Adhering to the literal teachings of Jesus, the Anabaptists emphasized obedience to God's will, adult baptism, pacifism, the separation of church and state, and a disciplined church community that remained distinct from the larger world. They were dubbed rebaptizers, or Anabaptists, because they insisted on baptizing adults who had already gone through the ritual as infants. Because adult baptism was considered both a religious heresy and a political threat, it triggered severe persecution. Thousands of Anabaptists died for their faith by drowning, burning at the stake, or decapitation.

The Amish splintered off from the Swiss Anabaptists in 1693 under the leadership of Jacob Ammann, from whom they derive their name. Hutterites, Mennonites and some Brethren groups also trace their lineage to the Anabaptists. The Amish share basic religious beliefs with other Christians, but put special emphasis on simplicity, community, obedience, humility, mutual aid, and separation from the world, a way of life galvanized by the persecution they suffered in Europe.

Large families: The Amish are flourishing in North America. From a small band of some 5,000 at the turn of the 20th century, they have grown to over 130,000. Their community has been doubling in size nearly every 20 years. Large families, averaging about seven children, provide a steady stream of members, since some 80 percent or more of their children join the Amish community. In addition to having a high birthrate, the Amish have constructed a variety of social fences around their community to protect it from the turbulent winds of modern life.

Except for family size, the Amish emphasize small-scale values. The Lancaster community revolves around 100 church districts consisting of 25 to 35 families. Worship services, held every other Sunday, rotate from home to home because the Amish have no church buildings. Worship, work, fellowship and mutual-aid activities, such as barn raisings, revolve around the church district, affording each person a social and emotional niche. Farms and businesses are also relatively small. Large operations employing more than a dozen people are thought to lead to arrogance and wealth that would disturb the relative equality of Amish life. The vir-

Left, there are 18,000 Old Order Amish in Pennsylvania's Lancaster County.

tues of humility and simplicity also stress a smallness of ego, which promotes cooperation with the community.

Social control is another fence that cordons off the community. Obedience is considered a virtue. Children learn at an early age to obey parents, teachers and elders. At baptism, in the late teens and early twenties, young adults promise to obey the *ordnung* – the discipline of the community passed across the generations by word of mouth. It prescribes the use of horses and traditional dress, and forbids high school, cars, TV, electricity and computers, among other things.

The flamboyant individualism of Ameri-

bishop enables the community to retain its sharp distinctions from the world. Each bishop typically is responsible for two church districts – about 50 to 60 households – enabling him to know the members quite well.

The bishops of the community gather periodically to coordinate activities and discuss troublesome issues such as the use of computers, eating in restaurants and embryo transplants in cattle. Individuals who violate community norms are asked to make a public confession in the church service. If they refuse, they are liable for excommunication and social avoidance, known as shunning.

Amish education provides another barrier

can culture threatens Amish ways. Submission to the community and concern for the corporate good takes priority over expressions of individualism, such as faddish dress, jewelry and personal photographs. The *ordnung* helps to insulate the community from the pressures of unbridled American individualism. It not only provides guidance for personal behavior but clarifies the importance of the community over individual whims and wishes.

The bishop of each church district interprets and enforces the rules of discipline. Respect for traditional authority held by the

around the community. Before 1950, most Amish children attended one-room schools. With the consolidation of public schools the Amish developed their own schools. Elders contended that eight years of education was adequate preparation for a successful life in the Amish community. After numerous legal battles in several states, the US Supreme Court in 1972 declared that Amish students could terminate their formal education at the eighth grade. Today, Amish youth complete their education in one-room schools operated by Amish parents.

Teachers are typically single Amish

women, products themselves of Amish schools, who teach without certification or a high-school diploma. The curriculum stresses practical skills but does not include science or religion. Indeed, religion is not formally taught in any sector of Amish society, including the church. Religious values are taught by example, not by formal doctrine. By limiting exposure to outside ideas and non-Amish youth, Amish education erects yet another wall around the community.

Other cultural fences protect Amish ways from the influence of modern life by regulating interaction with mainstream culture. Once burned by the fires of persecution, the Amish limits contamination by outside values. Avoiding membership in public organizations and political affairs also helps to draw boundaries with the larger world.

Although the Amish have built many fences around their community, they are also capable of reaching through them to strike bargains with the larger culture. These cultural compromises often seem like riddles or contradictions. Pragmatism permits the use and hiring of motor vehicles, for example, because that bolsters their economic well-being – but not the ownership or driving of vehicles, because such mobility would erode the integrity of the community. For the same

emphasize separation from the world, thus preserving the purity of Amish tradition. They believe that they are called out from the world to be a peculiar people. Although the Amish speak English, their Pennsylvania German dialect heightens group identity and stifles interaction with outsiders. The taboo on car ownership impedes mobility. The shunning of telephones, television, radio and other types of mass media in their homes

The Amish community has been doubling in size almost every 20 years. Left, Dutch Country produce. Above, Lancaster's Central Market.

reason, telephones are acceptable in shops or barns but not in homes.

Amish farmers typically use tractors around their barns for heavy-duty jobs, such as powering feed grinders and hydraulic systems. In the fields, however, modern farm machinery, designed for tractors, is pulled by horses. This distinction protects the horse, which has evolved as the prime symbol of Amish identity in the 20th century. Twelve-volt batteries are used to stir the milk in bulk tanks, but tapping into 110-volt power lines is forbidden – largely because this would bring into Amish homes the secular values transmitted by radio and television plus a variety of modern gadgets which would undermine the simplicity of Amish life.

The complexities don't stop there. Synthetic materials that require no ironing are used to make the Amish's traditional "plain" clothes. Carriages, made in Amish shops from fiberglass and vinyl, conform to customary colors and styles. Newer Amish homes appear remarkably contemporary with modern kitchens, bathrooms and gas appliances. But washing machines, and sometimes sewing machines and cake mixers, are powered by hydraulic pressure.

Struggles: The Amish of Lancaster County are among the most progressive Amish communities in North America. They have brokered more compromises with modern ways and accepted more technology than Amish settlements in more rural areas of the country. And even infringements of the rules are sometimes treated surprisingly leniently. A young farmer is given six months to replace the rubber tires on his tractor with steel wheels. A businessman is allowed several months to complete a project before getting rid of his illicit computer.

But the forces of urbanization and industrialization have squeezed Lancaster's Amish relentlessly. Shrinking farmland, sharply rising land prices and their own growing population have created a demographic crisis – too many Amish and too few acres.

To cope with the pressures, some families migrate to more rural areas. And whenever possible, farms are subdivided into smaller operations. But these moves are not enough, and the Amish face the big question: Would they leave their farms for factories? Once again, they compromise. Yes, they would leave the plow behind, but not for factory work, which they believe erodes the stability of family life. "The lunch pail," said one bishop, "is the biggest threat to our way of life." Cottage industries offered a way around the impasse. By starting small industries, the Amish earn a living surrounded by family and friends. Today, nearly half of Lancaster's Amish are employed in manufacturing a variety of crafts, equipment, quilts and cabinetry. Hundreds of these small shops have sprung up in the past decade, and now produce dozens of different products from doghouses to gazebos.

For the moment at least, the cottage industries are a happy compromise. They allow members of the community to leave their plows but stay close to ancestral roots and work in a congenial environment rich with ethnic values. But the cottage industries also pose a danger to the future of Amish society. They place Amish entrepreneurs in frequent contact with outsiders and expose them to the thinking of the larger world. Moreover, the shops are introducing a three-tier class system – farmers, day laborers and entrepreneurs – which in the long run could ruin the equality of Amish society.

Sense of belonging: The cost of being Amish is high, but there are benefits in return – fewer trips to the psychiatrist's office, lower rates of suicide, few drug and alcohol problems, no dependency on public welfare, and less environmental damage. Amish life offers a distinct sense of meaning, belonging and identity, a rare commodity these days.

These virtues require major concessions – forgoing unbridled individualism, giving up the pursuit of pleasure and convenience. But the Amish argue that true happiness and personal satisfaction are woven into the very fabric of a stable community, and that they discover themselves as individuals only when they yield to the wisdom of tradition.

As a result, some tensions between their community and the outside world are inevitable. The 1985 movie *Witness*, in which Harrison Ford played a Philadelphia cop who takes refuge in the Amish countryside, won two Oscars from Hollywood but received few plaudits from the Amish, who correctly foresaw a large influx of tourists arriving to indulge their wistful longing for simpler times and simpler lives.

Yet, at the same time, the 5 million tourists who visit Lancaster County each year spend a total equivalent to almost $30,000 for each Amish inhabitant – an invaluable boost to the prosperity of the entire community. Gasoline taxes paid by tourists, in fact, certainly exceed the amount the Amish would pay if they permitted themselves to drive cars.

Right, an Amish buggy.

Philadelphians like to think of their collective home as a "livable city" – not too hectic, not too crowded, manageable. It is a town with roots, old by American standards, but forward-looking, too – a colonial city with a modern attitude.

Thanks to William Penn, getting around Philadelphia is a snap. Center city, the river-to-river rectangle laid out by Penn in 1682, is designed like a giant checkerboard. North-south streets are numbered from the Delaware River to the Schuylkill River. East-west streets are named, mostly after trees, with house numbers corresponding to the numbered cross streets.

Philadelphia's historic heart is the colonial town – now known as Old City and Society Hill – where a young printer named Benjamin Franklin settled, the Liberty Bell rang out in celebration atop Independence Hall, and the Framers of the Constitution forged a new kind of nation governed by "We, the People." Around this colonial core is a jigsaw of neighborhoods, most within walking distance of each other. An afternoon stroll might take you from the art-gallery ghetto north of Market Street through the maze of charming alleys in Washington Square West to the high-octane shops and restaurants on South Street, the self-proclaimed "hippest street in town."

Beyond center city, Philadelphia is a study in contrast and color – from the ethnic enclaves of Chinatown and South Philadelphia to the diverse communities of University City and North Philadelphia. Envisioned by William Penn as a "greene countrie towne," the urban landscape is laced with open spaces. There are tree-shaded oases like Washington Square, Rittenhouse Square, the Morris Arboretum and 8,000-acre Fairmount Park, the largest municipal park in the country. Once known as the "Athens of America," the city exhibits its love of culture at distinguished universities, galleries and learned societies as well as the many museums along the Benjamin Franklin Parkway.

And there's more beyond the city limits. In little more than an hour, you can be strolling along New Jersey's windswept beaches, shooting craps at an Atlantic City casino, eating shoofly pie in Pennsylvania Dutch country, or soaking up Bucks County's stunning natural beauty.

This is a livable city indeed – a town of cobblestone alleys and gleaming skyscrapers, of hidden courtyards and bustling streets, of tight-knit communities and vital traditions. It is a treasure house of history, a modern metropolis, a "city to be happy in."

Preceding pages: Benjamin Franklin Bridge arches across the Delaware River; Society Hill's historic town houses; Logan Square in full bloom; Boathouse Row. **Left,** Rocky keeps an eye on Veterans Stadium.

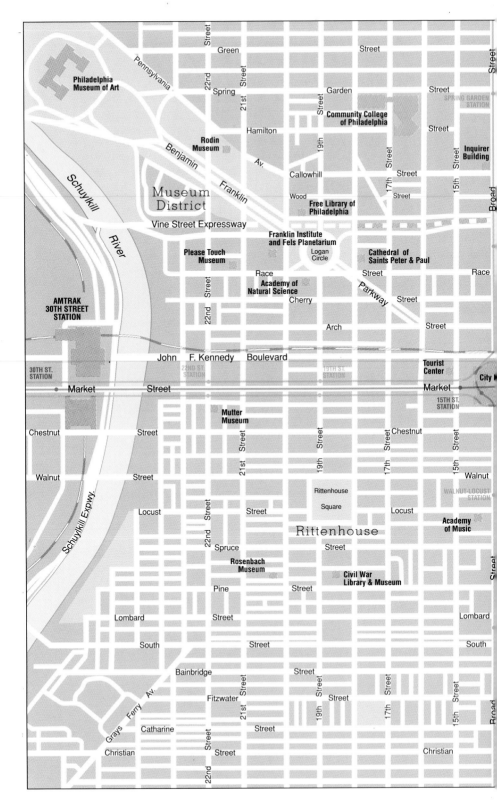

Philadelphia Museum of Art

Pennsylvania

Museum District

Schuylkill River

Rodin Museum

Benjamin Franklin

Green Street

22nd Street

21st Street

Spring

Hamilton

Av.

Callowhill

Wood

Vine Street Expressway

Please Touch Museum

22nd Street

Garden

Street

Community College of Philadelphia

19th Street

17th Street

15th Street

Street

Street

Street

Street

SPRING GARDEN STATION

Inquirer Building

Broad Street

Street

Free Library of Philadelphia

Franklin Institute and Fels Planetarium

Logan Circle

Academy of Natural Science

Race Street

Cherry

Arch

Cathedral of Saints Peter & Paul

Parkway

Street

Street

Race

Street

AMTRAK 30TH STREET STATION

30TH ST. STATION

Market Street

Chestnut Street

Walnut Street

Locust

Schuylkill Expwy.

John F. Kennedy Boulevard

22ND ST. STATION

Market

Mutter Museum

21st Street

22nd Street

19TH ST. STATION

Street

19th Street

Spruce

Rosenbach Museum

Pine

Lombard Street

South

Bainbridge

Fitzwater

Catharine

Christian

Grays Ferry Av.

21st Street

22nd Street

Street

Street

Street

Street

Tourist Center

Market

City

15TH ST. STATION

Chestnut Street

17th Street

15th Street

Walnut

WALNUT-LOCUST STATION

Rittenhouse Square

Rittenhouse

Locust

Academy of Music

Street

Civil War Library & Museum

Street

Lombard

South

Street

19th Street

17th Street

Street

15th Street

Christian

Broad Street

Green Street

Poe House

Spring

Garden Street

SPRING GARDEN STATION
Street

11th Street

9th Street

7th Street

6th Street

5th Street

3rd Street

2nd Street

Callowhill Street

Callowhill

Street

Street

St. Augustine's Church

St. George's Church

Chinatown

Franklin

Square

Old First Reformed Church

CHINATOWN STATION

Street

Race

U.S. Mint

Street

Cherry

Chinese Cultural Center

Street

Afro-American Museum

Franklin Penny Bust

Cherry Street

Betsy Ross House

Arch Street

Franklin's Grave

Old City

7th Street

Street

American Jewish History Museum

Delaware Expressway

1TH ST. STATION

8TH ST. STATION

Jacob Graff House

5TH ST. STATION

5th Street

Market Street

2nd Street

2ND ST. STATION

Balch Institute

Atwater Kent Museum

Independence Hall

Liberty Bell

Bourse Building

Maritime Museum

11th Street

9th Street

6th Street

Chestnut

Old City Hall

Carpenters Hall

Street

National Park Visitors Center

Congress Hall

Independence Square

Library Hall

Norman Rockwell Museum

Walnut

City Tavern

3rd Street

Street

Port of History Museum

Walnut Street Theatre

Washington

Old St. Joseph's Church

Forrest Theatre

Locust

Square

Bishop White House

Powel House

Penn's Landing

Washington Square West

Street

St. Mary's Church

Society Hill

Holy Trinity R.C. Church

Spruce

USS Becuna

Pennsylvania Hospital

Kosciuszko National Memorial

Street

USS Olympia

Mother Bethel Church

Old Pine Presbyterian Church

Pine

St. Peter's Church

Head House Square

New Market

Society Hill Playhouse

Lombard

Street

Street

Street

South

Street

11th Street

9th Street

7th Street

6th Street

Bainbridge

5th Street

3rd Street

2nd Street

Queen Village

Fitzwater

Street

Delaware Expressway

atharine

Street

Italian Market

Christian

Passyunk Av.

Street

Delaware River

Center City Philadelphia

0.8 miles / 1.3 km

OLD CITY

It's been called America's "most historic square mile" – Philadelphia's Old City – home to the nation's most sacred shrines and symbols. This is where a young journeyman printer named Benjamin Franklin set up shop, where Thomas Jefferson composed the Declaration of Independence, where the Constitution was drafted and a new kind of nation created.

But Old City is more than a journey into the past, it is a study in urban renewal. In the early 1950s, the National Park Service took over much of the district, cleared away the dreck and restored the area's historic sites. Rehabilitation spawned a generation of shops, galleries, restaurants and hotels. History remains the big attraction, however, and no matter where you go, you are liable to bump into a reminder of Philadelphia's illustrious past.

Colonial core: The best place to start a tour of Old City is at the **Independence National Historical Park Visitor Center** (3rd and Chestnut streets), where park rangers dispense free maps and information. Exhibits focus on various aspects of American history, and a short film, *Independence*, directed by John Huston, runs every 30 to 45 minutes.

The Visitor Center is surrounded by some of the city's most distinguished and dramatic buildings. Directly across 3rd Street, the **First Bank of the United States** stands in "lonely grandeur." Completed in 1797, this regal neoclassical structure is a monument to the political vision of Alexander Hamilton who, as the nation's first Secretary of the Treasury, insisted that government finances be handled by a central institution. The bank's charter lapsed in 1811 and was later purchased by a French-born merchant, Stephen Girard, a brooding, enigmatic figure who used his vast resources to finance the United States government during the War of 1812.

To the south of the Visitor Center is the **Philadelphia Exchange**, a magnificent Greek Revival structure designed by William Strickland and opened in 1834 as the nation's first stock exchange. Be sure to walk to the rear of the building for a look at the graceful curved portico. The wide cobbled way that wraps around the Exchange is **Dock Street**, formerly Dock Creek, where ships tied up to unload their cargo in the late 1700s.

A short walk along Walnut Street to the corner of 2nd Street brings you to the **City Tavern**, a fully functioning reconstruction of the 18th-century inn where Franklin, Washington, Adams and other luminaries wrangled over the issues of the day. Now run by the Park Service, the tavern is still a terrific place to enjoy traditional American cuisine (lunch and dinner only). Across 2nd Street, **Old Original Bookbinders**, a well-known seafood restaurant, is a big hit with tourists, although locals tend to shy away from the crowds and high prices. Around

ft, The Liberty Bell: "Proclaim ro' all the nd." Right, Idiers stand ard at dependence ll.

the corner on 2nd Street, **Welcome Park** is a tribute to William Penn, who occupied a slate-roof house on this site during his second and final visit to the colony. Designed by Philadelphia architect Robert Venturi, the park is a model of Penn's original plan for the city. Next door, the **Thomas Bond House** is an 18th-century restoration operated by the Park Service as a bed-and-breakfast inn.

Rising like an Art Deco fortress from the corner of 2nd and Chestnut Streets, the **US Customs Building** towers over the eastern end of Chestnut Street, Old City's unofficial restaurant row. There are some 15 eateries crowded into the two blocks of Chestnut Street between 3rd and Front streets and even more choices around the corner. Choices range from sushi to spaghetti, fish to French and high-class Italian, Middle Eastern and Afghan cuisine. The **Corn Exchange Building** situated at the corner of 2nd and Chestnut streets is an architectural confection of checkerboard Flemish-bond brickwork, fanciful pediments and a miniature clock tower.

Return to Walnut Street and turn right toward the lovely row houses and gardens between 3rd and 4th streets. The first is the **Bishop White House**, built in 1786 and occupied until 1836 by Episcopal Bishop William White, rector of Christ Church. Fully restored, the house is the very picture of 18th-century luxury and affluence, with a beautifully appointed dining room in which Washington, Jefferson, Franklin and other leading figures dined, the bishop's well-stocked library, and – a sign of real wealth – an indoor privy.

At the other end of the block, just past the fragrant offices of the Pennsylvania Horticultural Society, is the **Todd House**, built about 10 years earlier than Bishop White's house and, judging by the tiny rooms, modest furnishings and outdoor privy, meant for a family that was less privileged. John and Dolley Todd lived here for two years before John, an attorney, died in the great yel-

Fanciful Old City architecture

low-fever epidemic that swept through the city in 1793.

Dolley later married "the mighty little Madison" – James Madison, that is – "master builder of the Constitution" and the nation's fourth president. She was later renowned for her graciousness as a hostess in the nation's capital and also for her heroic evacuation of the White House during the War of 1812. Tickets to the Todd and Bishop White houses are free at the Visitor Center. Tours are limited to 10 people and begin about every half-hour.

The **Polish-American Cultural Center** – a modest exhibition space with displays featuring famous Poles, the Polish military and folk art – is among the row of handsome buildings across Walnut Street.

From the Todd House, it's a short walk through the Park Service's **18th-century Garden** into a lovely mall shaded by enormous willow and dogwood trees. Straight ahead is **Carpenters' Hall**, a beautifully proportioned

Georgian structure designed by Robert Smith and built in 1770–74 for the carpenters' guild. The First Continental Congress met here in September 1774 to air their grievances against George III, and the building later served as a hospital during the Revolutionary War. The hall is still owned by the Carpenters' Company; the first floor is open to the public and features an interesting display on the hall's construction.

At the front of Carpenters' Court, two smaller buildings face Chestnut Street. The **Marine Corps Memorial Museum**, a reconstruction of New Hall built in 1791 and used by the War Department until 1792, houses a modest collection of Revolution-era muskets, sabers, uniforms and cannonballs. The **Army-Navy Museum**, quartered in a reconstruction of a house built in 1775 by Quaker merchant Joseph Pemberton, details the development of the Army and Navy in the late 1700s with dioramas, a reconstruction of a frigate gun deck, and exhibits of flintlocks, mus-

e
hiladelphia
xchange.

kets, uniforms, flags and other instruments of 18th-century warfare.

A very good house: Directly across Chestnut Street, about 20 paces down a narrow alley between 3rd and 4th streets, is **Franklin Court**, site of Benjamin Franklin's last home. Franklin started work on the house in 1763 but didn't move in until 1785, when he retired from his diplomatic posts in Britain and France. All the while he sent letters home to his wife, Deborah, instructing her on everything from fireplace design to curtain hanging. "'Tis a very good house that I built so long ago to retire into," Franklin wrote. But even in retirement, Franklin had little rest. He served as president of Pennsylvania for three years and, at the ripe old age of 80, as a delegate at the Constitutional Convention. The house was torn down in 1812 by Franklin's grandchildren. Lacking plans for the structure, the National Park Service hired architect Robert Venturi to design a steel "ghost structure" representing the outline of Franklin's house and his grandson's printing office.

Beneath the steel frames, viewing bays let visitors peek down into the remains of Franklin's underground kitchen and privy pit. At the opposite end of Franklin Court, facing Market Street, a row of homes (Numbers 316, 318 and 322), built by Franklin in the late 1780s, now houses a park bookshop, the B. Free Franklin post office, the four-story archaeological display "Fragments of Franklin Court," and an 18th-century printing shop where Franklin's firebrand grandson, Benjamin Franklin Bache, once published an influential newspaper named *The Aurora*.

The exhibits continue in Franklin Court's fascinating underground museum, which features a portrait gallery, replicas of Franklin inventions like the glass "armonica" and library chair, a display detailing Franklin's life and work as a scientist, statesman, philosopher, printer and social organizer, an illuminated index of quotations, and an audio

Left, Carpenters Hall. Right, Second Bank of the United States.

"drama" explaining Franklin's part in the American Revolution and the Constitutional Convention. Best of all, you can pick up a telephone at the "Franklin Exchange" and hear what George Washington, Mark Twain, D.H. Lawrence and others had to say about "the wisest American" – not all of it kindly, either.

Walk back to Chestnut Street and turn right for the glorious, if somewhat graying, facade of the **Second Bank of the United States**, yet another of the park's Greek Revival jewels, designed by William Strickland in 1824. This is the house that Biddle built – and that "Old Hickory" Andrew Jackson tore down. A home-grown genius, Nicholas Biddle had administered the Second Bank for some 20 years when President Jackson, a fervent anti-elitist, launched a fierce campaign to close it down. Today, the bank serves as Independence Park's portrait gallery. Many of the works are by Charles Willson Peale, one of the premier American painters of his day. Works by James Sharples,

Gilbert Stuart, Thomas Sully and Peale's son, Rembrandt, are also part of the collection. During the summer, cool drinks are offered in a colonial-style tea garden at the side of the building. The trio of ornate buildings across the street once served as banks, too. This stretch of Chestnut Street, the city's financial center in the late 19th century, was known as Bank Row.

Library Hall stands next to the Second Bank. The original building was completed in 1789 for the Library Company of Philadelphia, destroyed in 1884 and then reconstructed in the 1950s as the library of the American Philosophical Society. The structure now houses all sorts of historical goodies, including letters and other documents written by Franklin, Jefferson and other eminent Americans. Most of the holdings are reserved for serious scholars, but visitors can sneak a peek at a few choice samples in the lobby.

Let freedom ring: Crossing 5th Street from Library Hall puts you smack in the

rriage in City.

middle of **Independence Square**, known in 1776 as the State House Yard. The two buildings hugging the corner are **Old City Hall** – home of the Supreme Court from 1791 to 1800 and to city government between 1800 and 1870 – and **Philosophical Hall**, headquarters of Ben Franklin's American Philosophical Society, which has occupied the building since 1789. Today, Old City Hall is exhibition space, focusing on the Supreme Court's early years and the daily life of Philadelphia's 18th-century craftsmen and laborers. Philosophical Hall is closed to the public.

Not to be missed is, of course, Philadelphia's **Independence Hall**, locus of the American historical experience. It was built between 1732 and 1756 as the Pennsylvania State House but was destined to play a key role in the birth of the nation. This is where the Second Continental Congress convened in 1775 to make their case against the British and, ultimately, to draft a revolutionary Declaration of Independence. Eleven years later, the Constitutional Congress met to amend the irresolute Articles of Confederation – and ended up forging an entirely new government. Tours of Independence Hall (every 15 minutes, 30 minutes in winter) start in the east wing and guide visitors into the Assembly Room, where John Hancock presided over his rebellious countrymen in 1776 and George Washington served as guiding light during the secretive proceedings of the Constitutional Convention in the steamy summer of 1787.

Although most of the original furnishings were destroyed by the British during the Revolutionary War, a few original touches remain, including the silver inkstand used to sign the Declaration of Independence and the Constitution, the "rising sun chair" used by Washington, and Thomas Jefferson's walking stick. The rest of the furniture dates to the late 1700s. Independence Hall also houses period restorations of the Pennsylvania Supreme Court and, on the second floor, the Governor's Cham-

The Great Clock on Independen Hall.

ber and the Long Room, which was used as a prison hospital for American soldiers after the Battle of Germantown, a reception hall for foreign dignitaries in the 1790s, and, later, as Charles Willson Peale's museum of art and science.

Now closed to the public, the bell tower was designed by William Strickland and erected in 1828, about 37 years after the unsteady original was torn down. The bell hanging in the steeple is not the famous Liberty Bell but a substitute – the John Wilbanks bell – installed in 1828 and still rung on national holidays. Finally, standing off Independence Hall's west shoulder, **Congress Hall** housed the United States legislature between 1790 and 1800. Inside, the Senate and House chambers are replete with fine studded leather, mahogany furnishings and other 18th-century fineries.

The real **Liberty Bell** has, since 1976, occupied a glass-and-steel pavilion in the plaza directly across Chestnut Street. This is probably the most famous bell in the world, which is somewhat ironic given its checkered history. First of all, there is that giant crack marring its face. Consider, too, that the colonial Philadelphians who lived nearby were wont to grumble about its insistent ring at inopportune moments. And later, in the 19th century, plans to scrap it as an antiquated heap of metal were considered on more than one occasion. Indeed, the circumstances surrounding the very making of the bell represent a kind of comedy of errors.

Intended for the State House tower, the bell was cast in London by the venerable Whitechapel Bell Foundry and sent to Philadelphia in 1752. Before it could be installed, someone decided to put it to the test and, perhaps ineptly, gave it a ring that promptly produced a crack. The bell was recast by two Philadelphia craftsmen, John Stow and John Pass. To their chagrin, bell number two sounded a rather unmelodious bong, and Pass and Stow recast it once again – in the process immortalizing themselves

ımodore
n Barry
Indepen-
ce Hall;
stand used
ign the
stitution
the
laration of
pendence.

with the inscription "Pass and Stow" on the bell's waist.

The bell tolled several times for the momentous events attending the American Revolution; for the joyous news of Cornwallis's surrender at Yorktown in 1781 and the signing of the Treaty of Paris two years later; for the sad news of George Washington's death in 1799 and Lafayette's in 1834. The bell cracked again in 1835 while being rung for the death of Chief Justice John Marshall. It tolled once more, on Washington's birthday in 1846, and since then it has stayed mute except for a handful of occasions on which it has been gently tapped.

To the east of the Liberty Bell Pavilion is the **Bourse**, a block-long Victorian beauty built in 1893–95 as a commodities exchange and now serving as a shopping mall and office building. Illuminated by a domed skylight, the three-tiered shopping arcade makes a convenient place to pick up a gift for the folks back home, grab a bite to eat or simply cool off on a hot summer day.

Western fringe: West of Independence Square, Old City begins to blend with the clang and clatter of downtown Philadelphia. The area is anchored at the corner of 6th and Walnut streets by the imposing mass of the **Curtis Center**, formerly headquarters of the Curtis Publishing Company, publisher of the *Saturday Evening Post*, the *Ladies' Home Journal* and other national magazines. Take a walk into one of the city's most spectacular lobbies for a look at Louis Comfort Tiffany's 100,000-piece mosaic, *The Dream Garden*, modeled after a painting by Maxfield Parrish. The **Norman Rockwell Museum**, featuring a collection of the artist's posters and *Saturday Evening Post* covers, beckons tourists into the building from a separate entrance on Sansom Street. It's really more of a gift shop than a true museum, but Rockwell lovers will find it interesting.

Crammed with jewelry stores of every type, **Jewelers Row**, located between 7th and 8th streets north of Walnut, is

Left, Thom: Jefferson. Below, Mar Place East.

Philadelphia's diamond district. North on 7th Street, the austere-looking **Atwater Kent Museum** details the history of Philadelphia from its Quaker roots to the present with exhibits drawn from a 30,000-object collection. A few steps away, the **Balch Institute**, one of the city's most imaginative and engaging new museums, is a glorious celebration of America's ethnic diversity. The Balch launched a long-term exhibit – "The Peopling of Pennsylvania" – in October 1992 in honor of the Columbus quincentennial. Changing exhibits in a second gallery usually focus on a particular theme or ethnic group; past shows have covered ethnic arts, rites of passage, immigrants in the media and various ethnic communities in Philadelphia.

Next door to the Balch, the **Graff House** is a reconstruction of the house in which Thomas Jefferson wrote the Declaration of Independence. When Jefferson rented the upstairs parlor in 1776, the house, built and owned by bricklayer Joseph Graff, was located on the quiet outskirts of town. A short film is shown on the first floor; Jefferson's rooms are recreated on the second.

Across Market Street, the old **Lit Brothers department store** is a magnificent block-long Victorian structure constructed of cast iron, brick and terracotta and slathered with a coat of bright white paint. In 1988, it was reborn as **Market Place East** with offices on top, retail space and restaurants below.

The first major museum devoted exclusively to African-American culture, the **Afro-American Historical and Cultural Museum** is two blocks away, at 7th and Arch streets. Five levels of changing exhibits will keep even repeat visitors interested. Previous shows have chronicled the history of the slave trade, the migration of African-American families to various Philadelphia neighborhoods, and the role of Philadelphia's community in the civil-rights movement. Space is also devoted to arts and crafts, with exhibits highlighting a particular theme, artist or medium.

Liberty
Pavilion.

Seventh Street continues past the awkward **Police Administration Building**, known as the Round House because of its curvy concrete design, and then leads to **Franklin Square**, one of William Penn's original five town plazas, now strangled by the entrance to the Benjamin Franklin Bridge, which arches more than 8,000 feet across the Delaware River. Isamu Noguchi's jolting stainless-steel sculpture, *Bolt of Lightning, a Memorial to Benjamin Franklin*, towers over the foot of the bridge, offering a rather peculiar welcome to motorists as they enter the city.

Gallery ghetto: On the opposite side of Independence Mall, Old City is quite clearly a neighborhood in transition, with handsome colonial buildings standing shoulder to shoulder with sooty, 19th-century warehouses, many of them transformed into artists' lofts, galleries and upscale condominiums. On the edge of **Independence Mall**, tucked into a quiet brick walkway between 4th and 5th streets, is the **National Museum of American Jewish History**. Most of the gallery is given over to an exhibit exploring the growth and diversity of the American Jewish experience from the establishment of the first Jewish community in New Amsterdam (later New York) in 1654 to the present. A side gallery is devoted to changing exhibits, including a yearly special on ceremonial art, "Contemporary Artifacts."

The **Free Quaker Meeting-house** and Christ Church Burial Ground face each other a little farther north on 5th Street. The homely brick meetinghouse was built in 1783 for the "Fighting Quakers," a splinter group that broke away from the pacifist Society of Friends in support of the American Revolution. Take a peek at the restored interior for a glimpse of the somewhat stark style characteristic of the Quakers.

Across the street, **Christ Church Burial Ground** is the final resting place of Benjamin and Deborah Franklin, Philip Syng Physick, Benjamin Rush, and several signatories to the Declara-

The Graff House, whe Jefferson wrote the Declaratio Independer

tion of Independence. The gates are usually locked, but you can steal a look at Franklin's grave from the corner of 5th and Arch streets. For an even better view of the cemetery, stroll over to the **US Mint** and take a free tour of Uncle Sam's money factory, where you can have a quick lesson in numismatics and watch as thousands of coins are cranked out every day. The windows in the visitors' gallery give a bird's-eye view of the burial ground, Independence Mall and the Liberty Bell Pavilion.

From the Mint, it's a short walk east on Race Street to the **Old First Reformed Church**, built in 1837, taken over by a paint factory, and now beautifully restored. A block north, the Benjamin Franklin Bridge intrudes on a pair of historic churches – **St George's United Methodist Church**, the oldest Methodist church in America, and **St Augustine's Catholic Church**, established in 1796, burned down by anti-Catholic rioters in 1844, and rebuilt to a fine standard just a few years later.

A two-block walk back to Arch Street brings you to the **Friends Meetinghouse**, built in 1804 on land granted to the Quakers by William Penn. A series of dioramas inside features scenes from Penn's life. Continuing down Arch Street – past the firehouse, the giant bust of Benjamin Franklin (it's made of thousands of pennies but looks like chopped liver), and the lovely homes hidden away in Loxley Court – is the **Betsy Ross House**. Did Betsy Ross actually live here? And did George Washington ask her to sew the first American flag? It's doubtful. Some people even question whether the bones interred in the front courtyard in 1975 are really those of Betsy Ross and her husband. Whatever the truth, the restored rooms give a fascinating glimpse into a seamstress's busy (and cramped) life in this tiny 18th-century house.

It's a short walk from the Ross House to **Christ Church**, at 2nd and Church streets just north of Market Street. With its soaring white steeple, elegant arched

h flying
ve
pendence
k.

windows and magnificent interior, Christ Church is one of Philadelphia's most handsome colonial buildings and the city's most prominent structure well into the 1800s. George Washington, Benjamin Franklin and Betsy Ross worshipped here, and several signers of the Declaration of Independence are buried in the brick courtyard. While you're in the area, be sure to explore narrow **Church Street**, where locals sip java at cozy little Old City Coffee.

Walking north on 2nd Street takes you past a few of the new art galleries that are turning Old City into Philadelphia's own SoHo. At last count there were about **33 galleries** in Old City. A number are housed in airy old factories, some with lovely cast-iron facades dating back to the 1890s. The Old City Art Association sponsors openings on the first Friday of every month except July and August – hence **First Friday**, a sort of freewheeling art fest that's become one of the hottest tickets in town. You'll find clusters of galleries on 2nd Street between Church and Race streets, and on 3rd and Cherry streets between Arch and Race. Nearly all specialize in contemporary works, many with an emphasis on local artists.

Elfreth's Alley, a hidden enclave of early 18th-century houses that is reputed to be the nation's oldest continuously inhabited street, is two blocks north of Christ Church between 2nd and Front streets. The homes are privately owned and, with the exception of the modest **Elfreth Alley Museum** at Number 126, are closed to the public.

Several galleries specializing in contemporary works are located just a few steps away on 3rd Street. And a few steps away, **Fireman's Hall** is packed with the stuff of schoolboy fantasy – historic fire engines, hand-pumpers, steamers, helmets, water cannon, a shiny brass fireman's pole and other equipment documenting the history of firefighting since Ben Franklin founded the Union Fire Company, the nation's first, in 1736.

Betsy Ross House courtyard.

BENJAMIN FRANKLIN

He walked into town an impoverished teenager in 1723, and in just 25 years Benjamin Franklin had turned himself into a Philadelphia celebrity. By his death in 1790, he had attained icon status, an international legend who had charmed the intellectual darlings of the Paris salons and helped steer the fledgling United States on their historic course.

Ben Franklin was the prototype for the Great American Success Story, a self-made man *par excellence* who embodied the essence of democratic meritocracy. He was a voracious improver, a child of the Enlightenment, a sort of early American Renaissance man who, as printer, journalist, scientist and statesman, potently combined common sense and inspiration.

Yet, despite all the mythology, Franklin the man has always seemed a puzzle. Is the Ben Franklin who, in *Poor Richard's Almanack*, espoused such pragmatic virtues as thrift, moderation and industry the same man whose flights of imagination gave us the Franklin stove, the bifocal lens and the kite-flying experiments in electricity? A genius he may have been, but where is the grandeur, the kind of reckless élan that appealed to the romantic fancies of hero-worshippers like Thomas Carlyle and D.H. Lawrence, also two of his severest critics. He was derided as a "crafty and lecherous old hypocrite" by William Cobbett. John Keats called him "a philosophical Quaker full of mean and thrifty maxims." And both Nathaniel Hawthorne and Herman Melville regarded him as something of a mountebank, a quack dispenser of warmed-over aphorisms.

He was crafty, cautious, and sometimes conformist. Even his celebrated remark at the signing of the Declaration of Independence – "Gentlemen, we must now all hang together, or we shall most assuredly hang separately" – bespeaks a certain timorous calculation. None of that "Give me liberty or give me death!" flair.

It is not easy to square the image of Franklin the moralist, the dour didact, the "maxim-monger," with the equally evocative image of Franklin the visionary, the audacious thinker, the "party-animal" who delighted French society, the lover of food, drink, and women who were not his wife.

His dalliances in France – especially with Madame Helvetius, a rich widow to whom he vainly proposed marriage, and the younger Madame Brillon de Jouy, who liked to perch coquettishly on the lap of her "*cher Papa*" – are legendary, if never fully disclosed in detail. His affairs in London produced at least one child, a son who, to his father's displeasure, became an ardent Loyalist in the colonies.

A self-satisfied, middle-class man preoccupied with material pursuits? Perhaps. But Franklin left his mark all the same. And despite conservative leanings, he was a man ahead of his time.

George Washington may have been first in the hearts of his countrymen, but Benjamin Franklin was Mr America to the world at large. When he died, aged 84, his funeral drew the largest crowd – 20,000 people – ever to assemble in early Philadelphia. He was, to borrow Horace Greeley's words, "the consummate type and flowering of human nature under the skies of colonial America." ∎

SOCIETY HILL AND PENN'S LANDING

Society Hill may very well be Philadelphia's loveliest neighborhood. Named for the Free Society of Traders, to whom William Penn granted land between Walnut and Pine streets, this chiefly residential neighborhood contains the largest concentration of 18th-century homes in the country. In the late 1700s, the neighborhood was shared by both working-class and wealthy families in a lively milieu of craftsmen, merchants, shopkeepers, shipwrights and seamen. The finest churches were within earshot of the rowdiest taverns, the most prestigious homes within smelling distance of the open-air market.

When well-heeled families started moving into more fashionable homes around Rittenhouse Square, the old neighborhood began a long decline that turned much of it into a slum. Had it not been for the efforts of preservationists in the 1950s, many of the historic homes would have fallen to the wrecking ball. The many years of rebuilding and renovating, painting and primping, have paid off grandly.

Today, Society Hill contains some of the most charming homes and priciest real estate in the city. It's a walker's paradise, honeycombed with cobbled alleyways and hidden courtyards, and filled with old houses that have been lovingly and accurately restored.

Sinful feast: You can slip into Society Hill through the iron gate of the **Rose Garden**, on the 400 block of Walnut Street behind the Second Bank of the United States. The brick walkway leads to the type of quiet courtyard that makes strolling through Society Hill such a delight. Follow the path across Locust Street into the even-more-secluded **Magnolia Garden**, where, in early spring, magnolia and azalea blossoms surround the flagstone walk with splashes of red, white and sherbet-pink. It's a wonderful place to read the Sun-

day paper and sip coffee, or to take a few restful moments before pressing on.

The **Philadelphia Contributionship** for the Insurance of Houses from Loss by Fire, the oldest fire insurance company in the country, founded by – who else? – Ben Franklin, is headquartered around the corner at 212 4th Street. Franklin and his pals started the "hand-in-hand" company in 1752. Its firemark – four hands locked in a fireman's carry – still hangs on buildings throughout Society Hill and Old City. The office was designed by renowned Philadelphia architect Thomas U. Walter and built in 1836. A free museum on the first floor contains a fascinating assortment of colonial firefighting equipment. Ask the guide to take you into the boardroom and living quarters for a look at the splendidly appointed interior.

Franklin's company refused to insure houses with trees nearby, so a competitor, the **Mutual Assurance Company** for Insuring Houses from Loss by Fire, the second oldest insurance company in

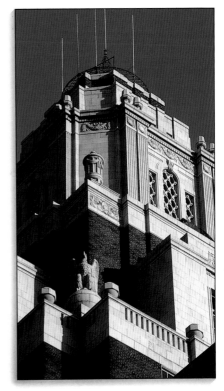

eceding
ges:
tting sail
m Penn's
nding.
ft, a man
Indepen-
nt means.
ght, US
stoms
ilding
wers over
ciety Hill.

America, filled the gap. The Green Tree Company – nicknamed for its firemark – is at Locust and 4th streets in buildings once occupied by the Shippen, Wistar and Cadwalader families, the very cream of Philadelphia society. It was frequented by the likes of John Adams, George Washington and a host of the city's most distinguished guests.

Next door, **St Mary's Church**, founded in 1763, is the oldest Catholic church still standing in Philadelphia and the second oldest congregation. Take a look inside for the two-tiered stained-glass windows. A brick walkway on the north side of the church leads to the cemetery, where Revolutionary naval commander John Barry is buried along with a number of other prominent Philadelphians.

Across the street from St Mary's Church, narrow St James Place leads into **Bingham Court**, a generous plaza surrounded by modern town houses designed by the noted architect I.M. Pei. The north entrance leads across Willings

Alley to the inner courtyard of **St Joseph's Church**. Founded in 1733, St Joseph's is Philadelphia's oldest Catholic parish. As an inscription at the door explains, St Joseph's was the only place in the British empire where the Catholic Mass was permitted by law – a tribute to William Penn's policy of tolerance. Although enjoying legal status, Catholics were looked on with suspicion if not outright contempt. According to tradition, Ben Franklin advised the Catholic fathers to confine their church behind an iron gate for protection.

Return to Bingham Court and follow St James Place across to 3rd Street. To the right, just past two handsome houses adorned with ornate wrought-iron balconies, is the **Powel House** (1765), one of the grandest colonial homes in Philadelphia and a classic example of Georgian style. As mayor of Philadelphia and one of the wealthiest men in town, Samuel Powel entertained George Washington, John Adams, the Marquis de Lafayette and other friends in the lavish reception room, dining room and ballroom. And the Powels knew how to party. John Adams – always the starched-collar Bostonian – described a Powel fête as "a most sinful feast… [with]… everything that could delight the eye or allure the taste; curds and creams, jellies, sweetmeats of various sorts, twenty sorts of tarts, fools, trifles, floating islands, whipped sillibub, &c., &c."

Nearly demolished in the 1930s, the Powel House has been restored in painstaking detail from the splendid crystal chandelier, Chippendale chairs (George Washington liked them so much he ordered 20 for Mount Vernon) and Nanking china (a gift from the Washingtons) to the rack upon which Samuel hung his wig before going to bed. Before leaving, be sure to stroll through the 18th-century garden in the rear courtyard.

Take a few steps south on 3rd Street for a look at the beautiful old brownstones once owned by Michel Bouvier, great-great-grandfather of Jacqueline Kennedy Onassis, and then retrace your

The father of the country

steps to **Old St Paul's Episcopal Church**, built in 1761, redesigned by William Strickland in 1830, and now used as office space for the Episcopal Church. St James Place continues past St Paul's along a row of modern town houses to I.M. Pei's **Society Hill Towers**, a trio of wind-beaten apartment buildings that are conspicuously out of sync with the neighborhood's colonial style. The Society of Free Traders once kept an office on this knoll overlooking Dock Creek, where ships arriving from Britain and the West Indies unloaded their freight. Years later, the area was occupied by the rancid sprawl of Dock Street Market, since relocated to a modern facility in South Philadelphia.

Heading downhill on 2nd Street brings you back to the 18th century in a hurry. The first brick building on your right is **Abercrombie House**, a handsome Georgian home built for a Scottish sea captain in 1759 and kept in excellent repair. Across the street, the modest brick building that seems to lean to one side is **A Man Full of Trouble Tavern**. Constructed in 1759 and, sadly, now closed, this homely but endearing little building was typical of the taverns that once huddled around the waterfront where a sea-dog could find dinner, a few mugs of grog and, if he didn't mind a lumpy and sometimes crowded bed, a place to stay for the night.

Delightful detour: Before continuing to Head House Square – the bustling old marketplace you see in the distance – take a stroll down Spruce Street into the residential heart of Society Hill, where lovely 18th- and 19th-century homes have been brought back to life with all sorts of interesting contemporary touches. Some of the larger houses, like the **Davis-Lenox House** (No. 217) and the **Wharton House** (No. 336), were occupied by the well-to-do. But many homes are fairly modest, with two or three stories, dormers on top, and relatively tight interior space. Be sure to peek down the cobbled alleyways at Philip and American streets (between

ead House
quare.

2nd and 3rd streets). On the next block, St Joseph's Walkway returns to Bingham Court, passing a quaint pocket of houses on the left named **Bell's Court**, with an informal garden in front. These homes have only one room on each of three stories – Philadelphians call them Father, Son and Holy Ghost, or Trinity houses – and are typical of working-class dwellings in the early 1800s.

On the opposite side of Spruce Street, St Peter's Way crosses to a lovely shaded playground between Cypress and Delancey streets. **Delancey Street**, one of the most charming and secluded in the city, is lined with 18th-century homes such as the **Alexander Barclay House** and **Trump House**, tiny private courtyards (**Drinker's Court**) and imaginative modern conversions.

The metal brackets you see outside second-story windows hold "busybody mirrors," which let upper-floor occupants see who is at the front door. It is said that Ben Franklin invented the mirror so he could see his wife coming

down the street while he "entertained" young ladies in the upstairs parlor. Boot scrapers – those metal bars you see at entrances throughout the older neighborhoods – were a necessity before the city's muddy streets were paved.

Farther along Spruce Street, between 4th and 5th streets, next to the impressive white mass of the **Society Hill Synagogue** (1829), Lawrence Street leads into a snug courtyard with modern town houses.

Two alleyways – Cypress Street and Lawrence Court Walkway – lead out of Lawrence Court to 4th Street, where the grand **Hill-Physick-Keith House** has stood for more than 200 years. This magnificent freestanding mansion – one of the finest Federal-style homes in the country – is fully restored and open to the public. Furnishings date to 1815–37, when the house was occupied by Philip Syng Physick, "father of American surgery."

Among the good doctor's many innovations are a number of surgical devices displayed upstairs, including a rather ghastly-looking gall bladder remover that was used, it should be remembered, without the benefit of anaesthesia. But Physick obviously knew his trade. Among the fine Federal furnishings are a number of gifts from grateful patients, including a silver wine cooler from the Chief Justice of the United States, John Marshall, and a painting from Joseph Bonaparte, Napoleon's brother.

South of Spruce Street, Society Hill is graced with a number of historic churches. From the Hill-Physick-Keith House, it's a short walk to the corner of Pine and 4th streets, where **Old Pine Street Presbyterian Church** has stood, in one form or another, since 1768. Originally, the church looked like its Georgian-style neighbor, St Peter's Church, but a renovation in the 1800s turned it into a Greek Revival temple, with prominent Corinthian columns and a grand second-story entrance. John Adams worshipped here on occasion and, during the British occupation, redcoats used the church as a hospital and

A view of Penn's Landing from the Jersey side.

stable. A number of Revolutionary War veterans are buried in the cemetery, including 100 Hessians – German mercenaries hired by the British to put down the rebellious Yanks. Visitors should make a point of catching Jazz Vespers, a musical treat offered at the church every third Sunday of the month.

A block away, at 3rd and Pine streets, **St Peter's Episcopal Church** retains the simple dignity of its original Georgian design. Built between 1758 and 1763 by Robert Smith, master builder of both Carpenters' Hall and Christ Church, this "chapel of ease" was established for well-to-do parishioners who were tired of slogging through the mud to Christ Church. Apart from the six-story steeple, which was added in 1852 by William Strickland, St Peter's looks much as it did more than 200 years ago. The high-backed box pews are original (Washington sat in No. 41), and the church's unusual layout, with the chancel in the east end and the pulpit in the west, remains intact. Outside, a brick path

wanders through weathered tombstones past the silent graves of painter Charles Willson Peale, naval hero Stephen Decatur, financier Nicholas Biddle, and a delegation of Indian chiefs who died in the yellow-fever epidemic of 1793.

Across the street, the **Thaddeus Kosciuszko National Memorial** commemorates the Polish patriot who aided the American cause in the Revolution. After an illustrious career as a military engineer in America, Kosciuszko led a failed revolt against the Czarist occupation of Poland. Wounded, imprisoned and later exiled by the Russians, he returned to Philadelphia and boarded at this house between 1797 and 1798, where he received distinguished visitors, among them Vice-President Thomas Jefferson. The exhibit, which includes a slide program and a recreation of Kosciuszko's bedroom, details the career of the man who, in Jefferson's words, was "as pure a son of Liberty as I have ever known."

Around the corner on Lombard Street,

e *USS*
ympia and
:S Becuna
Penn's
nding.

there are three church buildings of note. The **Presbyterian Historical Society** is a beautifully balanced Federal structure set in a walled garden at 5th and Pine streets. About a block west, **Congregation Bnai Abraham** is housed in an imposing building with an arched arcade and stained-glass rosette over the entrance.

Around the corner, **Mother Bethel African Methodist Episcopal Church** was built in 1889 in the Romanesque Revival style. The church was founded in 1787 by Richard Allen, a former slave and preacher who broke with Old St George's Methodist Church when he and other black parishioners were relegated to the upstairs gallery. The new congregation's first church was an old blacksmith shop that Allen had hauled to the site on a horse-drawn wagon.

Allen and his followers won the city's respect for their selfless efforts during the yellow-fever epidemic of 1793. And later, as the center of Philadelphia's largest black neighborhood, Mother Bethel hosted abolitionists like Frederick Douglass and spirited runaway slaves along the Underground Railroad. Allen's tomb is in the basement.

From Mother Bethel, it's a short walk down Pine or Lombard Street to **Head House Square**, Society Hill's only shopping area. In colonial times, the brick shed in the center of 2nd Street (1745) sheltered the town's newest market. The little brick house at the end – the Head House – was added in 1804 and used as a meeting place for volunteer firemen. A fire bell once hung in the green-capped cupola. Today, Head House Square has been splendidly refitted with smart shops and restaurants. And on summer weekends, the old market shed is given over to a lively crafts fair.

Unfortunately, much of the **New Market** complex – a terraced, glass-walled shopping area just off Head House Square – has lain vacant on and off for several years, although efforts to use the space for a theater, gallery and cabaret have had some success. Incidentally, the bank directly across 2nd Street from the Head House – strikingly out of place with its arched windows, ornate cornices and cast-iron pilasters – was modeled after the Loggio Consiglio in Padua, Italy, although it is now greatly altered.

Penn's Landing: In Benjamin Franklin's day, Philadelphia's waterfront was a bustling hive of sailing ships, warehouses, taverns, sail makers and counting houses. But, like New York, Baltimore and Boston, Philadelphia tore down the rotting piers and seedy whiskey joints that once choked its historic waterfront and turned it into a riverside park dubbed Penn's Landing. The big attraction here is an open-air stage where pop groups perform free concerts almost every weekend during the summer and where the Philadelphia RiverBlues Festival, Jambalaya Jam and other special events are held each year.

The angular concrete structure near the stage is the **Independence Seaport Museum**. The collection focuses on the history of the port, with displays on 19th-century shipbuilding and navigation and a fascinating array of nautical gizmos, model ships, scrimshaw and other artifacts associated with the life of early-American mariners. South of the museum, an international sculpture garden leads toward the marina, where visitors can watch traditional wood boatbuilding at the **Workshop on the Water**. The *USS Becuna*, a guppy-class World War II submarine, and the *USS Olympia*, a 19th-century cruiser pressed into service during the Spanish-American War, are berthed a few steps away and open to the public. Nearby, the **Philadelphia Vietnam Veterans Memorial** is modeled after the now-famous "Wall" in Washington DC.

If time allows, consider taking a side trip on the **Riverbus** ferry from Penn's Landing across the Delaware to the **New Jersey State Aquarium** in Camden. It is possible to purchase a special River Pass which covers the cost of the ferry, the aquarium and the Independence Seaport Museum inclusively.

Right, Four of July fireworks over the Benjamin Franklin Bridge.

SOUTH STREET AND QUEEN VILLAGE

When Philadelphians talk about South Street, they aren't referring to its entire river-to-river stretch, which forms the unofficial southern border of center city. They're talking about the strip from Front Street to about 6th Street where on weekends the pedestrians move faster than the bumper-to-bumper "cruisers." It's this stretch, the self-proclaimed "hippest street in town," where the action is – shops, restaurants, music, and assorted characters. Here are the graying hippies, punks, androgynes, hip-hoppers, gays, college kids questing for fun, teenagers looking for trouble, singles hunting for love, and local parents somehow trying to raise healthy urban kids in this quirky milieu.

Pushcarts to punks: Towards the end of the 19th century, this was the commercial center of the city's largest Eastern European Jewish neighborhood. Pushcarts and storefronts lined the street. These days, you can still get a hint of the old neighborhood around 4th Street, filled with old-fashioned fabric shops, tailors and dressmakers. The so-called South Street renaissance got rolling in the 1950s, when Philadelphia planned a crosstown expressway that was slated to wipe out everything along the street from the Delaware to the Schuylkill rivers. Residents complained, but had little luck fighting City Hall.

Reluctantly, many of them packed up and moved on to greener pastures. But like most civic projects in Philadelphia, the expressway debate dragged on for years, never quite resolving one way or the other. Meanwhile, artists discovered this low-rent district and started moving in, ignoring the possibility that the bulldozers might be rumbling toward their doorstep at any moment.

But thanks to a vocal rainbow coalition made up of blacks, Irish and hippies, the bulldozers never came. By this time, too, many of the artists, artisans and alternate-lifestylers were buying their own studios and buildings, which is one of the reasons why South Street has retained much of its artsy, edgy attitude and hasn't sprouted a fast-food joint on every corner.

There are chain stores now – Tower Records, The Gap, Workbench – and they have helped add stability to the revolving door of businesses that often seem to close before they open. However, South Street doesn't get its high-octane mystique from peddling the sort of run-of-the-mill merchandise you can find at any suburban shopping mall. It is South Street because it's one of the few strips in Philadelphia that is genuinely exciting to walk, especially on Friday and Saturday night when all the crowds hit the pavement. It is South Street because the merchants and workers who live here make it as much a community as a marketplace. It is South Street because the yuppies who discovered the area in the 1980s seem to have adapted to the neighborhood rather than forcing

ceding
es: party
e on
th Street.
, flower
dor at
ival.
ht, red
chili
pers.

the neighborhood to conform to their upscale liking.

The action begins on the 200 block, just past Head House Square. Here weekend visitors often find themselves pressed elbow to elbow on the sidewalks outside the many cafes, galleries and funky little shops. If you're looking for a bite to eat, consider paying a visit to the **Knave of Hearts**, a romantic little nook and South Street pioneer with a faithful following for Sunday brunch. A few steps away, **Bridget Foy's South Street Grill** is no gastronomical wonder but offers dining on a front porch that's perfect for people-watching on a sunny afternoon. The **South Street Diner** is simple and cheap but a favorite among late-night partiers who want to munch on burgers, fries and a few Greek specialties. If you prefer takeout, stop at **Chef's Market**, one of the best gourmet shops in town with a savory selection of prepared foods.

The businesses are packed tighter on the 300 block. For gazing and grazing,

you can't beat **Jon's**, where the comfortable outdoor patio gives you a prime view of the South Street carnival. At night, you are likely to hear music blasting from **J.C. Dobbs**, a down-and-dirty rock club where graying local legends who never made the big time keep wailing away with apologies to no one.

Other prime eateries on the block include **Ishkabibble's**, the best place in the city for chicken cheesesteaks; **Café Nola**, for days when fiery jambalaya is the only thing to get your motor revving; and **Copabanana**, the street's undisputed hamburger king.

At the center of the block is the **Theatre of the Living Arts**, a South Street landmark that has survived a number of incarnations. During the hippie heyday, it was a theater operated, for an infamous season, by André Gregory of *My Dinner with André* fame. It later became a revival house showing foreign and domestic movies. After a failed attempt to turn it back into a playhouse, it's now one of the city's prime venues **Street beat**

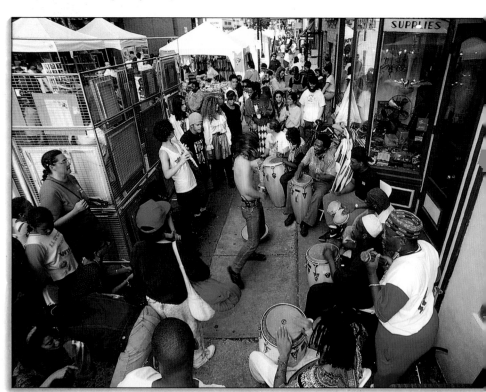

for touring bands that can't quite fill the city's larger concert halls.

Shopping highlights on this block include **Xog**, one of the best and longest-lived of the "fashion-with-an-attitude" boutiques that populate South Street; **American Pie**, a hodgepodge of crafts, jewelry, chimes and other handcrafted goods; and **The Works Gallery**, both featuring exquisitely crafted furnishings, pottery, sculpture and other *objets d'art*.

Before you even cross 4th Street, your nose will let you know you're approaching **Jim's Steaks**, South Street's sandwich king. It's usually placed in the second tier of the cheesesteak hierarchy (behind Geno's and Pat's King of Steaks, both in South Philly), although converts claim it's right up there among the very best. Across the street, the place with king-sized plastic ants crawling over the storefront is **Zipperhead**, another South Street original where fashionable punks and would-be punks come to check out the scene and to find the latest in the studs-and-leather look.

The 400 and 500 blocks are South Street's literary hub. **Tower Books** is one of the larger bookshops in the city, with thousands of titles and a knowledgeable staff. At the corner of 5th Street, the **Book Trader** offers a wide range of used books and terrific posters; there's a gallery featuring the work of prominent local photographers, and an annex in the rear with used records (remember them?). The block also has **Garland of Letters**, a New Age bookstore with enough crystals to choke Shirley MacLaine; the subject matter tends toward spirituality, astrology, philosophy and methods of healing that do not require a physician.

Heading toward 6th Street, you'll find **Tower Records** and the **Tower Records Classical Annex**. Together, the stores offer the most comprehensive selection of tapes and CDs in the city.

Queen Village: South Street is the main thoroughfare of an area that, since the 1960s, has been known as Queen Village. Before that it was Southwark, and

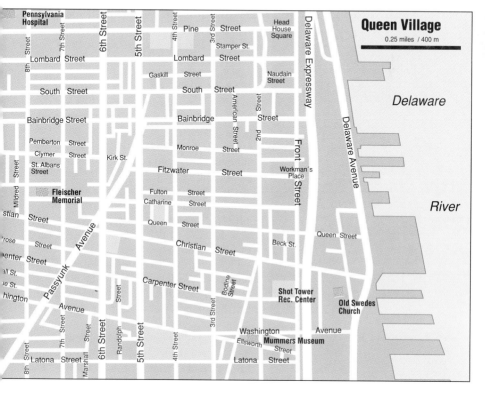

before that Wiccaco. Whatever the name, it's the oldest settled part of the city. As early as 1640, more than 40 years before William Penn arrived with his Quaker immigrants, Swedish settlers erected log cabins in this area as well as a crude blockhouse that served as the area's first church.

Stretching from Lombard Street to Washington Avenue and from Front to 5th streets, the neighborhood claims some of Philadelphia's oldest houses and churches. Like South Street, the area has been greatly affected by highway construction plans. But here, the highway, I-95, was actually built, clearing away much of what had become a slum while leaving historic buildings relatively intact.

In the far southeast corner of Queen Village, at Delaware Avenue and Christian Street, stands **Old Swedes' Church** (also known as Gloria Dei). Now a national historic site, this is Pennsylvania's oldest church, dating back to 1700. The courtyard encompasses a well-kept

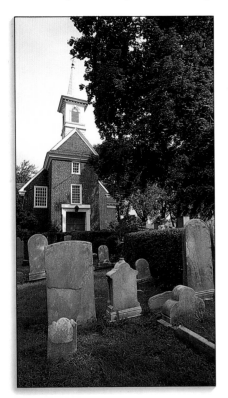

cemetery, the 18th-century **Guild House**, Parish Hall, caretaker's house and rectory. The church itself features carvings brought from Gothenburg, Sweden, in 1642, models of the *Key of Kalmar* and the *Flying Griffith* (two ships that carried early Swedish settlers to "New Sweden") hanging from the ceiling, and a pair of wooden angels that were part of another ship.

Other houses of worship worth noting are the somewhat austere **St Philip de Neri Roman Catholic Church** on Queen Street, which survived an attack during the notorious anti-Catholic riots of the 1840s; **Neziner Synagogue**, an unadorned stone structure on 2nd Street built in 1810 as a Baptist church; and, across from Philip de Neri Church, pretty little **Mario Lanza Park** – the late tenor still has worshippers in his native South Philly. Lanza has another memorial at the nearby **Settlement Music School**, where the singer used to study. The museum, a collection of Lanza paraphernalia, was recently included on the *Philadelphia Daily News'* bad-taste list. Tasteful or not, the school itself sponsors a series of concerts, teaches 3,000 students, and has always been a major force in nurturing the city's up-and-coming musical talent.

Also serving as both classroom and museum is the **Samuel S. Fleisher Art Memorial** on Catharine Street, one of those places that even the locals don't know much about. Closed during the summer, the free art school features five exhibitions a year of emerging local talent. These shows are supplemented by a collection of Russian icons and 14th- to 16th-century European paintings housed in the odd, Italian-style Fleisher Sanctuary.

Other Queen Village sites worth the walk are Workman's Place and the Sparks Shot Tower. In 1748, George Mifflin, grandfather of the Fort Mifflin namesake, built the homes now known as **Workman's Place**. A group of houses built around a central courtyard between Fitzwater and Pemberton streets, it was

Gloria De
Old Swed
Church.

134

bought, expanded and given its name by John Workman in 1812. In 1906, Workman's Place was taken over by the Octavia Hill Association, a private company dedicated to improving low-rent housing. Although renovations have been done on both the exteriors and interiors of the Workman's Place homes, the flavor of the American Revolution permeates the area.

Unless you look above the buildings, you might miss **Sparks Shot Tower** at Front and Carpenter streets. The 142-foot tower is all that remains of an early 19th-century ammunition plant. In order to make shotgun bullets, workmen dropped molten lead through a series of screens and into barrels of cold water, where it hardened into balls. Sparks's partner, a Quaker pacifist named John B. Bishop, suffered a crisis of confidence and sold his half of the business when, during the War of 1812, he became sickened by the factory's product being used to shoot down people instead of game, as he originally thought.

And finally, you shouldn't leave Queen Village without trying one of the neighborhood's excellent restaurants. There is Dmitri's for savory Mediterranean fare; Judy's Café for an eclectic menu with a homey, hearty feel; Walt's King of Crabs for no-holds-barred crustacean cuisine; Hikaru for sushi, tempura and other Japanese specialties; Sala Thai for a delectable selection of traditional Thai dishes and interesting desserts in an informal setting; the intimate Alouette Restaurant for thoughtful French dishes with an Asian accent; Cedars for spicy but inexpensive Middle Eastern fare; and many others.

But for sentimental reasons, you may want to stick with the Famous 4th Street Delicatessen which, despite the occasional circus-like atmosphere, wins accolades for its fabulously rich chocolate-chip cookies and overstuffed corned beef sandwiches. The Pink Rose Pastry Shop, a pretty little cafe at 4th and Bainbridge streets, is the perfect place to finish with pastries and coffee.

WASHINGTON SQUARE WEST

Washington Square West isn't as quaint or historic as Society Hill, but it's certainly no slouch in the character department. More daring in spirit than its genteel neighbor, and a bit rougher around the edges, this 36-block checkerboard is a lively mix of bohemians, business people, shopkeepers and householders. There are historic sites, charming antique shops, cozy restaurants and a labyrinth of hidden alleyways. Add a dollop of fine architecture and a dash of jazz and you'll begin to see why this is one of Philadelphia's most varied and colorful neighborhoods.

A placid patch of green shaded by sky-high walnut and sycamore trees, **Washington Square** anchors the neighborhood at the northeast corner. One of William Penn's original town plazas, the square served as a potter's field during the American Revolution. The 5,000 British and American soldiers who were laid to rest here are memorialized by the **Tomb of the Unknown Soldiers of the Revolution**, where an "eternal flame" burns below an inscription: "Liberty is a light for which many men have died in darkness." Later, during the tragic yellow-fever epidemic of 1793, hundreds of victims were interred in the square in unmarked graves.

By the middle of the 1800s, Washington Square had become a high-class residential neighborhood. A few of the fine old homes still stand on Washington Square West and Walnut Street, although most are now occupied by businesses. Some years later, the square became the center of Philadelphia's prestigious publishing industry. The massive **Curtis Center**, once the headquarters of the *Ladies' Home Journal*, the *Saturday Evening Post* and other magazines, still dominates the northeast corner. Lea and Febiger, the oldest publishing house in the country, was once lo-

cated in the gorgeous *palazzo* on Washington Square South now occupied by the Marian Locks Gallery's collection of contemporary art. J. B. Lippincott, one of the nation's leading medical publishers, operates out of a handsome brick building on 6th Street, and the Farm Journal and W. B. Saunders are across the park in the southwest corner.

The grand Renaissance-style palace on 6th Street is the **Athenaeum**, a private library built in 1845 and one of the country's foremost repositories of Victorian design and architecture. Filled with antique art and furnishings, the building looks much as it did 100 years ago, when well-heeled bibliophiles came here to read, study and chat with other members. A changing exhibit is displayed on the first floor, and tours of the magnificent reading room are given upon request. The Colonial-style reconstruction next door to the Athenaeum was the residence of the late Mayor Richardson Dilworth, a Democratic reformer described by a colleague as

Preceding pages: Pennsylvania Hospital was America's first. Left, the Athenaeum reading room. Right, an Antique Row bicycle shop.

"D'Artagnan in long pants and a double-breasted suit." The **Penn Mutual Building**, located at Walnut and 6th streets, is a rambling, classically-oriented composition with a towering glass-and-concrete addition. (Note the original Egyptian Revival facade of the old Pennsylvania Insurance Company still standing on Walnut Street.) And the Italianate bank directly across the square was built for the **Philadelphia Savings Fund Society** in 1869.

Rotten eggs and riots: A quick walk west on Walnut Street brings you to two theaters. The **Walnut Street Theater**, at 9th Street, is the oldest continuously used theater in America. Before Broadway stole the show, great thespians like Edwin Forrest, Edwin Booth, Sarah Bernhardt and Ethel Barrymore regularly walked the boards at this venerable old hall, now fully modernized. These days the Walnut Street Company keeps busy with a series of dramas, musicals, Shakespeare and an occasional new or experimental work. Before moving on,

be sure to catch the *Starman in the Ancient Garden* statue across the street, a spacey confection of stone and steel by Brower Hatcher.

Farther along Walnut, the **Forrest Theater** packs in the crowds with big-time Broadway road shows like *Phantom of the Opera* and *Les Misérables*. The Forrest is named after stage idol Edwin Forrest, a Philadelphian whose passionate style and fiery disposition made him a national sensation. It's difficult to imagine just how popular Forrest was in his day. When he was panned by London critics, for example, his fans in Philadelphia retaliated by pelting a rival British actor, William Macready, with rotten eggs and tomatoes. When Macready later appeared in New York City, Forrest partisans stormed the theater, sparking a riot that killed 22 people in the blackest moment in American stage history.

Return to 8th Street and walk south for a look at some of the neighborhood's architectural landmarks. The town house at No. 225 S. 8th Street is the **Morris House**, built in 1786 when this area was still on the outskirts of town. The large fanlight over the door, heavy cornices, and black-and-red brickwork – known as Flemish bond – are hallmarks of the late-Georgian style.

The **Musical Fund Hall**, just around the corner on Locust Street, was designed by noted Philadelphia architect William Strickland in the 1820s. In its brief career as the city's main concert hall, it sponsored engagements by Charles Dickens, William Makepeace Thackeray, singer Jenny Lind, "the sweet nightingale of Europe," and many other artists of note. The building has since been converted into condominiums.

A block south – at 8th and Spruce streets – **St George's Greek Orthodox Church** is housed in a striking Greek Revival structure originally designed for an Episcopal congregation by the well-known Philadelphia architect John Haviland, who is entombed beneath the church. The interior is a heady Byzantine

Starman in the Ancient Garden.

transformation of the original conservative Episcopal style, replete with gold-foil iconography, ornate woodwork and glowing stained glass.

Walking east on Spruce Street will take you past two blocks of beautifully restored 19th-century houses. At least they look like houses. In actual fact, the houses between 7th and 8th streets are facades only, with a modern office building behind. **Trinity Roman Catholic Church**, erected by German immigrants in 1789, stands at 6th and Spruce. The church's small cemetery contains the graves of Acadian (French-Canadian) refugees who were kicked out of Nova Scotia by the English in 1755 and sheltered in Philadelphia.

To the west on Spruce Street, between 8th and 9th streets, is tiny **Mikveh Israel Cemetery**, consecrated in 1740 and one of America's oldest Jewish cemeteries. Haym Salomon, an exiled Polish Jew who helped finance the American Revolution, is buried here, as is Nathan Levy, whose ship, the *Myrtilla*,

transported the Liberty Bell from England. The cemetery's most celebrated occupant is Rebecca Gratz, a friend of Washington Irving and model for the character of Rebecca in Sir Walter Scott's popular novel *Ivanhoe*.

The handsome brick houses on the 900 block of Spruce Street – each with a marble portico at the entrance – are known as **Portico Row** and were designed by the distinguished Philadelphia architect Thomas U. Walter. Around the corner at 260 S. 9th Street, the **Bonaparte House** was the residence for two years of Joseph Bonaparte, Napoleon's brother and the deposed King of the Two Sicilies.

You can begin to explore the neighborhood's cozy alleys farther along Spruce Street, past the weathered brownstones between 10th and 13th streets. Try Quince Street, where the University of Pennsylvania's **Mask & Wig Club** (No. 310) – a bizarre yellow chateau – is tucked away amid tiny brick homes and ivy-covered cul-de-sacs. To the north of

uiet
ment at
rivate
lery.

Spruce Street, Quince leads into the labyrinth of Sartain, Manning, Irving and Jessup streets. To the south, it cuts across Pine Street to a corridor of trim homes at Waverly Street and another at Addison Walk.

The maze of alleyways entered at **Camac Street** (between 12th and 13th) is even more complex, with side alleys branching off every few steps. In the late 1880s, this sheltered byway was considered "one of the meanest and most disreputable streets in the city." According to the *WPA Guide to Philadelphia*, published in 1937, it was "the scene of brawls by day and crimes by night… lined with brothels and taverns (and) rotted in a mire of debauchery."

It was also known for the many clubs that kept meeting places here, including the defunct **Sketch Club** (No. 235), which once boasted artists N.C. Wyeth and Thomas Eakins among its members. The **Charlotte Cushman Club**, founded in 1907 as a residence for visiting actresses, is located in a snug town

house at No. 239. The club is best known for its prestigious Charlotte Cushman Award; among its recipients have been Richard Burton and Helen Hayes. An appointment is needed for a tour of the building, but theater-lovers will certainly be tickled by the offbeat collection of memorabilia.

You can follow narrow Panama Street to 13th Street, where the **Church of St Luke and the Epiphany** (1839) stands in Greek Revival splendor. A short walk north to Locust Street brings you to the **Historical Society of Pennsylvania**, which features one of the city's best exhibits on local history, "Finding Philadelphia's Past: Visions and Revisions," as well as smaller changing exhibits.

Antique Row: You can wrap up this tour by walking two blocks south to Pine Street, known in this neck of the woods as Antique Row. There are about **25 antique shops** between 13th and 8th streets, not to mention a number of shops specializing in jewelry, folk art and vintage clothing. Serious collectors will find first-rate selections and expert advice at Albert Maranga Antiques (1100 Pine Street), Schaffer Antiques (1032 Pine Street), M. Finkel and Daughter (936 Pine Street) and Reese's (928–930 Pine Street), among others. Indigo carries a colorful collection of folk art from the Americas, Africa and Asia; Maide Franklin features a fine collection of jewelry; and Giovanni's Room is a bookstore specializing in gay, lesbian and feminist material.

If all this shopping has your stomach growling, try one of several funky little eateries (including a pizzeria and cafe) that cater to the neighborhood's bohemian crowd. And yes, there is more than just ice cream at Not Just Ice Cream, but you can't go wrong with the mountainous apple pie smothered in two huge scoops of French-vanilla ice cream. And finally, Zanzibar Blue, around the corner on 11th Street, is Philly's hippest jazz joint, with a menu as electrifying as the music. **Headline news.**

A quick detour south on 10th Street

brings you to the **Henry George School**, birthplace of the visionary economist whose *Progress and Poverty* was a best-seller in the 1880s. George believed that a "single tax" on land would narrow the gap between rich and poor. At the height of his single-tax movement, he nearly became mayor of New York City. Although few people remember George these days, there are still faithful Georgists who feel that the self-educated economist's ideas are as valid now as 100 years ago. The school houses a modest museum and offers a series of classes and seminars.

Backtrack on 10th Street just north of Pine for a quick look at **Clinton Street**, one of the neighborhood's loveliest and most exclusive. The walled complex of buildings at Clinton and 10th streets is **Pennsylvania Hospital**, the oldest in the country, founded in 1751 by chronic overachiever Benjamin Franklin. You can get a good look at the original buildings by walking along the iron fence on Pine Street and then entering through the 8th Street gate. The east wing was completed in 1775. The west wing and stately central pavilion – a masterpiece of Federal architecture – were finished about 30 years later. The statue of William Penn was given to the hospital by Penn's grandson John, who found this rendering of his dear departed grandfather in a London junkyard and had it shipped to Philadelphia. It's said that at the stroke of midnight on New Year's Eve, the statue steps off its pedestal for a stroll around the grounds.

A tour of the hospital (by arrangement only) takes you through the historic medical library and surgical amphitheater where distinguished physicians like Benjamin Rush, Philip Syng Physick and Caspar Wistar made breakthroughs in the healing arts. The hospital's treasures include a collection of surgical instruments, a chair used by William Penn, a Rittenhouse grandfather clock, several Sully portraits, and Benjamin West's painting, *Christ Healing the Sick in the Temple.*

ladelphia
medical
:ca.

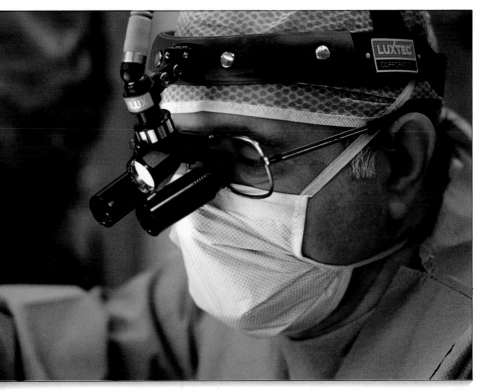

RITTENHOUSE

Rittenhouse is the *grande dame* of Philadelphia – a few years past her prime, perhaps, but still handsome, haughty and resolutely upper-crust. This is the Philadelphia of old families and old money, an enclave of Victorian splendor in a sea of "Quaker gray," a place where one finds, in Henry James's polished description, a "bestitching of the drab with pink and green and silver."

At the heart of the neighborhood is **Rittenhouse Square**, named in honor of colonial clockmaker-astronomer David Rittenhouse who, like his predecessor Ben Franklin, was president of the American Philosophical Society and a major figure in both science and government. Rittenhouse Square hit its stride in the late 1800s when the wealthy families that once occupied the narrow streets of the colonial city moved into more spacious and stylish homes west of Broad Street.

It was a period of explosive growth in Philadelphia. Energized by the meteoric rise of an industrial elite, a new breed of architects like John Notman, Wilson Eyre and Frank Furness were compelled toward ever more exuberant and eclectic designs that were more in keeping with the city's new status as an industrial giant.

Most of the well-to-do residents have long since moved away to the suburban comforts of the Main Line, but a few old families are left to keep the home fires burning. And although many of the grand Victorian mansions that once surrounded Rittenhouse Square have been replaced by faceless apartment buildings, this is still one of the most prestigious addresses in the city.

Today, Rittenhouse Square is both a geographical and social crossroad that brings together a cross-section of neighborhood residents. Young professionals can be seen power-walking in the morning and power-lunching in the af-

ternoon; fur-clad dowagers walk their dogs; homeless people hang out in the shade; mothers watch their kids play on the bronze goat and dip their feet in the reflecting pool. During the **May Flower Market**, the square is a rainbow-colored sea of petals and pollen. In spring, the **Clothesline Exhibit** transforms it into an enormous open-air gallery where artists pin up their work in the hope of catching a collector's eye.

Blast from the past: As you walk the perimeter of the square, it's not difficult to spot traces of the glory days. At 18th and Walnut streets, the **Fell-Van Rensselaer House**, one of the country's great Beaux Arts mansions, is currently occupied by clothier Urban Outfitters. Although much of the interior has been gutted, the ornate mantels, domed stained-glass skylight and the unusual ceiling portraits of the Roman Catholic popes (Mrs Fell, *née* Drexel, was a devout Catholic) are still intact. While you're on this corner, be sure to take a peek at the extraordinary Beaux Arts

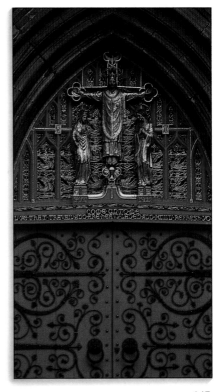

ceding es: above enhouse are. **Left**, sic ker. ht, St k's rch.

town house across 18th Street at No. 131, the former nutshell palace of the Baer family, which made its fortune as undertaker to the very wealthy.

Back to the square, the **Presbyterian Ministers' Fund**, the oldest life insurance company in the country, is housed in the dignified Alison Building. The well-fixed members of the exclusive **Rittenhouse Club** still keep a low profile at their private palace next door, despite talk of relocating or disbanding. And around the corner, John Notman's Romanesque **Church of the Holy Trinity**, once the city's most fashionable congregation, is overshadowed by the modern sawtooth profile of the **Rittenhouse Hotel**, where afternoon tea is a tradition at the cozy Cassatt Tea Room.

A row of Victorian town houses (including the home and private gallery of the late art collector Henry McIlhenny) still occupies the southwest corner of the square adjacent to the **Ethical Society**, a "humanist religious fellowship" that offers "Sunday platforms" on a

wide range of topics and issues. At the southeast corner, the posh **Barclay Hotel** is still a favorite among the Social Register crowd. And guests at the Barclay get an added treat: they are occasionally serenaded by the strains of Mozart, Bach and other composers that drift over from the **Curtis Institute of Music**, a world-renowned conservatory established by Mary Louise Curtis Bok Zimbalist, daughter of publishing magnate Cyrus Curtis. Among Curtis's well-known alumni are Leonard Bernstein, Gian-Carlo Menotti and Samuel Barber. Performances, including free student concerts, are held at the Curtis's lovely little concert hall.

A half-block away, the **Philadelphia Art Alliance** is housed in the grand old Wetherill mansion. Exhibits change about every six weeks and range freely over the spectrum of fine arts – painting, sculpture, crafts, photography, drawing – by well-known artists, unknowns, even children. Check with the Alliance for its published schedule of free readings, recitals, performances and lectures.

Moving east of the square, you'll find a bevy of smart shops on **Walnut Street**, including Rodier, Laura Ashley, Burberry and Ann Taylor. If you're a booklover, be sure to stop at Borders Book Shop (1727 Walnut Street), where you can browse through some 100,000 titles, sip a frothy cappuccino at the espresso bar, and maybe catch one of the first-rate authors who come here to read their work. The shopping continues around the corner on narrow **Sansom Street**, which, with its edgy attitude, basement shops, bookstores, little theaters and restaurants, is like a slice of New York's Greenwich Village.

The neighborhood also offers prime gallery-hopping. There are more than 20 galleries in the Rittenhouse Square area, and, like the galleries of Old City, they have banded together for **Second Saturday**, an artsy gala with lots of wine, cheese and highbrow chitchat held on the second Saturday of each month between December and June. And where

Petals and pollen brighten the square.

can you go for a post-gallery repast? There's a restaurant for just about every taste and budget in this neighborhood, but there's no matching Le Bec-Fin (1523 Walnut Street), one of the country's finest French restaurants, or Susanna Foo (1512 Walnut Street), cited by critics for consistently imaginative Chinese cuisine. Neither place is cheap, so be prepared.

A short jaunt south on 17th Street past the opulent **Warwick Hotel** brings you to Locust Street, where **St Mark's Church**, a Gothic Revival masterpiece designed by John Notman, has stood since 1851, when the area was first developing. The handsome buildings across the street, including the exclusive Locust Club, are the handiwork of several prominent architects, including Notman and Wilson Eyre. You can't miss the beautiful old **Cadwalader mansion** at No. 1602. It's now the Magnolia Café, a popular Cajun restaurant. The tree in front is decorated with hundreds of colorful mardi gras beads.

Continue south on 17th Street and detour into narrow Latimer Street, where you'll find changing exhibits of prints and photographs at the **Print Club**, founded in 1915. Be sure to check the gift shop for one-of-a-kind prints, stationery and handmade books. Latimer Street is occupied by a number of other well-known clubs, including the Cosmopolitan Club and the Pennsylvania Society of the Colonial Dames of America, and is a great place to peek into some of the lush gardens that are tended behind mansion walls.

Old bones: To the south of Rittenhouse Square, the neighborhood is largely residential, with an occasional florist, antique shop or doctor's office at street level. **Spruce Street** is the most interesting architecturally, with a fine row of brownstones between 20th and 21st streets, and extraordinary homes by Frank Furness (2132–34 Spruce Street and 235 S. 21st Street), Wilson Eyre (315–317 S. 22nd Street) and George Hewitt (2100 Spruce Street). The **Tenth**

Presbyterian Church, a combination of styles and materials, is a paragon of Victorian eclecticism, with a magnificently ornate iron gate and prominent bell tower. The extraordinary mansion behind the church was once owned by Harry K. Thaw, who, in a scandalous episode, shot his wife's lover, the distinguished New York architect Stanford White. It seems that White flaunted the affair by using Mrs Thaw as the model for his nude sculpture *Diana*, which once stood atop New York's old Madison Square Garden and is now housed at the Philadelphia Museum of Art.

A block away, at 18th and Spruce streets, **Temple Beth Zion-Beth Israel** is an imposing and picturesque structure built of a lustrous local stone.

The 2000 and 1800 blocks of **Delancey Place** – the quietest and most exclusive street in the neighborhood, if not the entire city – have long been associated with Philadelphia's oldest families. The genteel atmosphere makes a perfect setting for the **Rosenbach**

Museum (2010 Delancey Place), a collection of some 30,000 rare books, 275,000 manuscripts, and a houseful of art and antiques gathered by brothers Philip and A.S.W. Rosenbach, considered the foremost rare-book expert of his day. Tours are led by extremely knowledgeable house guides and are tailored to visitors' interests. If there is something special you would like to see, call a few days in advance and the curators will try to have it on display.

Exhibits change frequently, but highlights are likely to include original drawings by Honoré Daumier, William Blake and children's book author Maurice Sendak; 15th-century illuminated manuscripts of *The Canterbury Tales*; a page or two of James Joyce's handwritten draft of *Ulysses*; the *Bay Psalm Book* (first book printed in America); the only known first edition of *Poor Richard's Almanack*; and rare editions of Melville, Defoe, Carroll and countless others. Not to mention drafts of poetry by Ezra Pound, Wallace Stevens and Marianne

Gracious living on the square

Moore; letters by Cortéz, Pizarro, Franklin, Washington, Jefferson, Franklin Roosevelt and hundreds of others. Elsewhere on Delancey, you'll find the premises of **Plays and Players** (1714 Delancey), the city's oldest community theater group and an intimate venue for an evening of theater.

Another of Philadelphia's little-known jewels resides about two blocks away at 1805 Pine Street. It's the **Civil War Library and Museum** of the Military Order of the Loyal Legion of the United States, a three-story repository of Civil War artifacts, documents and paraphernalia, and a 12,000-volume library. Over the years, the Loyal Legion has accumulated hundreds of firearms, swords, broadsides, photographs and paintings as well as such curiosities as Ulysses S. Grant's death mask, a lock of Abraham Lincoln's hair, and the stuffed head of Major General George G. Meade's trusty war horse, Old Baldy, wounded five times in battle and now the museum's mascot.

To the west, **Pine Street** runs past town houses and shops to a tidy pocket park called **Fitler Square**. **Schuylkill River Park** – a pleasant little patch of trees and benches – is just two blocks beyond. Dubbed Judy Garland Park by local gays, it's become the source of some controversy as an after-hours rendezvous. If you're in the area, you can wander through some of the neighborhood's quiet alleyways. **Panama Street**, between 18th and 19th streets, is a tree-lined hideaway of ivy-covered homes (check out the magnificent Tudor conversion at No. 1920), and tiny Addison, Smedley and Croskey streets are worth exploring, too.

Head north on 22nd Street, turn right on Spruce Street and then left on Van Pelt, which is lined with imaginatively renovated carriage houses. Follow Van Pelt across Locust Street and pass through the archway into **English Village**, a hidden enclave of Tudor-style homes built around a flagstone plaza. Return to 22nd Street and continue north

past the rambling Gothic structure of the former **Swedenborgian Church** at the corner of Chestnut Street. A half-block away, at 22nd and Ludlow streets, is yet another of Philadelphia's little-known, and somewhat grisly, treasures: the **Mutter Museum**.

Founded in 1858 as a medical teaching aid, the Mutter Museum – housed at the College of Physicians of Philadelphia – is a collection of medical instruments, artifacts and specimens. This is not a museum for the faint of heart – "the thinking man's *Texas Chainsaw Massacre*," *Philadelphia Magazine* aptly put it. There are exhibits on technology – an early heart-lung machine, a collection of obstetrical instruments, and a doctor's office from the early 1900s, among other things – all fairly innocuous. And then there's the study of pathology. If you're the squeamish type, this is the time to head for the door.

There are graphic displays of just about every eye and skin disease one would care to imagine, a plaster cast made at the autopsy of Chang and Eng, the original Siamese twins, a mummified "Soap Lady" from the early 1800s, an ovarian cyst the size of a bowling ball, a ghastly display of fetal anomalies, a human horn (that's right, a horn), the skeleton of the so-called Kentucky giant, and a variety of organs, limbs and decapitated heads pickled in formaldehyde, including the brain of murderer John Wilson and the liver shared by Chang and Eng.

And if you think that's weird, how about hundreds of foreign objects (buttons, pins, bones and bullets, all neatly organized in a filing cabinet) that Dr Chevalier Jackson pulled from his patients' throats with a special device invented for the task, vesicles removed from Chief Justice John Marshall's bladder by renowned Philadelphia doctor Philip Syng Physick, a chunk of John Wilkes Booth's thorax, and a tumor removed from President Grover Cleveland's jaw during a secret operation performed aboard a yacht.

Street-corner cuisine.

Pretzel Logic

A pretzel is more than a twisted biscuit, it is a storied knot of dough – as much a part of Philadelphia gastronomy as cheesesteaks, scrapple, water ice and hoagies.

Its pedigree stretches all the way back to 7th-century France. While preparing unleavened bread for Lent, a French monk twisted scraps of dough into a shape resembling arms crossed in prayer. The tasty twists were given to children as a reward for learning their prayers. Hence the Latin name *pretiola*, meaning "little gifts or prayers," or perhaps *brachiola*, "little arms." By and by, German bakers got the knack of the doughy delights, which they dubbed *brezel*. By the time German-speaking immigrants settled the countryside outside Philadelphia, they were more commonly known as pretzels.

While it was the Pennsylvania Dutch who brought pretzel-making to the New World (Lancaster County is still known as the "Pretzel Basket of America"), it was, in the words of one journalist, "Philadelphia who civilized it and made it into a household pet." At last count there were about 10 pretzel bakeries in the metropolitan area, turning out, by a conservative estimate, more than a million pretzels daily.

You can't walk far in Philadelphia without bumping into a pretzel cart, or hearing the call of a roaming vendor – "Pretzels, four for a dollar." "In Philadelphia, pretzels are a staple," says Edward Ermilio, owner of Northeast Soft Pretzel in Tacony. "You see people run up to a cart, grab a pretzel and then go about their business." Mind you, these are soft pretzels, the pliant, doughy variety with shiny salt-kissed skins usually smeared with mustard – quite different from the crusty, crunchy hard tack you're likely to find at the supermarket. Ermilio turns out about 20,000 pretzels a day, all hand-twisted. A first-class pretzel-bender, he says, can twist 800 pretzels an hour – 13 per minute. The world record is said to be 57 a minute.

How to tell a good pretzel from the mediocre? "What you want to look for is a golden-brown color, freshness, and the proper amount of salt," says Thomas Conley, baker at the Philadelphia Pretzel Museum (312 Market Street), where aficionados can bone up on the history, lore and traditions of the "Wonderful World of Pretzels." Conley's recipe turns out a puffy, bagel-like concoction that comes in a variety of shapes and sizes – nuggets, braids, hearts and rings, most hand-twisted – as well as the standard pretzel knot.

Pretzel paramours might also seek out Fisher's Pretzels at the Reading Terminal Market, where Amish girls twist foot-long strands of dough with a flick of the wrist. The finished product is less salty and a bit firmer than Conley's, but always served hot from the oven and drenched in butter.

Fresh pretzels are not only delicious, they're good for you (OK, so butter and salt aren't exactly health foods). They're low in calories, and almost fat-free. They are said to prevent motion sickness, nausea and bed-wetting in young children, and, according to a doctor's report published in the *Reading Times* in 1927, they "prevent constipation," strengthen the "power of the teeth," and "increase the flow of the digestive fluids." ∎

ly's
:eries
1 out
:e
1 a
lion
:zels
ay.

CITY HALL AND DOWNTOWN

They started working on it back in 1871, it took no less than 30 years to complete, and about halfway through the project somebody tagged it "the biggest and ugliest building in America."

City Hall, at once monstrous and magnificent, sits squarely on the bull's-eye of downtown Philadelphia like an urban version of some inscrutable Egyptian pyramid, evoking ambivalent awe. Walt Whitman sized it up as "a magnificent pile… weird, silent, beautiful," and the American Institute of Architecture later pronounced it "the greatest single effort of late 19th-century architecture."

Love it or hate it, you'll find it hard to ignore this endearing hangover from the gaudy age of architectural excess. It stands right in the heart of center city, at Broad and Market streets, former site of William Penn's eight-acre Centre Square. To the west is Philadelphia's business district, bristling with a fresh wave of glass-and-granite skyscrapers. To the east is a cavernous new convention center and the city's largest shopping area. And to the north and south are some of the city's finest cultural institutions, including the oldest opera house and art school-museum in America.

Designed by John McArthur and Thomas U. Walter, and adorned with hundreds of sculptures by Alexander Milne Calder, Philadelphia's **City Hall** is the largest municipal building in the country. Its style is classified as French Empire, whatever that means – a puffed-up sense of optimism, perhaps, that bespeaks the American romance with Victorian architecture in the latter part of the 19th century. Its massive granite walls are 22 feet thick at the base, and its central tower, the world's tallest masonry structure without steel reinforcement, rises 510 feet above street level – and Calder's famous 27-ton statue of William Penn adds another 37 feet. Until recently, a gentlemen's agreement prevented the construction of any building whose height would exceed the top of William Penn's hat, but with modern skyscrapers shooting up on Market Street, such niceties have quickly fallen by the wayside.

The observation deck atop **City Hall Tower** is just below William Penn's toes, and though it is no longer the highest point in the city, the view is still breathtaking. To reach the **observation deck**, take the elevator from the northwest corner (15th Street and Kennedy Boulevard) to the seventh floor and then follow the red lines. A second elevator takes you the rest of the way. But be prepared to wait. During peak season and weekends, it can take an hour or more before you get lifted into the heavens. If you'd like a closer look at some of City Hall's splendid public rooms, a free one-hour tour is offered weekdays at 12.30pm. It includes, among other sights, Conservation Hall, the City Council Chambers, the Supreme Court, and the Mayor's Reception Room.

eceding
ges:
erty Place
vers over
Benjamin
anklin
rkway.
t, inside
y Hall.
ght,
ristmas on
oad Street.

The imposing medieval-style building to the north of City Hall is **Masonic Hall**, headquarters of the Right Worshipful Grand Lodge of Free and Accepted Masons of Pennsylvania and one of the most spectacular Masonic structures in the world. Designed in 1868 by 27-year-old James Windrim, the building is a monumental patchwork of architectural styles. A free tour guides visitors through seven lavishly decorated lodge halls, each reflecting a major architectural style – Oriental, Gothic, Ionic, Egyptian, Norman, Renaissance and Corinthian. The scale of the place is dazzling, the workmanship is masterful, and the Masons' predilection for arcane symbols is evident just about everywhere in the building.

The tour ends at the **Masonic Museum**, which features all sorts of Masonic paraphernalia, much of it owned by historic figures like the Marquis de Lafayette, Andrew Jackson, Ben Franklin and George Washington.

Walk north on Broad Street past the

Gothic spires of the **Arch Street Methodist Church**, erected in 1868, to the **Pennsylvania Academy of the Fine Arts**, the oldest art school and museum in the country. Frank Furness's Victorian *tour de force* is as much a work of art as the paintings it contains (*see picture on page 74*). Highly eclectic and idiosyncratic, this building is a fine example of the stylistic mix-and-match that became Furness's hallmark. The interior is a riotous counterpoint of deep-blue ceilings, red-veined marble floors, Moorish arcades, gilt accents and purplish walls with a gold floral pattern. You might expect the building to overpower the art, but it doesn't. That's because the Academy of Fine Arts owns one of the strongest collections of early-American art in the country.

Exhibitions change regularly, but you're likely to find work by Charles Willson Peale, Benjamin West, Gilbert Stuart, Washington Allston, Mary Cassatt, Winslow Homer, Andrew Wyeth and the Academy's most celebrated student and teacher, Thomas Eakins, who was dismissed from the faculty for his insistence on using female nude models in a class that included women. The Academy also shows contemporary work, much of it by students or faculty, particularly in the first-floor Morris Gallery. Call ahead for details on gallery talks, receptions and daily tours.

Avenue of the Arts: Retrace your steps to City Hall, looping around 15th Street for a look at downtown's best-known (if not best-loved) public sculptures, including Joseph Brown's *Benjamin Franklin, Craftsman*, Jacques Lipchitz's *Government of the People*, Claes Oldenburg's colossal *Clothespin*, and Robert Engman's pretzel-like *Triune*. Much of the artwork in this area is a product of Philadelphia's 1-percent rule, which earmarks a fraction of municipal construction costs for public art.

Heading south on Broad Street, you'll pass the domed neoclassical **Girard Trust Company** (now Mellon PSFS), a

Reflection
William Pe
statue ato
City Hall.

loose adaptation of the Roman Parthenon designed by Stanford White and Frank Furness. The **Land Title Building**, an early skyscraper built in 1897, is on the next corner. And the **Union League** (1865) – a private club organized by well-to-do patriots during the Civil War – is housed in a majestic Second Empire mansion with a sweeping double staircase at the corner of Sansom Street.

A block away, the venerable old Bellevue-Stratford Hotel has been re-born as the **Hotel Atop the Bellevue**. After a multimillion-dollar face-lift, the lower levels have been converted into high-class retail space where a handful of upscale stores like Ralph Lauren's Polo, Gucci, Rizzoli bookstore and Tiffany & Co. do business in marble and mahogany digs.

The hotel also accommodates several fine restaurants including **The Palm**, a fancy steak house known for gargantuan slabs of beef and high-profile clientele (including the late Frank Rizzo), and on the top floor, Founders, sky-high and ultra-elegant with thrilling views of center city.

Opened in 1857, the **Academy of Music**, at Broad and Locust streets, is the oldest concert hall in America still in use. Designed by Napoleon Le Brun and Gustave Runge, and renowned for its fine acoustics, the Academy has welcomed a host of famous speakers and musicians, including Abraham Lincoln, Tchaikovsky, and former conductors of the Philadelphia Orchestra, among them Leopold Stokowski, Eugene Ormandy and Riccardo Muti. After years of prodding, plans are now underway to move the orchestra to a new $95-million Orchestra Hall at Spruce and Broad streets.

Orchestra Hall will be one of the major new players on South Broad Street now known as the **Avenue of the Arts**. The **Wilma Theater** (currently at 2030 Sansom Street) is also planning to relocate to Broad and Spruce. The new halls will be joining the **Arts Bank**, which offers theater and rehearsal space in a renovated bank; the **Merriam Theater**, which features Broadway shows, concerts, opera, pop music and the Pennsylvania Ballet and Pennsylvania Opera Theater; and the **University of the Arts**, which is housed in one of John Haviland's stark Greek Revival structures at Pine and Broad streets. The school shows work by faculty, students and guest artists in the main hall and at the Rosenwald-Wolf and Mednick galleries across the street.

Corporate muscle: Big changes have been made in the business district west of City Hall, too. A fresh crop of office towers on Market Street is pumping new vigor into an area that hasn't seen much action since the early 1960s, when the **Penn Center** complex rose from the ruins of the old Chinese Wall. The twin towers of I.M. Pei's **Commerce Square** at 20th and Market streets, site of the snazzy Cutter's Grand Café, and the granite-and-glass towers of both the **Mellon Bank Center** and **1919 Market Street** are among the most con-

es
lenburg's
ossal
thespin.

spicuous additions to the skyline. But the real head-turner is **Liberty Place** (17th and Market), a pair of glass-plated towers designed in a sort of neo-Art Deco style reminiscent of New York City's Chrysler Building.

The two-level shopping arcade at **Two Liberty Place** is a welcome newcomer, with lots of polished marble tile, shiny brass trim and a sunlit central rotunda. The shops and eateries are predictably trendy, although Sfuzzi, a swank Italian restaurant and bar, and the Rand McNally travel bookstore are worth a special look.

You can watch the wheels of capitalism turn two blocks away at the **Philadelphia Stock Exchange**, the oldest in America. The trading floor is built around a sunny eight-story atrium where visitors can follow the action through plate-glass windows while lounging in a small forest complete with waterfalls, fountains and thousands of plants.

Market East: To the east of City Hall, Market Street is dominated by discount shops and department stores. The granddaddy of them all is the former **John Wanamaker**, a Philadelphia institution since the 1870s, when department-store pioneer John Wanamaker moved his first dry-goods shop into the old Pennsylvania Railroad depot. Alas, Wanamaker was sold in 1995 and renamed **Hecht's**.

The current building was completed in 1911 and features a magnificent five-story **Grand Court** where Wanamaker's old mascot, a giant bronze eagle, keeps an eye on shoppers queuing up at the gourmet counter. The airy Grand Court is the site of spectacular Christmas light shows and a great place to stroll during the daily organ concerts, performed on a 30,000-pipe organ – said to be the largest in the world. The fate of the organ under new ownership remains uncertain, however.

St John the Evangelist Church is located around the corner on 13th Street. Built in 1832, it was the second Roman Catholic cathedral in Philadelphia. A

Philadelph Stock Exchange, the oldest America.

block away, at 12th and Market, the **PSFS Building** (1930–32) – best-known for its giant neon sign – was the first American skyscraper to be built in the International style, forerunner of the glass-skinned monoliths that sprang up in the 1950s and '60s.

The shopping then picks up again at **The Gallery**, a three-block mall stretching from 11th to 8th streets with three major department stores and some 200 shops and restaurants set in an airy, skylit atrium. Between 8th and 7th streets, the old Lit Brothers Department Store – a beautiful white cast-iron structure – has been transformed into **Market Place East**, a mixed-use complex of shops, restaurants and offices (*see page 113 for details*). You'll find even more shopping opportunities a block away on Chestnut Street, which is closed to all traffic except buses between 18th and 6th streets.

Big changes are under way north of Market Street, too. The $523 million **Pennsylvania Convention Center**, encompassing 1.3 million square feet, recently opened at 13th and 11th streets. The new facility encompasses **Reading Terminal Market**, a boisterous food bazaar housed in a 100-year-old train shed where vendors offer a bewildering array of everything from sushi to scrapple, bok choy to baclava. In addition to fresh produce, meats and seafood, you'll find a slew of Philadelphia specialties: chocolate-chip cookies from the Famous 4th Street Deli, cheesesteaks from Olivieri's (owners of Pat's King of Steaks), Bassetts' irresistible ice cream and Termini Brothers' scrumptious Italian pastries – not to mention hearty meats, sweets and baked goods brought to Philadelphia by members of the Pennsylvania Dutch community.

And that's only the beginning. In the mood for seafood? Try Pearl's Oyster Bar. Fancy a blue-corn enchilada? Have a bite at the 12th Street Cantina. How about an ice-cold brew at the Beer Garden? Rib-sticking Southern cuisine at the Down Home Diner? Scrapple and

pping at Gallery.

eggs at the Dutch Eating Place? And be sure to save enough room for one of Fisher's famous pretzels – soft, warm and smothered in butter.

If you're still hungry, drift over to **Chinatown**, where about 45 restaurants are packed between 9th and 11th streets on one side, and Vine and Arch streets on the other. Nearly all are Chinese, of course, but there are also excellent Vietnamese and Thai places, and most are reasonably priced. Gift shops and grocery stores carry a bonanza of exotic Asian goodies. You can stock up on fortune cookies at the Chinese Cookie Factory, Chinese pastries at Diamond Bakery (232 N. 10th Street), or Chinese noodles at the East Asia Noodle Company (212 N. 11th Street) and New Tung Hop (133 N. 11th Street).

While you're in the neighborhood, be sure to see the 40-foot **Chinese Friendship Gate** at 10th and Arch streets, built by craftsmen in 1984 as a sign of friendship between Philadelphia and Tianjin. The **Chinese Cultural and Community Center** (125 N. 10th Street) is also worth a look. The building is modeled after a Mandarin palace and is the site of a traditional 10-course banquet in celebration of the Chinese New Year. Call the center for reservations.

If all this walking is making your feet hurt, pay tribute to the traveler's best friends – your feet! – at the Pennsylvania College of Podiatry's **Shoe Museum**. This modest but lovingly-tended collection is a testimony to the cobbler's art. There are exotic shoes (3-inch slippers for the bound feet of aristocratic Chinese women, Egyptian burial sandals), historic shoes (black pumps worn by Nancy Reagan, loafers worn by husband Ron, and other First-Lady footwear), sports shoes (Reggie Jackson's baseball cleats, Julius "Dr J" Erving's enormous basketball sneakers), celebrity shoes (Lucille Ball's pink dancing shoes), and a fascinating look at "Footwear Through the Ages." Visitors are welcome on Wednesday and Friday. Call ahead to make an appointment.

The Chinese Friendship Gate in Chinatown

WILLIAM PENN

Like some benevolent *padrone*, William Penn has perched serenely atop City Hall since 1894, overseeing the real estate he acquired in 1681 from Charles II in satisfaction of a debt the king owed Penn *père*. But if this statue – 37 feet tall, 547 feet above ground – strikes the visitor as precarious, it is an apt impression: Penn's grip on Philadelphia was never too firm. Who owned what, how the place was to be governed, theological hairsplitting that pitted Quaker against Anglican and Quaker against Quaker – it was at times an unbrotherly stew that mired the affairs of the Founder, who didn't spend all that much time here anyway.

Turmoil was nothing new to Penn. He lived through civil strife and regicide, fire and plague. Born in 1644 in London, he was sufficiently nonconformist (after embracing Quakerism, he was expelled from Oxford) to merit Admiral Penn's dispatching his upstart son on a Continental tour. But Quakerism stuck with young Penn, providing the touchstone for his utopian designs on Pennsylvania.

A religious liberal, Penn preached and pamphleteered and got into familial and civil hot water. Confined to the Tower of London for a spell, he churned out more tracts in prison. In 1672, he married Gulielma Maria Springett, who was pregnant eight times in their first 13 years of marriage. She died in Penn's arms in 1694. Two years later he married another Quaker, 24-year-old Hannah Callowhill, begetting seven children by her.

Penn first visited his colony in 1682, just after his 38th birthday. He had promoted it so well that a couple of thousand settlers were already on hand to greet him. Penn named Philadelphia and shaped its block pattern along orderly grid lines, did land deals with the Indians, and went back to England in 1684. He returned for his second, and final, visit 15 years later.

Although remembered for his tolerant leanings, Penn had his complexities. The freeholding aspirations of his settlers, for instance, clashed with his own seigneurial impulse. Although he insisted on fair-dealing with Indians, he regarded them as little more than noble savages. While Quakers were among the earliest to denounce slavery, Penn himself was a slaveholder. And yet, for all this, Penn's "holy experiment" laid the foundation for America's first melting pot, predating by nearly a century Jefferson's declaration that "all men are created equal."

From the very beginning, however, Penn was vexed by changing political and economic fortunes. Mired in debt, he considered selling the burgeoning colony back to the British crown in 1712 for less than its original value, but the deal was dropped when he suffered a stroke. It would take another 64 years and a revolution to bring an end to the Penn arrangement.

The statue atop City Hall of this English Quaker, crafted by Scottish-born Alexander Calder, adorns a French Renaissance-style building presided over by a succession of hyphenated Americans tending the affairs of a polyglot community. The city is the legacy of a man who, with mixed emotions, took his final leave of it in 1701. In all, Penn had spent less than four years in Pennsylvania. ∎

ng
liam
n.

MUSEUM DISTRICT AND FAIRMOUNT PARK

Philadelphia's museum district is located along **Benjamin Franklin Parkway**, a grand European-style boulevard that runs from City Hall to the Philadelphia Museum of Art, urging travelers toward the bucolic spaces of Fairmount Park. This is Philadelphia's Champs Élysées, a bold swath through William Penn's orderly street grid adorned with fountains, flags, flower beds and more than 25 outdoor sculptures.

Designed by French-born architects Jacques Greber and Paul Philippe Cret – exponents of the City Beautiful movement of the early 1900s – the Parkway was conceived as a sign of civic maturity, a declaration that the Quaker City had shed her mundane persona and was poised to take on the trappings of a great urban center.

The Parkway starts at **John F. Kennedy Plaza**, a favorite spot for people lunching outdoors. The plaza, adjacent to City Hall, is the site of Robert Indiana's word-sculpture *Philadelphia LOVE*, said to be "the most plagiarized piece of artwork in the country." (*See pic on page 77.*) The mushroom-shaped building at the corner of 16th Street is the **Philadelphia Visitors Center**, where maps and brochures are available and tourists can purchase tickets for a variety of events.

Mind games: From JFK Plaza, it's a 10-minute walk to **Logan Square**, one of William Penn's original town plazas, now girdled by a busy traffic circle. Originally the site of a cemetery and gallows, old Northwest Square was renamed in 1825 in honor of James Logan, who had come to Pennsylvania as William Penn's secretary. Logan was not only a first-rate businessman – he made a killing in the fur trade and in real estate – but a man of uncommon learning. His personal library was one of the most extensive in the colonies and is now maintained by the Library Company of Philadelphia. At the center of Logan Square is **Swann Memorial Fountain**, an evocative rendering of three reclining nudes (representing Philadelphia's three rivers – the Delaware, Schuylkill and Wissahickon) executed by Alexander Stirling Calder. His father, Alexander Milne Calder, sculpted the statue of William Penn atop City Hall. Stirling Calder's son, Alexander Calder, continues the tradition. His mobile, *Ghost*, hangs in the Museum of Art, and local wits have said this makes the Calder family the Father, Son and Holy Ghost of the Parkway.

On the east side of the square is the **Cathedral of Saints Peter and Paul**, a venerable Italian Renaissance structure designed by Napoleon Le Brun and John Notman. Begun in 1846 when Logan Square was still on the outskirts of town, the cathedral is one of the only major buildings on the square that predates the Parkway. The twin neoclassical structures on the north side of the square are the **Free Library of Philadelphia** and

eceding ges: the **iseum of t. Left, peye ats down e Parkway. ght,** *The inker* at e Rodin **iseum.**

Municipal Court, built between 1917 and 1927 and modeled after matching palaces on the Place de la Concorde in Paris. Bibliophiles should check for special exhibits at the library's Rare Book Department as well as an excellent collection of Dickens memorabilia at the William Elkins Library.

Walk clockwise around the square to the **Franklin Institute**, one of the premier science museums in the country. With acres of exhibit space and hundreds of interactive displays, the institute is a playground for the mind. Everywhere you turn, there's something to touch, explore, discover or play with. The **Science Center** is the core of the museum, covering ecology, aviation, astronomy, physics, mathematics and just about everything else of interest to young, budding Einsteins. Walk through a giant heart, climb into a jet fighter, "freeze" your shadow, have a look at "liquid air," and see how a four-story Foucault's pendulum demonstrates the Earth's rotation. At the **Mandell Fu-**

tures Center**, visitors can explore the trends and technologies that will shape the 21st century. Walk into an immune cell, design a futuristic car with a touch-screen computer, step aboard a space station, and teach a computer how to play tick-tack-toe.

Don't miss the **Tuttleman Omniverse Theater**, which shows spectacular 70mm films on a four-story domed screen. And if you've got the time, go stargazing at the state-of-the-art **Fels Planetarium**. The institute is also home to the **Benjamin Franklin National Memorial** (free admission), which, in addition to a fascinating collection of Frankliniana, features an enormous marble statue of the institute's namesake and inspiration.

Around the square, past the ground-floor galleries of the **Moore College of Art**, is the **Academy of Natural Sciences**. If you're a bit lost, just look for a pair of bronze dinosaurs near the entrance. They were installed in 1987 as part of the Academy's efforts to update its image. Founded in 1812, the Academy is the nation's oldest museum of natural history and has striven in recent years to modernize its exhibits. The "Discovering Dinosaurs" exhibit has been thoroughly reworked in order to incorporate the latest thinking about the prehistoric beasts, and a video display has been added to explore the role of "Dinosaurs in the Movies."

Space for the Academy's excellent temporary exhibits has also been renovated. The rest of the Academy is dedicated to traditional wildlife dioramas, covering animals around the world. There's also an impressive gem collection, an Egyptian mummy, and Outside/In, a hands-on learning center where kids can explore local habitats, examine fossils and handle live animals.

Child's play: If you're traveling with young children, be sure to put the **Please Touch Museum** on your list, the first museum in the country dedicated to kids aged seven years and younger. Located behind the Franklin Institute near

The
Cathedral o
Saints Pete
and Paul.

the corner of 21st and Race streets, this former warehouse has been transformed into a three-story romper room where kids can let their imagination run wild. Children can make fairy tales come to life, crawl inside a giant Space Geode, see themselves on television, get behind the wheel of a bus, and much more. The Education Store carries all sorts of nifty items for busy hands and inquisitive minds and is a great place to shop for the kids back home.

While you're in the neighborhood, make a short detour to **St Clement's Episcopal Church** (Cherry and 20th streets), a picturesque brownstone structure designed by John Notman in 1855. About four blocks away, the **Arch Street Presbyterian Church** (18th and Arch streets) is also worth a look. Built in 1855, the church is a harmonious blend of styles brought together with massive Corinthian columns, copper dome and cheerful orange trim. Be sure to step inside; the interior is a study in classical proportion.

Across the street, the splendid **Bell Atlantic Tower** steps skyward in a cascading series of setbacks. Its spiffy neighbors – **One** and **Two Logan Square** – are worth a look, too. Parched travelers may want to stop at the Dock Street Brewery and Restaurant at Two Logan Square for a Philadelphia hometown brew. A block away, the **Cigna Corporation** (17th and Arch streets) displays antique fire engines, pumpers, fire marks and other firefighting apparatus in the lobby of its office tower.

Back on the Parkway, just past Logan Square, the twin pylons of the **Civil War Soldiers and Sailors Memorial** stand sentinel on either side of the boulevard, acting as a gateway to the Philadelphia Museum of Art. A block farther, the **Rodin Museum** is an island of tranquility behind an elegant portal, a replica of the gateway Rodin constructed for his own home. Given to the city by movie-house mogul Jules Mastbaum, who commissioned Paul Cret and Jacques Greber to design the building,

the museum houses the largest collection of Rodin's work outside France, including *The Thinker*, *The Gates of Hell* and *The Burghers of Calais*.

The Rodin Museum is administered by the **Philadelphia Museum of Art**, which stands like a modern-day acropolis atop Faire Mount, its monumental staircase (the same stairs on which Sylvester Stallone made his triumphant trot in the wildly popular film *Rocky*) inviting visitors into the cavernous lobby. At the heart of the museum is an extensive collection of European art.

On the first floor, the John Johnson collection features European paintings from the 14th to 19th century with highlights like Van der Wyden's *Crucifixion with Virgin and St John* and Van Eyck's *Saint Francis Receiving the Stigmata*. European holdings are fleshed out on the second floor, starting with a fine medieval collection, which features a 12th-century French abbey, through to Peter Paul Rubens's *Prometheus Bound*, Poussin's *The Birth of Venus*, Renoir's

njamin anklin tional morial.

The Bathers and Van Gogh's *Sunflowers*, not to mention works by Rousseau, Monet, Gauguin, Manet and other latter-day masters. Elsewhere in the museum, an entire wing dedicated to 20th-century art traces the influence of innovators like Picasso, Klee, Brancusi and Duchamp on the postwar work of Warhol, Oldenburg, Johns, Stella and others. A renowned American collection features the work of Pennsylvania Dutch and Shaker craftsmen, period rooms, and well-known Philadelphia painters such as Charles Wilson Peale, Thomas Eakins and Mary Cassatt.

A 16th-century Hindu temple and Japanese teahouse are but a few of the treasures in the Asian wing. A fascinating gallery of arms and armor details the extraordinary talents of Renaissance metalworkers, and an excellent photography exhibit features the work of Alfred Stieglitz. It's impossible to see everything in a single visit, so be selective. A good way to start is to join one of the free hourly gallery tours or a "spotlight" tour of a particular work or artist. Check the schedule for films and lectures. And visit the museum shop for the city's best collection of art books.

Into the woods: The museum's backyard is the **Azalea Garden**, a four-acre bouquet of azaleas, rhododendrons and magnolias that opens on to Fairmount Park. Spreading over 8,000 acres on both sides of the Schuylkill River, **Fairmount Park** is the largest municipal park in the country, with 100 miles of hiking trails and bridle paths, 3 million trees, hundreds of statues, 105 tennis courts, 73 baseball fields, 6 pools, 6 golf courses, amphitheaters, a zoo and more than 20 historic homes, most of them built in the late 1700s. The park is so large, it's necessary to drive or take the **Fairmount Park trolley-bus**, which departs from the JFK Plaza visitors center every 20 minutes most days of the week. The trolley-bus makes regular stops along the 17-mile loop.

If you're walking, you can wander down to the **Fairmount Waterworks**

Fairmount Park is the largest municipal park in the country.

(1812–15), a glorious old pumping station that looks like a cluster of Greek temples perched on the river's edge, and then follow the river path to **Boathouse Row**, home to the sculling clubs that make up the so-called Schuylkill Navy. It's a five-minute walk beyond the boathouses to the **Samuel Memorial**, a terraced sculpture garden featuring the work of several artists, including Jacques Lipchitz and Waldemar Raemisch.

If you plan to remain on foot, you can continue along the river or take Lemon Hill Drive to **Lemon Hill**, the only historic home within walking distance of the museum. The property was originally owned by Revolutionary financier Robert Morris until he ran afoul of his creditors and landed in debtor's prison. Henry Pratt bought the estate at a sheriff's sale and built the present house in 1800. Named after Pratt's hothouse lemon trees, the property is a particularly graceful example of Federal design with large, lacy fanlights, unusual oval parlors overlooking the river, and a fine collection of period furnishings. Lemon Hill is supposed to be open Wednesday through Sunday, but, as with other houses on this tour, hours occasionally change. It's best to check ahead.

From Lemon Hill, it's a short drive along the river (turn at the Grant Monument) to **Mount Pleasant**, a majestic Georgian mansion constructed in 1761 by Scottish sea captain John Macpherson, who made his fortune as a "privateer" – a pirate in service of the monarch – a line of work that cost him an arm. A tireless entrepreneur, Macpherson occupied his later years as a farmer, publisher and inventor of a "vermin-proof bed." In 1779, Benedict Arnold bought the house for his bride, Peggy Shippen, but was convicted of treason before either could move in. Described by John Adams as "the most elegant seat in Pennsylvania," Mount Pleasant remains a masterpiece of Georgian style, with beautifully restored woodwork, Chippendale furniture, portraits by Benjamin West and Charles Willson Peale, and a lush rear garden.

You'll pass more modest **Rockland** (built in 1810) and **Ormiston** (1798) along the curvy road to **Laurel Hill**, a pretty summer estate built in 1760 with additions on either side. Farther along the loop, **Woodford** is a stately Georgian manor house built in 1756 by William Coleman, a member of Franklin's Junto, and later occupied by David Franks, who turned the house into a center of Tory activity during the British occupation. Home of the Naomi Wood collection of American antiques, Woodford is brimming with 18th-century furnishings, including scores of household items like foot warmers, wind harps, wick trimmers, even a bookcase filled with antique volumes.

Nearby, **Strawberry Mansion** was built in two stages: the central section in 1798 and the matching wings in the 1820s. The largest house in the park, Strawberry Mansion got its name in the 1840s when strawberries and cream were served to visitors. Today, the house is

Fairmount Park

1.5 miles / 2.4 km

East Falls
Cresson St.
Henry St.
Ridge Av.
Schuylkill Expressway
Roosevelt Expressway
Cynwyd
City Avenue
River Park
Monument Rd
Hunting Park Av.
Belmont Avenue
West Park
Chamounix Drive
Laurel Hill Cemetery
Paradise
ula
FAIRMOUNT PARK
Strawberry Mansion
Huntingdon St.
Cumberland St.
ynnefield Av.
Belmont Mansion
Schuylkill River
Woodford Mansion
33rd Street
Vynnefield
Mann Music Centre
Horticultural Center
East Park Reservoir
Sedgley Av.
Glenwood Av.
Japanese House
Cedar Grove
Mt. Pleasant
Memorial Hall
Sweetbriar Mansion
Letitia St. House
Jefferson St.
llestonville
Lancaster Av.
Solitude
40th Street
34th Street
Boat House Row
Lemon Hill Mansion
Fairmount
Vestminster Av.
Zoo
Azalea Garden
Brown
Street
Mantua
Fairmount Av.
Baring
Museum of Art
53rd Street
Haverford Av.
Powelton Village
Market Street
Powelton Av.

fully restored with a variety of period furnishings, including an attic filled with antique toys and knick knacks.

Before heading across Strawberry Bridge, you may want to detour to **Laurel Hill Cemetery**, a sprawling Victorian necropolis with elaborate monuments and temples designed by the best architects of the day. Graveyards aren't much of an attraction these days, but in the 19th century a day at the cemetery was considered quite an outing. The house tour continues on the west side of the Schuylkill River at **Belmont Mansion**, which was built about 1743. Closer to the river, **Boelson Cottage**, built in the 1680s, is the oldest structure in Fairmount Park and possibly the oldest surviving house in Pennsylvania.

About a mile away, the **Horticultural Center** contains a greenhouse complex, a fine 22-acre arboretum, and **Japanese House**, a replica of a 16th-century Japanese home sequestered behind a lovely walled garden. Guides are available to show you around, and tea ceremonies are occasionally conducted.

The huge green dome you see looming over the trees belongs to **Memorial Hall**, a monumental exhibit hall built in 1875 for the Centennial Fair and one of only two buildings that remain from the celebration. The other is **Ohio Hall**, a modest Victorian structure made out of Ohio stone located about a mile away at States Drive and Belmont Avenue. Both buildings are now used for office space, but visitors are welcome to view Memorial Hall's breathtaking central hall.

Exiting from the rear of Memorial Hall, it's a short way on North Concourse Drive through the twin spires of the **Smith Civil War Memorial** to two very different historic homes. **Cedar Grove**, a fieldstone farmhouse built in 1745 and moved stone by stone from its original Northern Liberties site, is a fine example of rustic Quaker simplicity. A short walk away, **Sweetbriar** is a refined Federal manse built in 1793 as a sanctuary from the yellow-fever epidemics sweeping the city.

The last stop on the tour is yet another Philadelphia first. Opened in 1874, the **Philadelphia Zoological Gardens** is the oldest zoo in the whole of America. The 42-acre site is home to nearly 2,000 animals, many in recreated habitats. Major exhibits include the 5-acre African Plains, free-flying Jungle Bird Walk, Bear Country, World of Primates, and Children's Zoo. Special exhibits featuring particularly rare or exotic species are brought in each season. To get an overview of the park, try the elevated **Monorail** Safari, which gives riders a bird's-eye view right along the mile-long track.

While at the zoo, keep your eyes peeled for two other historic houses. **Solitude**, a sturdy country house built by William Penn's grandson in 1785, is on the zoo grounds. **Letitia Street House,** a tidy colonial bandbox built in 1715, is hidden behind hedges across 34th Street. Originally located on the Delaware waterfront, it was moved from the site in 1883 on the mistaken belief that William Penn had built the house for his daughter Letitia. Both houses are closed to the public.

Finally, if you're looking for a quiet getaway, head for **Wissahickon Creek** in the upper reaches of the park. **Forbidden Drive** – a gravel path prohibited to motor vehicles – provides miles of hiking, biking and horseback riding along the stunning **Wissahickon gorge**.

Keep your eyes peeled for the Thomas Mill Covered Bridge, America's only covered bridge within city limits. **Rittenhouse Town**, a cluster of stone buildings dating from the 1690s, is located near a trailhead on Lincoln Drive. Originally a paper mill town, the old village includes the birthplace of Philadelphia clockmaker-astronomer David Rittenhouse, for whom Rittenhouse Square is named.

Lunch or dinner at the **Valley Green Inn**, a lovely 19th-century restaurant overlooking the creek, is a wonderful way to start, or finish, an afternoon in this near-urban wilderness.

Philadelphia Zoo's feathered friends.

UNIVERSITY CITY

The saga of the **University of Pennsylvania** begins in 1740 with the campaign for a Charity School at 4th and Arch streets "for the instruction of Poor Children Gratis… and also for a House of Publick worship." Unfortunately, the school never did get solidly off the ground, financially speaking, and a few years later the ubiquitous Benjamin Franklin stepped in to spearhead a drive to transform the benevolent school into a less secular, more public-oriented institution. The Academy that was founded evolved into the College of Philadelphia and then into the nation's first university in 1779; it shifted its place of operations in 1802 to 9th Street, between Chestnut and Market.

This second home sufficed for seven decades, until a new provost took over and denounced the location as a "vile neighborhood, growing viler every day" – fashionable Philadelphians had already begun abandoning center city and heading west. And so did the university. "Penn" shifted its campus across the Schuylkill River to the west bank, some 15 blocks from the paternal glance of William Penn atop City Hall. Construction of a permanent bridge in 1805 had opened the way to easier access from the east, but it was the university's relocation that quickened the developmental pace. And in 1892, the founding of what became Drexel University nearby gave impetus to the designation of the area as University City.

School spirit: A walk through the neighborhood, following a roughly circular route, discloses much of the area's character – the cloistered campus, ivy-covered halls, exuberant collegiate atmosphere, grand Victorian architecture, and ethnic and racial diversity – a bit like a little college town surrounded by the city. The boundaries of the neighborhood run roughly from the Schuylkill River to 45th Street and from

Baltimore Avenue to Market Street. Here, as in center city, the sreets are laid out in a grid, making finding your way fairly simple.

The **30th Street Station** on Market Street, which can be reached by any SEPTA (Southeastern Pennsylvania Transportation Authority) subway-surface trolley or Market Street subway train (or, for the energetic, by a stroll across the river from center city), acts like a sort of reception hall for University City. Occupying nearly a full city block, the station, of Greek design and faced with Alabama limestone, was opened in 1933 by the once mighty but now vanished Pennsylvania Railroad. Today, the newly renovated station has been handed over to Anttrak and is that line's second-busiest depot.

Evidence of the University of Pennsylvania can be seen almost as soon as one steps outside the door of the 30th Street Station. The university's athletic facilities include an ice-hockey rink a block south of the station on Chestnut

ceding
ges:
tumn
ves. **Left,**
duation
. **Right,**
porting
ile.

Street across from the Main Post Office; the **Palestra**, the university's indoor basketball and track arena; and **Franklin Field**, a capacious pile of brick that is the site of Penn's exploits in Ivy League football, the Penn Relays and other outdoor sports. They more or less line the Schuylkill south of the railroad station.

Of particular interest in this area is the **University Museum**, located near 34th and Spruce streets. The museum boasts one of the most distinguished archaeological collections in the world, with special emphasis on the arts and cultures of the classical old-world civilizations as well as the native people of Polynesia, Africa and the Americas. The museum is housed in a huge, though never completed, 19th-century building that was designed in an almost dizzying variety of architectural styles.

Hair of the dog: A visitor who has walked past just a few of these buildings has caught some of the flavor of the University of Pennsylvania. For contrast, the block on Sansom Street just west of 34th Street offers a charming respite from purely academic vistas. The south side of the block (the university's **law school** is on the north side of the street) is occupied by **row houses** built around the time of the Civil War. No. 3420 was for a time the home of the famous 19th-century spiritualist and founder of the Theosophical Society, Madame Helena P. Blavatsky.

The building, divided into small dining rooms that are at once charming and eclectic, now houses the **White Dog Café** (named in honor of the anonymous white dog Madame Blavatsky successfully draped over her infected leg as a cure), and is perhaps the finest and most stylish restaurant in University City, and among the most characteristic of the neighborhood's colorful milieu. About a block west, at 36th and Sansom, the **Institute of Contemporary Art** features cutting-edge photography, performance and plastic arts.

The **Penn campus** begins in earnest just around the corner from the White

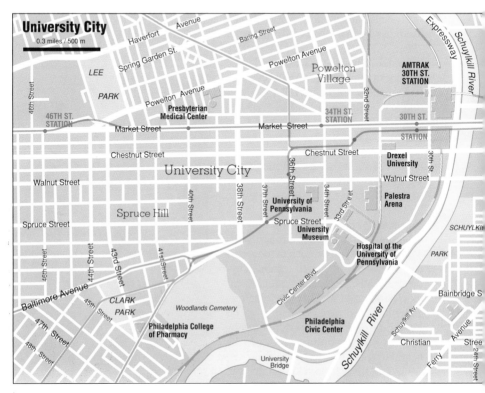

Dog at 34th and Walnut. A stroll down **Locust Walk**, an eastward pedestrian extension of Locust Street, offers a splendid way to examine the university's central portion. Architecturally, the campus is a patchwork of many styles. It is as if the school's trustees had decreed that each building had to represent an entirely different school of design. The result is a little like sorting through an architectural grab bag, whose contents, even if pleasing individually, are somewhat unsettling in the mass.

Some of the most intriguing university buildings are clustered at the east end of Locust Walk. Notable among them is the old University Library, built in 1888–90, and now the **Fine Arts Library**. The building, perhaps the masterwork of noted local architect Frank Furness (whose buildings dot University City), is so richly ornamented that it seems like a fairy-tale castle constructed of a warm, almost glowing, reddish stone. Named a National Historic Landmark in 1985, part of the

library is devoted to the **Arthur Ross Gallery**, which features changing exhibits drawn from the university's wide-ranging art collection. In sharp contrast to the Furness library is its replacement, the starkly modern **Van Pelt Library**, across the walk.

The somewhat odd-looking sculpture directly in front of the library, only one of many pieces on campus, is Claes Oldenburg's *Split Button*. **College Hall**, an exemplary model of the Victorian Gothic style, lies across the court from the Van Pelt Library. It was built in 1871–72 to house the university upon its move from 9th and Chestnut streets, and reflects the influence of John Ruskin, the eminent English art historian and critic, who long championed the decorative use of contrasting colored stone and other materials. Behind College Hall is **Houston Hall**, a heavy Tudor-style structure completed in 1896 and funded by Chestnut Hill developer Henry Howard Houston. The unusual, ziggurat-like building next door is **Irvine Audi-**

h Street
tion.

torium, designed by Horace Trumbauer and erected in 1929.

Locust Walk is paralleled two blocks to the south by **Hamilton Walk**. Another of the many leafy walkways that cut through the Penn campus, Hamilton Walk is bordered by the former **Men's Dormitories**, which run along Spruce Street from 36th to 38th streets. A lumpy, sprawling structure adorned with gables, gargoyles and unusual stone figures, the building is a beautiful evocation of a medieval English university.

Across the walk are the starkly vertical lines of the **Alfred Newton Richards Medical Research Laboratories**, designed in 1959 by the noted local architect Louis Kahn. Hidden away just south of the Richards building is a **botanical garden**, an unexpected pleasure in this otherwise urban academic environment and a great place for footsore tourists to take a breather or break for lunch.

From the end of Hamilton Walk, it's a short jaunt to charming **Delancey Place**, a handsome enclave of row houses hidden away between 39th and 40th streets just south of Spruce Street. About three blocks away, the quiet and well-preserved residences of **Woodland Terrace** are crooked between Woodland and Baltimore avenues. And across Woodland Avenue is **Woodland Cemetery**, burial ground for many of Philadelphia's most distinguished families.

The site is open to walkers; among the pleasures to be had in crisscrossing the grounds are unparalleled views of the Schuylkill River near the **Woodlands**, a refined Federal-style mansion built in the mid-1700s by early settler William Hamilton. Farther down Woodland Avenue is the Philadelphia **College of Pharmacy and Science**. It is located (at 43rd Street and Kingsessing Avenue) amid the sort of widespread urban blight that is more characteristic of West Philadelphia in general than of University City proper.

The far western area of University City, though poised delicately between decay and renewal, has undeniable

Crew teams compete on the Schuylkill River.

charms. Spruce, Pine and Locust streets (which comprise what is sometimes called the **Spruce Hill** neighborhood) all offer shady rambles down brick sidewalks past mostly well-maintained Victorian row houses and more imposing freestanding residences. Many of the dwellings closest to 40th Street have threadbare couches shoehorned on to the porches, a sure sign that the units have been converted into student rentals. Most of the houses farther west are either well-restored or show signs of impending rehabilitation.

A row of 19th-century houses on Spruce Street just west of 42nd is particularly handsome. The buildings sport the sort of dark-green wood porches that you see throughout the neighborhood. Across Spruce Street is the former **Philadelphia Divinity School**, an Episcopal seminary that has been recycled as a children's day-care center. Around the corner of Locust Street, a true residential gem, **St Mark's Place**, is a virtually unaltered street of row houses attributed to Frank Furness. A stroll up the street reveals what the area looked like in the 1890s.

Chestnut Street, though it has become somewhat run-down in the westernmost portion of University City, is still lined with fine churches of various styles. **Christ Memorial Church**, at 42nd and Chestnut, is a massive pile of stone designed at the very height of the Victorian Gothic style. The church, built in 1887 by the Reformed Episcopal Church, a denomination that went its own separate way in the 1870s over objections to perceived Catholic tendencies in the parent Episcopal Church, is still in use, though the building and grounds need some refurbishment.

Next door is the breakaway denomination's **Philadelphia Theological Seminary**, located in a much more modern but comparatively pedestrian building. Farther east along Chestnut Street are such large houses of worship as the Roman Gothic limestone structure housing **St Agatha-St James**

Roman Catholic Church at 38th Street, the **Episcopal Cathedral of Our Savior** (half a block north of Chestnut Street on 38th), and, a block to the east at 37th Street, the English Gothic **Tabernacle Presbyterian Church**.

A walk of four additional blocks to the east puts you at the doorstep of University City's other institution of higher learning, **Drexel University**. Much of the campus is newly but unimaginatively constructed. The most important of Drexel's original buildings remains in use – the **Main Building** at 32nd and Chestnut streets, now a National Historic Landmark. The structure, built in a classic Renaissance style with terra-cotta decorative touches and a truly heroic interior court, is a stunning example of late 19th-century design. The **Drexel Museum**, featuring antique furnishings, porcelain, 19th-century art and a historic Rittenhouse clock, is located on the third floor.

The **Powelton neighborhood** is tucked into the northeast corner of University City, several blocks directly north of the Drexel campus. The area is characterized by large Italianate and Victorian homes, some of which are imposing mansions, as well as several blocks of exquisitely designed and decorated row houses.

A walk through Powelton's streets paints a picture of what an upper-middle-class, turn-of-the-century Philadelphia neighborhood must have looked like. While conditions of the houses today range from dilapidated to completely restored, an energetic rehabilitative spirit is obvious throughout most of the area. Many of the dwellings are occupied by students, and a number of the larger houses have been turned into fraternities and sororities. A stroll through the Powelton neighborhood can be followed by a quick ride back to center city on a subway-surface car, which runs through the neighborhood on Lancaster Avenue and 36th Street.

Right, fall colors outside College Hall.

183

PHILADELP

Ita

SAU

MA'S FINEST

lian

SAGE

KS CHOPS FILETS
for your
FREEZER

SOUTH PHILLY

It's almost midnight at the Melrose Diner. And, as usual, the place is packed and buzzing with life. A bunch of teenage boys makes a ruckus in a corner booth, trying to attract the attention of the girls with the teased-up hair at the counter. Waitresses whiz by like they're on roller skates, doing a juggling act with meat loaf and apple pie. A group of night-shift guys swab gravy off their plates, toss down a second cup of coffee, then drag themselves to work.

A few blocks away, a couple of shirtless kids slap a handball against a brick wall. Their buddies hang out on the corner, staking out the turf. Over at Victor Café, opera-singing waiters serve up heaping bowls of fettuccine, and then belt out an impromptu version of *Il Pagliacco*. And at 9th Street and Passyunk Avenue, the late-night crowd lines up for the neighborhood's famous cheesesteaks at Pat's and at Geno's.

Grandma's tale: And somewhere in South Philly, in one of the thousands of anonymous row houses that crowd the streets, an old woman tucks her grandchildren into bed with stories of the Old Country. She tells them about her long voyage across the ocean, and the day she first stepped foot on American soil. It's an American story. A story of immigration. And in so many ways, the essential story of South Philadelphia.

On balance, Nietzsche said, the most admirable of all Europe's people are the Italians, the most perfect humanists. Their American cousins have exhibited this genius for humanism in enclaves like South Philadelphia since around 1880, when the migratory urge began the depopulation of Italy's Mezzogiorno. These ragged *paesani* were poor in material possessions but rich in culture, determination and family spirit.

Lots of others – Irish, Germans, Jews from Eastern Europe, blacks from Dixieland – came to South Philly, too,

and in recent years there has been a steady influx of new faces from Asia – Vietnamese, Cambodians and Chinese sinking roots into the row-house terrain, struggling to build new lives in a strange land. But it is the Italians who have left the most indelible mark here.

South Philly is a tight-knit community. Kids play stickball in the streets, old folks perch on stoops and gossip, church bells chime all day. Old men play *bocce* in tiny **Bardascino Park** at 10th and Carpenter streets, elderly ladies traipse to Mass, and the smells of countless delis, bakeries, pastry shops and pizzerias permeate the air.

***Rocky* road:** At the heart of the neighborhood, in all of its bustling, ramshackle glory, is the **Italian Market**, six blocks of butchers, bakers and pastamakers strung along 9th Street between Catharine and Wharton. There's a slew of discount stalls, too, hawking everything from bootleg videos to cut-rate shoes. And yes, this is the market Sylvester Stallone jogged through in the original *Rocky*. (At Rocky's Gym, located a block from the market at 8th and Carpenter streets, aspiring pugilists prove Oscar Wilde's observation that life imitates art.)

Touring this **Little Italy** in the early 1920s, Christopher Morley wrote that the market "breathes the Italian genius for good food." And so it does, although these days you're likely to find Chinese, Vietnamese and black hucksters right alongside the Italians. Whoever does the selling, the merchandise is much the same as it was 70 years ago. There are piles of fruit and vegetables, bushels of wriggling crabs, miles of fresh linguine, and everything from 6-foot salamis to suckling pigs hanging in the storefront windows. Most shops are open Monday to Saturday, but the best time to visit is Saturday morning. That's when local chefs, amateur and professional, stock up for a week of cooking, and the vendors, eager to get rid of produce before the weekend, offer the best deals. Starting at the top of the market, a quick tour

eceding
ges: prime
ts. Left, a
uth Philly
her.

might include a taste of crusty, brick-oven bread at **Sarcone's Bakery**, a sample of homemade pasta at **Superior Ravioli**, a sackful of herbs, seeds, teas and coffee beans at **Spice Corner**, a wedge of provolone at **Di Bruno Brothers' House of Cheese** or a bowl of moist mozzarella at **Claudio's Italian Market Cheese**, a look at the latest culinary gadgets at **Fante's**, and then a pound or two of fresh linguine at **Talluto's**.

At the end of the market, reward yourself with one of **Geno's** or **Pat's** "world-famous" cheesesteaks (*see page 191*). Or, if you're looking for a regular restaurant, there are several within walking distance of the market, including Osteria Romana (exceptional but pricey northern Italian cuisine), The Saloon (a boisterous steak and pasta place), Victor Café (where waiters and waitresses serve up a bit of opera with dinner), Dante's and Luigi's (stripped-down and inexpensive, but a recent Mafia hit adds mystique), as well as several Vietnamese places around 8th and Christian streets.

The shopping continues at a less hectic pace farther south along **Passyunk Avenue**, where a mix of clothing stores, restaurants, ice cream parlors and barbershops tend to do a brisk neighborhood business. Passyunk Avenue swerves through the street grid and intersects Broad Street, which, as any true-blue South Philadelphian can tell you, is the path of the Mummers' **New Year's Day Parade**. The Mummers have a long history in the city. Derived from the English and German traditions of costumed pantomimes and New Year's revelry, Mummer clubs were active in South Philadelphia as early as the 1840s.

Today, the area's many Mummers organizations number hundreds of members, and the Mummers Parade – one of the largest in the country – stretches for more than 2½ miles north along Broad Street to City Hall. If you can't wait until New Year's Day to see the Mummers do the high-step down Broad Street, you can get a taste of the Mummer experience at the **New Year's Shooters**

Cheesesteak champion.

and Mummers Museum, located seven blocks from the Italian Market at the corner of Washington Avenue and 2nd Street. Housed in an unusual (and oft-maligned) building that is supposed to represent the strutters' flamboyant outfits, the museum chronicles the tradition and history of Philadelphia Mummery with exhibits of elaborate, feathered costumes, video and audio displays, and plenty of explanatory panels. The famous Mummers string bands offer weekly concerts at the museum between April and September and at special events throughout the city.

Before Penn: Of course, Italians weren't the first immigrants to settle in these parts. Way back in the 1640s, four decades before William Penn ever stepped foot on American soil, a hardy bunch of Swedish pioneers hacked out farms and built log cabins in the very place where row houses and mom-and-pop grocery stores now stand.

After years of shooing away pesky Dutch interlopers, the Swedes, led for many years by a lusty and rather rotund character known as Printz the Tub, readily accepted Penn's tolerant Frame of Government. "I must needs commend the Swede's respect to Authority, and kind behavior to the English," wrote Penn. "And I must do them that right, I see few young men more sober and laborious."

You can learn more about the brief but fascinating history of New Sweden, as well as achievements of later Swedish-Americans, at the **American Swedish Historical Museum**. Set on the edge of Roosevelt Park in a building modeled after Sweden's 17th-century Eriksberg Castle, the museum features a fine collection of artifacts and art works displayed in galleries that are designed in a variety of Swedish architectural styles. The museum also sponsors two annual festivals: *Valborgsmassoafton*, in April, and *Lucia Fest*, in December. Both feature folk dancing, traditional Swedish food and holiday music.

While you're in **Roosevelt Park**, you might also want to take a peek at the **Bel Aire** mansion (on the golf course next to the museum), a sturdy early Georgian house with narrow windows and a steep gable roof. Like the mansions of Fairmount Park, Bel Aire was built as a country manor between 1714 and 1729, making it one of the oldest in the city. It was probably built for a Philadelphia mayor, Samuel Preston.

History buffs may want to travel even farther south to old **Fort Mifflin** (near the airport off Highway 95), site of the gallant but failed defense of Philadelphia during the American Revolution. Construction of the fort was started by the British in 1772 on what was then known as Mud Island, but it was abandoned to the Americans after the Declaration of Independence. In 1777, the rebel force at Fort Mifflin was instrumental in preventing the British fleet from reaching Philadelphia and re-supplying the redcoats occupying the city. Hundreds of Americans died during two weeks of constant bombard-

furling the g at old rt Mifflin.

ment, and the redcoats finally broke through. But the delay was sufficient to protect General Washington's army at Valley Forge. Winter had set in, and the British were unable to mount an assault on Washington's camp.

The fort was rebuilt in 1795, and used as a prison for as many as 300 Confederate soldiers during the Civil War. Now a National Historic Landmark, many of the historic buildings inside the thick stone walls have been restored, and guided tours, which are usually led by costumed soldiers and include the firing of 19th-century cannon, are offered Wednesday through Sunday from April through November.

The **John Heinz National Wildlife Refuge** at Tinicum is a short drive from Fort Mifflin, on Lindbergh Boulevard near 84th Street. Hard to believe that there's a wilderness preserve within city limits, much less in this area of oil refineries, air traffic and heavy industry, but thanks to the efforts of local conservationists, 900 protected acres have been set aside along the woods, tidal marshes and mud flats of Darby Creek. **Tinicum** was first settled in 1643 by Johann Printz, who put his village on what was then an island at the mouth of Darby Creek. Even then, draining and landfilling the low-lying marshes was considered an effective way of reclaiming fertile alluvial soil for planting. Much of the development in the area, including **Philadelphia International Airport**, stands on landfill.

Today, Tinicum is among the last unspoiled areas in the environmentally rich wetlands around the metropolitan area. The reserve serves as a nesting ground for more than 70 species of bird as well as a stopover for migratory birds like hawks, owls, shore birds and hordes of waterfowl. Check in at the visitors center for information on the latest bird sightings and ask for directions to the observation tower. Or, if you want to get a closer look, the 3-mile loop trail and boardwalk lead hikers across the lagoon and into the woods and thickets.

Fresh fruit and fish at the Italian Market.

THE GREAT SOUTH PHILLY CHEESESTEAK WAR

They have been locking horns for more than 25 years: Pat's King of Steaks and Geno's, South Philly's cheesesteak champs, facing off like opposing chess pieces across the intersection of Passyunk Avenue and 9th Street. There are other – some heretics even say better – cheesesteak stands in Philadelphia, but the long-standing rivalry between Pat's and Geno's has catapulted them to legendary status. Publicly, the owners downplay the grudge match. "There's a subtle rivalry between the two of us," says Frank Olivieri, Jr, grandson of one of Pat's founders. "Sure, we're always looking out the window to see what the other guy is doing, but it's mostly media hype. We're friends on the battlefield and we're friends off the battlefield."

Geno's owner agrees. Competition is healthy, Joe Vento says. "It keeps you on your toes." But the rivalry is "not what people think. We're friends."

Still, like longtime sparring partners, the two can't help but throw a few jabs. Olivieri says his cheesesteaks are the people's choice. He claims to outsell Vento 12 to 1. The secret, he says, is the well-seasoned, 64-year-old grill. Vento counters by pointing out his place's cleanliness. "Some people say that I've lost the atmosphere, but I don't buy that greasy spoons make better steaks."

About the only thing the two agree on is who started selling steak sandwiches first. "Pat's did it first," concedes Vento, who opened his stand in 1966 – although who first added cheese is still debatable. It all began in 1930. Pat's founders, brothers Pasquale and Harry Olivieri, then working as hot-dog vendors, slipped grilled chopped beef into a hot-dog roll for a hungry taxi driver. The cabbie liked the newfangled sandwich so much he came back for more, and pretty soon Pasquale and Harry knew that they had a hot item on their hands. Years later, after the brothers opened shop at their Passyunk Avenue stand, one of the cooks got bored eating plain steak on a bun, so he melted some cheese on top. The rest was history.

Since then, the cheesesteak has proved a remarkably adaptable concoction. Imaginative chefs substitute pork or chicken, melt in mozzarella or provolone, pile on mushrooms, hot sauce, tomatoes, hot peppers, grilled eggplant and, of course, mounds of fried onions. A few have even come out with a vegetarian variety.

But in South Philly, a cheesesteak is still a cheesesteak. The only choice you have to make is Pat's or Geno's. And loyalty is a very serious matter. "Geno's is the best," a group of customers chimes, hoisting hefty sandwiches toward their mouths. "Tastes better, friendly people. No contest. They're not chintzy with the onions either."

"Pat's is number one," customers on the opposite side of the street say. "The first, the original, the best."

Says Olivieri: "When people come to Philly they do three things. First they go to Pat's, then they go to the Liberty Bell and Independence Hall." "They don't all go to Pat's," Vento rebuts. "There are lines on both sides of the street. Plenty of people go to Geno's first." ∎

's King Steaks, ventor of cheese- ak.

THREE URBAN VILLAGES

Philadelphia is often described as a city of neighborhoods, each with its own identity. And you couldn't ask for a better example than the three "urban villages" clustered in the city's northwest corner – Germantown, Chestnut Hill and Manayunk. Established at different times and under very different circumstances, the trio have little more in common than their general location. **Germantown** is the oldest of the three. It was founded just two years after Philadelphia and is filled with historic sites and buildings. **Chestnut Hill** began as a real-estate development for well-to-do Philadelphians and remains an enclave of beautiful homes and ritzy shops. Working-class **Manayunk** started as a mill town and has recently undergone sweeping gentrification along its trendy, boutique-lined Main Street.

Three neighborhoods, three very different personalities. Taken together or separately, they make a terrific day trip "outside" the city without really leaving Philadelphia. Although public transportation is available from center city, driving (but not necessarily parking) may be the most convenient, especially if you plan on visiting more than one neighborhood.

Germantown: Lying about 6 miles northwest of Philadelphia, Germantown was founded in 1683 by Quaker and Mennonite immigrants who were invited by William Penn to join his "holy experiment" in the New World. Led by Pietist scholar Francis Daniel Pastorius, the original 13 families – most Dutch or German-speaking Swiss – laid out the village on a gentle rise along **Wissahickon Creek**. The little town grew quickly, gaining an early reputation in weaving, printing and publishing. When the British captured Philadelphia in 1777, Lord Howe stationed the bulk of his army in Germantown. General George Washington launched a daring four-pronged attack against the redcoats, but dense fog and poor timing scuttled the plan, and despite fierce combat along Germantown Avenue, Washington was forced to retreat to Valley Forge. Philadelphians fled to Germantown 16 years later to escape a different sort of invader – the devastating yellow-fever epidemic of 1793. Many of them returned, often building sumptuous summer retreats in the surrounding countryside.

Today, Germantown is a treasure of 18th- and 19th-century architecture, most of it on a 3-mile stretch of **Germantown Avenue** between Windrim and Phil-Ellena streets. Although sections of the old village are suffering from 20th-century decay, there are still tranquil tree-lined side streets like **Walnut Lane**, **Tulpehocken** and **Pelham streets**, where gracious colonial and Victorian homes are lovingly maintained. Hours at historic homes are maddeningly irregular (*see Travel Tips*), so call in advance if you would like a guided tour. Most are open Tuesday,

•ceding
ges:
•trait of
•nayunk.
ft,
estnut
•'s
storius
•k.
•ht, the
•estates
•e.

Thursday and Saturday afternoons; a few are open by appointment only.

William Penn's brilliant secretary, James Logan, was among the first to build a Germantown retreat. **Stenton Mansion** (18th Street and Windrim Avenue, two blocks east of Germantown Avenue), a magnificent Georgian house built in 1728, was Logan's refuge from his many professional obligations. Stenton was Logan's sanctuary, a place where he could entertain Indian friends, indulge his interest in science, and delve into his 2,000-volume library, one of the largest in the colonies.

Only five of the original 500 acres remain in this partially blighted neighborhood, but the barn, orangery, weaving shed and much of the Logan family's furnishings are intact. Washington camped here with the Continental Army before confronting the British at the Battle of Brandywine, and the British commander, General Howe, chose the estate as his headquarters before the Battle of Germantown.

A short drive up Germantown Avenue takes you to **Loudon** (4650 Germantown Avenue), a regal Greek Revival mansion erected on a promontory 30 feet above street level. Built in 1801 by Thomas Armat, a wealthy merchant, the house contains furnishings collected over five generations of family history. Be sure to ask about "Little Willie," Loudon's ghost-in-residence.

The **Germantown Historical Society Museum Complex**, housed in six historical structures at 5214 Germantown Avenue, offers an overview of local history with a large collection of 18th- and 19th-century tools, toys, household goods and textiles. Across the street, **Grumblethorpe** (5267 Germantown Avenue) is a solid stone house built by John Wister in 1744 employing a style of Georgian architecture unique to the Germantown area.

Two blocks north, the 18th-century **Deshler-Morris House** (5442 Germantown Avenue) sheltered President Washington during the yellow-fever epidemic

The eyes have it.

Urban Villages

1.5 miles / 2.4 km

of 1793. Washington liked the place so much, he returned the following summer with wife Martha and her two grandchildren. Now maintained by the National Park Service, the house has been beautifully restored with period furnishings and a lovely rear garden. Across the street, **Market Square** was once the village center, site of the firehouse, stocks and market shed. The square is now occupied by an imposing Civil War monument. A Presbyterian church dating from 1888, and the Federal-style **Fromberger House**, which dates from the late 1790s and is now used by the offices of the Germantown Historical Society, face the square on either side.

Continue north on Germantown Avenue past majestic **Vernon Mansion** (5708 Germantown Avenue, closed to the public) to **Wyck** (6026 Germantown Avenue), a modest Quaker home built in 1690 with original furnishings and a fascinating 200-year-old garden. The **Green Tree Tavern** (6023 Germantown Avenue, closed to the public), a typical

18th-century public house, is across the street. If you're in the area on Tuesday, be sure to stop at the **Farmers Market** on nearby West Haines Street for scrapple, cinnamon buns and other Pennsylvania Dutch delights.

About a half-block north, the **Mennonite Information Center** (6117 Germantown Avenue) is located in a meeting-house built in 1770 on the site of the sect's first American house of worship. Around the corner, at 200 West Tulpehocken Street, is the **Ebenezer Maxwell Mansion**, an elaborate Victorian home built in 1859 and furnished with a clutter of Philadelphia-made furniture and late-Victorian decor.

Back on Germantown Avenue, the **Johnson House** (6306 Germantown Avenue, by appointment), a typical Georgian home built in 1768, saw heavy fighting during the Battle of Germantown and was a safe house in the Underground Railroad before the Civil War. Across the street, the one-room **Concord Schoolhouse** (6309 Germantown Avenue, by appointment), constructed in 1775, contains original desks, chairs – even books – as well as the old school bell. The **Upper Germantown Burying Ground** is adjacent, with weathered headstones dating to the colonial and Revolutionary War period.

A block away, **Cliveden** (6401 Germantown Avenue), Germantown's most lavish 18th-century mansion, occupies a six-acre park. Built in 1763 by Benjamin Chew – a prominent lawyer, Loyalist, and the last Chief Justice of the colonial period – the house was transformed into a fortress by the British during the Battle of Germantown.

Cliveden's two-foot-thick walls still bear pockmarks left by American musket balls and grapeshot. The house is beautifully maintained and, thanks to the reams of documentation saved by the Chew family, a thoroughly accurate renovation. During the assault on Cliveden, Washington placed his artillery on a knoll across the street, where the lovely Federal-style **Upsala** has

ttle of
rmantown
-enacted at
veden.

stood since 1798. Two churches are worth a look about four blocks north. **The Church of the Brethren** (6611 Germantown Avenue, by appointment), erected in 1770, is the first of the Dunkard sect, a branch of the Mennonites named for their distinctive practice of baptism. Nearby, **St Michael's Lutheran Church** (6671 Germantown Avenue, by appointment), founded in 1717, is the oldest Lutheran congregation in the country. The existing structure is the third on the site, although the Lutherans' schoolhouse, built in 1740, still stands.

Chestnut Hill: If you continue north on Germantown Avenue through the Mount Airy neighborhood, you'll come to Chestnut Hill, the city's most exclusive residential district. Known as Sommerhausen in the early 1800s, Chestnut Hill was a remote area of farmland and forest until Henry Houston, a director of the Pennsylvania Railroad and the area's largest landholder, arranged to put a commuter line through in the 1880s. Houston constructed a grand country

inn (now **Chestnut Hill Academy**) and church (**St Martin's in the Field**), both on West Willow Grove Avenue, as well as scores of fashionable homes intended to lure well-heeled Philadelphians to the suburbs. Houston's son-in-law, Dr George Woodward, continued the work well into the 1900s. Woodward drew inspiration from English and French country homes in an effort to develop comfortable housing for both affluent and working families. Among the best examples of the Houston/Woodward style are **French Village** at Elbow and Gates lanes; the **Benezet Street** and **Winston Road** houses; Houston's private castle, **Drum Moir**, at West Willow Grove Avenue; and the court houses around **Pastorius Park**.

If you prefer shopping to architecture, stay on Germantown Avenue, where you'll find upscale boutiques, friendly bookstores, art galleries and excellent restaurants, some with outdoor dining. **Woodmere Art Museum** (9201 Germantown Avenue), housed in Charles Knox Smith's magnificent Victorian mansion, features changing exhibits from the permanent collection of 19th-century art as well as work by contemporary Delaware Valley artists. The museum also sponsors a yearly concert and lecture series.

Farther north, at the very edge of Chestnut Hill, the University of Pennsylvania maintains the serene 175-acre **Morris Arboretum** (100 Northwestern Avenue, between Germantown and Stenton). Developed by John and Lydia Morris (heirs to the Morris Iron Works fortune) in the late 1800s on their former summer estate, the arboretum maintains nearly 2,000 kinds of plants, including a fragrant rose garden, azalea meadow, medicinal plants and exotic specimens as well as a contemporary sculpture garden and a formal English garden.

Manayunk: It's a big jump from blue-blooded Chestnut Hill to blue-collar Manayunk, but not quite as much as you might expect. Since upscale stores and eateries have opened on Main Street,

Stenton, James Logan's country retreat.

this compact working-class burg has been drawing a fresh crowd of big-spending, high-style yuppies. Built on a steep hillside rising from the Schuylkill River, Manayunk was once one of Philadelphia's most productive industrial neighborhoods. With the swift current of the Schuylkill River to power its factories and the mule-drawn barges of the Schuylkill Canal to transport materials, **Main Street**'s 14 mills turned out blankets, upholstery, cloth and other textiles by the ton.

Although the textile industry was decimated by the Great Depression, a few manufacturers survived and many of the massive old mills are now serving as fancy condominiums or office buildings. The sons and daughters of the original Polish, Irish and Italian immigrants are still here, occupying the same modest row houses. Take a look at the top of the hill and you'll see the mansions that were once occupied by the wealthy mill-owners, too. Usually quiet, Manayunk's back streets are crowded

with spectators who come to watch cyclists conquer the grueling "Manayunk Wall" during the annual **Corestates Pro Cycling Championship** in June.

But, of course, the big attraction in Manayunk is Main Street, a strip of trendy shops and galleries tucked into a parade of colorful storefronts. The bars and restaurants have been garnering terrific reviews, too. Manayunk, it should be noted, is a Lenape Indian word meaning "the place we go to drink," and with food-and-drink lovers packing local eateries like Sonoma, the Main Street Café, the River Café, and Jake's, the name is as fitting today as it was 300 years ago. If you need even more incentive to break out of center city, keep two other special events in mind, both usually held in June: the **Main Street Stroll** and the **Annual Manayunk Arts Festival**. Both events provide a great opportunity to see Manayunk at its best and to meet the old and new "Yunkers" who have transformed a graying mill town into a thriving urban village.

pping up the plate.

NORTH PHILADELPHIA

North Philadelphia is a vast urban sprawl that covers everything north of center city and east of Germantown Avenue. This is a rather indistinct, amorphous expanse that takes in a wide range of ethnic enclaves, sprawling suburban housing, faded industrial centers, inner-city blight and a wooded city park.

Faded glory: In the mid-1800s, parts of North Philadelphia were considered quite fashionable. North Broad Street in particular was a magnet for the burgeoning class of industrialists seeking large lots for sumptuous new homes.

Unfortunately, North Broad has long since fallen on hard times, but there are still signs of its former grandeur – houses like the **Gaul-Forrest Mansion** (now occupied by Moore College of Art, 1346 N. Broad Street), where the famed American actor Edwin Forrest once lived, and ecclesiastical structures like the magnificent French Gothic-style **Church of the Advocate** (located at 18th and Diamond).

Also in the neighborhood are the monumental **Church of the Gesu** (18th and Stiles), which features a stunning interior as well as **Rodeph Shalom Synagogue** (615 N. Broad Street), the oldest American Ashkenazic congregation in existence, now standing on the site of a synagogue built by Frank Furness; and the **Baptist Temple**, built in 1889 by minister Russell H. Conwell, the founder of Temple University, centered on Broad and Berks streets.

Nearby is the little-known **Wagner Free Institute of Science** (17th and Montgomery), built in 1860. Its founder was William Wagner, a wealthy merchant with a penchant for stones, bones and stuffed animals. He hired John McArthur, Jr, architect of City Hall, to design the impressive Greek Revival building. But the amazing thing here is that the museum remains almost exactly the same as it was more than a century ago – a museum frozen in time. Farther north on Broad Street, you'll find an even more unusual collection of artifacts at the **Temple Dental Museum** (Broad and Allegheny).

Here visitors can peruse a rather ghastly array of primitive drills, extractors, dental chairs and other pain-inducing tools, as well as anatomical models, ancient toothbrushes, all sorts of advertisements, photographs and cartoons relating to early dentistry, and a bucket filled with thousands of teeth yanked by one of the most colorful figures in dental history, Dr Edgar "Painless" Parker.

Big bucks: Closer to center city is **Girard College** (Girard and Corinthian), a compound of classically inspired structures centered around **Founder's Hall**, a building of breathtaking scale designed by 29-year-old Thomas U. Walter in 1833 and regarded as one of the finest examples of Greek Revival architecture in the country. Founder's Hall houses the **Girard Collection** (open Thursday afternoon and by appointment), which

ft, a editative oment. ght, urch of e Gesu.

preserves the furnishings, housewares, art works and other personal belongings of Stephen Girard, the college's founder and one of America's first millionaires.

Girard was born in Bordeaux, France, to a family of merchant mariners. At the age of 14, he signed on as a cabin boy aboard a merchant vessel and remained at sea for several years. He was only 23 when he became a captain on a ship that traded in the West Indies, and he then took part in the American coastal trade, building up his own business at the same time that he represented a New York mercantile company.

Britain's blockade of American ports during the stormy political period before the Revolution led the French-born Girard to settle in Philadelphia, where he launched a successful business career. He built a fleet of merchantmen that was to provide him with a great fortune. In 1812, he acquired the building that had been the Bank of the United States, along with its assets, and transformed it into the Bank of Stephen Girard. Girard and the German-born John Jacob Astor – both destined to become the richest men in America – spearheaded a drive to sell government bonds to finance the War of 1812 against Britain.

At the age of 75, Girard began carefully planning the administration of his estate, including large bequests to both Philadelphia and Pennsylvania, and setting aside $6 million of his fortune for the establishment of a school for white male orphans.

The school, Girard College, was opened in 1846, 17 years after its founder's death. Legal battles challenging the terms of Girard's will had been fought before the school was opened, and another protracted legal conflict ensued in the mid-20th century over the stipulation that admission was restricted to white entrants. Finally, in 1968, non-whites were admitted following a ruling by the US Supreme Court.

Nevermore: To the east of Broad Street, just north of Old City, is a neighborhood known as the **Northern Liberties**, part

Freewheelin through Philly.

of the "Liberty Lands" that William Penn parceled out as bonuses to people who bought building lots in the city proper. Gentrification has crept up from center city, but the area is still peppered with factories, warehouses and vacant lots. Many come to pay homage to a literary genius at the **Edgar Allan Poe National Historic Site** at 7th and Spring Garden streets.

The site encompasses two structures, one occupied by Poe between 1842 and 1844 and the neighboring house, which now contains a modest display on this famous author's life and work and where rangers show you around a bit before letting you explore on your own. The Poe House itself seems to have been left much as it was found – bare and unfinished from the upstairs bedrooms to the spooky dark basement. Even the walls are stripped down to the plaster. Poe moved often when in Philadelphia, and sold most or all of his furniture when he eventually left town.

Poe had come to Philadelphia in 1837 to do editorial work for *Burton's Gentleman's Magazine*, having already established a reputation in literary circles as a poet and short-story writer. A year earlier he had married his 13-year-old cousin Virginia Clemm, the inspiration for his immortal poem *Annabel Lee*, and they lived here with Poe's mother-in-law, Maria Clemm, and their beloved cat, Catterina.

It was in the house on North 7th Street that this sensitive man of letters – Poe's actress mother had died when he was only two years of age, and his childhood was an unhappy experience – composed some of his famous stories, among them *The Fall of the House of Usher*, *The Murders in the Rue Morgue* and *The Gold Bug*. And it was here in Philadelphia that he enjoyed success as a literary critic of the first order and found the greatest domestic contentment.

Poe lived at several different addresses during his Philadelphia years, but this house is the only one that has survived. It was a happy menage: "Eddy" (as Poe

e Anti-
raffiti
etwork in
tion.

was called by the family), his beloved "Sissy" with her gentle bearing and pale complexion and raven hair, and her mother, Poe's Aunt Maria, whom he called "Muddy." Alas, in 1842 Virginia suffered her first attack of consumption, the family moved to New York two years later, and the poet lost his "beautiful Annabel Lee" there on January 30, 1847. She was only 24.

The poet wrote these haunting lines in her memory:

It was many and many a year ago,
*   In a kingdom by the sea,*
That a maiden there lived whom you
*   may know*
By the name of Annabel Lee;
And this maiden she lived with no
*   other thought*
Than to love and be loved by me.

The blow was devastating, and it wasn't long before the disconsolate widower was gone as well. Poe was found lying on a Baltimore street corner on October 3, 1849, and four days later he died in a Maryland state hospital.

Across the street, the **German Society of Pennsylvania** houses one of the largest German-language libraries in the country. Founded in 1764 to help immigrants adjust to the New World, and now of interest mainly to scholars and German-Americans curious about the city's rich German heritage, the society's headquarters is a handsome late-19th-century town house.

The lustrous gold dome you may see over the roof-line across the street belongs to the nearby **Church of the Immaculate Conception**, headquarters of the Ukrainian Orthodox Church in the United States and the largest Ukrainian cathedral in the world. It is open for Mass only.

To the north, the area gets dicey for travelers. Known by local cops as the "badlands," this section of North Philadelphia is a wide swath of devastation where burned-out row houses stand like blackened teeth surrounded by a jigsaw of empty lots choked with weeds, rubble and trash, and where just about every surface has been "tagged" by spray-can wielding graffitists. In some spots, the **Philadelphia Anti-Graffiti Network** has covered the scroll with beautiful murals, some covering an entire side of a building. But for the most part, this is an area of depressing and dangerous urban blight.

A bright spot here is **Taller Puertorriqueño**, a cultural center and community workshop located at 2721 N. 5th Street in this Hispanic neighborhood's colorful business district. A brilliant three-story mural is painted on the side of the building. A gallery shows an occasional traveling exhibit and work by local artists. Ask about upcoming lectures, workshops and seminars.

The Great Northeast: The scene is somewhat different to the east of 5th Street in the old manufacturing centers like Frankford, Richmond, Fishtown and Tacony along the Delaware River. In the early days these were small agrarian villages separated from Philadelphia by farms and pastures. But by the late 1600s,

Edgar Allan Poe moved Philadelphi, in 1837.

204

small mills and workshops were already springing up along Pennypack Creek, providing the area with flour, lumber, textiles and iron tools.

The steam engine freed factories from swift-running streams and, at the onset of the Industrial Revolution, this northeastern area flourished, cranking out iron, steel, textiles and other manufactured goods, and attracting thousands of immigrant laborers.

Philadelphia lost much of its manufacturing after World War II, and the loss is clearly evident. In the area near **Penn Treaty Park** (E. Columbia Avenue and Beach Street) where William Penn had his legendary meeting with the Lenape Indians – romantically depicted by Benjamin West's painting *Penn's Treaty with the Indians* – factories stand silent and vacant, chimneys no longer belch smoke and warehouses are empty.

Thanks to the Fairmount Park Commission, there is a patch of green in these post-industrial neighborhoods;

1,300-acre **Pennypack Park** runs 8 miles along Pennypack Creek, with miles of hiking and biking trails, picnic areas, peaceful woods, a 150-acre bird sanctuary and, near Veree Road and Bloomfield Avenue, an environmental center with many interesting exhibits on the wildlife and ecology of this inner-city wilderness.

The **Grand Army of the Republic Civil War Museum** is also in the area. One of the city's forgotten jewels, the museum provides knowledgeable costumed guides who lead visitors through a collection of flags, firearms, broadsides, uniforms and various wartime novelties, including a pair of handcuffs once owned by Abraham Lincoln's assassin John Wilkes Booth, and a few blood-soaked threads plucked from Lincoln's deathbed.

The museum is housed in a late-18th-century mansion at 4278 Griscom Street. It is only open one Sunday a month (every Sunday in January), but well worth the wait for Civil War buffs.

ading out town.

PENNSYLVANIA DUTCH COUNTRY

There are two kinds of tourists: those who hate being identified as such, and those who don't care what other people think as long as they are taking enough pictures. If you happen to be in the former category, you may have a problem in **Lancaster County**, the heart of Pennsylvania Dutch country.

Out here, it's easy to tell the tourists from the locals. It's not just the black-clad, buggy-driving, barn-raising, Amish and their half-a-step-farther-into-the-20th-century neighbors, the Mennonites, who quickly make you feel like an invader from another world; it's the other locals, too. The religious dissenters who settled this land in the early 1700s were an independent group, and they've managed to hang on to their beliefs, traditions and language despite the encroachment of mainstream culture. Adding to the confusion is the fact that they were German-speaking people and not Dutch at all – immigration officials, trying to ascertain their nationality, misheard their answer, "*Deutsch.*"

In any case, Lancaster County is not a place where you blend into the scenery. And, because the scenery is so beautiful – rolling fields, the occasional one-room schoolhouse popping up after an unexpected turn, simple and charming homes – you may feel compelled to take out your camera and snap along with the rest of the crowd.

Once you've accepted the fact that you are a tourist, your difficulties haven't ceased. For Lancaster County is a minefield of both tourist attractions and tourist traps, and sometimes the difference is subtle. This confusion is compounded by the fact that the tourism industry tries to capitalize, sometimes shamelessly, on the Amish way of life (*see chapter on the Amish, pages 87–91*).

The road to Paradise: Given all these caveats, how do you have an enjoyable time? If you've taken the 90-minute drive from Philadelphia along the **Pennsylvania Turnpike**, you've overcome the first obstacle – the tourist traps that litter the alternate road from Philadelphia, **Route 30**. There, billboards ruin the countryside with come-ons for "genuine Amish" attractions and smorgasbord restaurants. Instead, by taking the Pennsylvania Turnpike and jumping off at exit 21, you'll enter through the far more subtle town of **Ephrata**.

The town is home to the **Ephrata Cloister** (632 W. Main Street), where 300 celibate followers of German Pietist Conrad Beissel built a community of log-and-stone buildings between 1732 and 1750. Known for printing, basket-making and milling, the cloister founded a school in the 1740s, nursed 500 wounded soldiers during the Battle of Brandywine, but had lost most of its importance by the 1800s. Then as now, there isn't much of a future in celibacy.

Ephrata also houses the **Artworks at Doneckers** (100 N. State Street), a clever scheme for marketing the work of 50

ceding
ges:
nnsylvania's
artland.
t,
ncaster
unty lad.
ht, Dutch
untry
vest.

artists and artisans by having them work and sell in one location, a former shoe factory. The Doneckers complex also features a top-of-the-line French restaurant (perfect for Sunday brunch), a hotel, fashions and housewares.

Just outside downtown **Lancaster**, you can learn about 250 years of local history at the **Lancaster County Historical Society** (230 N. President Avenue), where the staff can help you locate the kind of sites you are looking for. History buffs will be most interested in nearby **Wheatland** (1120 Marietta Avenue), the home of James Buchanan, the only Pennsylvania native to become President of the United States. Listed on the National Register of Historic Places, the 19th-century estate is a showcase of early Victorian furnishings and contains quite a few of Buchanan's personal possessions.

About 3 miles east of town on Route 462, the **Amish Homestead** is among the best of the many "authentic" Amish attractions. A guided tour through parts

of this working farm lets visitors eavesdrop on the day-to-day life of Amish families. And a short drive northeast of town on Route 272, the **Landis Valley Museum** is a tiny village occupied by stores, workshops and houses where guides attempt to recreate the crafts, skills and day-to-day chores of 19th-century country life.

Convenient parking in downtown Lancaster puts you within walking distance of **Central Market** (Penn Square), the nation's oldest publicly-owned farmers' market and a prime place to get a look at how the farmers and townfolk do business. There's also the **Heritage Center of Lancaster County** (13 W. King Street), a decorative-arts museum, with furniture, rifles, silverware and the area's famous Pennsylvania Dutch quilts. Entrance is free.

If you're a news hound, check out the **Lancaster Newspaper's Newseum** (28 S. Queen Street), and then see what's on the bill at the **Fulton Opera House** (12 N. Prince Street), which has been offer-

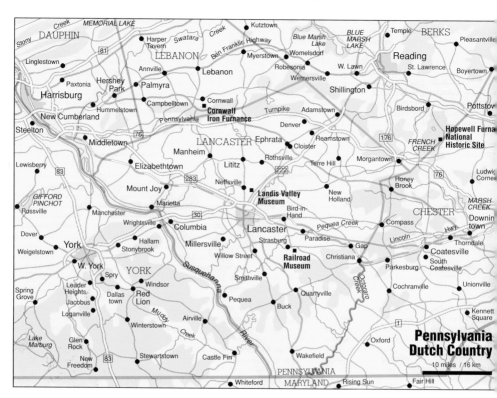

Pennsylvania Dutch Country

ing local and touring talent on its Victorian stage since 1852. For a more detailed look at downtown, you can join one of the costumed guides of **Lancaster Walking Tours** (100 S. Queen Street), who lead visitors on an excursion of the houses, churches and markets of historic Lancaster. If you are still around after dark, try dinner at the stylish **Press Room** (26–28 W. King Street).

East of Lancaster are small towns with the oft-punned names of **Bird-in-Hand**, **Paradise** and **Intercourse**. All have become overrun with tourists abandoning any attempt at originality by sporting "Intercourse is for Lovers" T-shirts. It's unfortunate, since this part of the county features some of the area's most beautiful scenery.

For the best views, take the back roads, and be patient if you get stuck behind a slow-moving buggy. For an informative stop, try the **People's Place** on Main Street in Intercourse, where a collection of arts and artifacts and a 25-minute film explore Amish history and customs. Try ascertaining the origin of the town's name and you'll find there's no accepted explanation. Some think the entrance to an old racecourse just outside town was known as "Entercourse" and that the name became corrupted. Others believe the village grew up at the intercourse of two famous roads, the Old King's Highway from Philadelphia to Pittsburgh (now the Old Philadelphia Pike) and the road from Wilmington to Erie.

About 10 miles south, on Route 741 in **Strasburg**, you can learn about the development of America's railways at the **Railroad Museum of Pennsylvania**, and then hop aboard the **Strasburg Railroad's** historic steam locomotive for a 45-minute round-trip to Lancaster. The town has a number of other attractions, from an "Amish village" to buggy rides and miniature golf.

At some point, though, if you are going from Intercourse to Paradise (double-entendres are hard to avoid here), you have to cross Route 30. Skip the

e
rasburg
ailroad.

wax museums and anything that features a diorama of Amish life on the brochure or billboard. An exception is **Zinn's Diner** (Route 272), a heavily advertised eatery/gift shop/recreation park that serves up respectable local food under the watchful eye of a giant papier-mâché Amish gentleman. Kids may talk you into stopping at **Dutch Wonderland** (2249 Route 30 East), a tolerable low-tech amusement park skewed to the younger set. If you want serious rides, you'll have to leave Lancaster County and visit **Hersheypark**, home of the world-famous chocolate-maker, where you not only get to ride the spine-tingling roller coasters, you can also walk through the 11-acre **ZooAmerica**, visit the lush **Hershey Gardens** (Hotel Road), and take a ride through **Hershey's Chocolate World** (800 Park Boulevard).

Around Lancaster itself, keep in mind that any place with a pile of brochures can call itself an information center. Two genuine organizations are the

Pennsylvania Dutch Tourist Bureau's Visitors' Information Center on Route 30 and the **Mennonite Information Center** on Mill Stream Road just off Route 30. At the former, you can also rent an audio-tape tour, which gives you an in-car guide to the area's major sights and attractions.

West of Lancaster, you'll have to search even harder in order to find the more sophisticated attractions. In Mount Joy, a local legend, Groff's Farm Restaurant (Pinkerton Road), offers chicken Stoltzfus and other Pennsylvania Dutch specialties. Fancier is the **Cameron Estate Inn** (Donegal Springs Road), a historic country seat once owned by Abraham Lincoln's Secretary of War, Simon Cameron, and now a lovely inn and restaurant. The **Cornwall Iron Furnace** (Rexmont Road) in nearby Cornwall was constructed in 1742 and now impresses tourists as a working historical site where the forges still burn every day.

Serious lovers of antiques won't re-

Left, friends on the farm. Below, craft at the Kutztown Fo Festival.

gret going even farther west to **Columbia**, near the Susquehanna River, where the C.A. Herr Annex (3rd and Walnut), Partner's Antiques (403 N. 3rd Street) and many other local businesses can keep you hunting for hours. The town's other big attraction is the **Watch and Clock Museum** (514 Poplar Street), which will delight some and tick others off. For great fishing, head about 30 minutes south of Columbia to **Muddy Run Recreational Park**.

For shoppers more interested in designer clothes than in quilts, the area is littered with factory outlets selling everything from brand-name clothing and dinnerware to power tools. Of course, it doesn't make much sense to drive hundreds of miles just to save a few dollars on a pair of shoes, but the outlets help make Lancaster a place where you can enjoy more than just the slender "Dutch Country" offerings.

The gentle people: The best way to get up close to, if not personal with, the Amish is to take in a public auction. The two most popular auction houses in the area are **Howard Shaub, Inc.**, and **Kreider and Kline**. With either company, you're likely to see Amish people bidding against Philadelphia antique dealers on an assortment of items – practical and otherwise. Remember that here, as is the case in all dealings with the Amish, photography is not appreciated. Among conservative Amish, appearing in photographs is prohibited.

You can also see the locals at one of the many fairs which are scheduled throughout the year. The most popular of these include the April **Pennsylvania Relief and Auction** sponsored by the Mennonite Central Committee, **Heritage Days** in August, and the **Kutztown Folk Festival** in June.

The fact that **Kutztown** isn't in Lancaster County is just a technicality – it's still one of the best ways to experience Amish culture without feeling as though you were trespassing. The Pennsylvania Folklife Society, sponsor of the event, manages to do a good job of keeping this

ish quilts.

from becoming another tourist affair. Horseshoeing, glass blowing, sheep-shearing, ox-roasting and other country-fair activities fill the days.

For bawdier fare, the summer months also bring the **Pennsylvania Renaissance Faire**. Here, a troupe of costumed actors, musicians and other performers turn the grounds of the **Mount Hope Estate and Winery** (just off the Pennsylvania Turnpike at exit 20) into a tourist-friendly version of a 16th-century English country fair complete with jousting, Shakespearean performances (significantly abridged), and dancing. In the winter, the estate reopens for an **Edgar Allan Poe Halloween** and a **Charles Dickens Christmas Past** with similar actor/audience interaction.

History of a very different period comes to life at **Hopewell Furnace National Historic Site**, just over the Lancaster County line near Pottstown, where an entire iron-manufacturing village has been restored to its early 19th-century appearance. In the summer months, costumed guides demonstrate the various skills and occupations necessary to keep the community running and the furnace at full blast. The site is almost completely surrounded by the lovely wooded vales of **French Creek State Park**, with lakes, campsites and miles of hiking trails.

And finally, if you plan on spending a few days around Lancaster, you may want to take a long side trip across the Susquehanna River to **Gettysburg National Military Park**. In the summer of 1863, Confederate and Union forces met here in a terrible three-day battle that claimed more than 50,000 casualties, the bloodiest engagement in American history. In November of that year, Abraham Lincoln dedicated the adjacent cemetery, delivering his famous Gettysburg Address ("government of the people, by the people, and for the people…"). Guided walks, lectures and audio-visual presentations are on offer, as well as a self-guided tour of the park tracing the evolution of the battle.

Pennsylvania sunflower.

VALLEY FORGE

There were no battles fought at Valley Forge, but more Continental soldiers died here than in any single engagement during the American Revolution. The enemies at this grueling six-month encampment were hunger, cold, fatigue, disease. Of the 12,000 who retreated to Valley Forge under the command of George Washington in December 1777, some 2,000 never returned. Only loyalty to Washington and to the cause of American independence held the camp together. Yet, despite heavy losses, desertions and rumors of mutiny, the ragtag Continental Army was transformed at Valley Forge into a capable, cohesive fighting force.

Valley Forge was preceded by a series of engagements against the better-equipped, better-organized British. Hoping to stop Sir William Howe's advance on Philadelphia, Washington was repelled at the Brandywine and at Germantown. Unable to stop the redcoats, the beleaguered rebels pulled back to Valley Forge.

Freezing, half-starved and demoralized, Washington's men set about the backbreaking work of building the camp. A thousand log huts were erected, earthworks were constructed, foraging parties scoured the countryside. Dogged by food shortages, soldiers sustained themselves on "firecake," a bland mixture of flour and water. Without proper shoes, clothes or blankets, and holed up in cramped quarters, hundreds of men came down with dysentery, pneumonia and typhus. At times, nearly a third of Washington's men were unable to report for duty. "Unless some great and capital change suddenly takes place," Washington lamented, "this Army must inevitably... starve, dissolve, or disperse, in order to obtain subsistence in the best manner they can."

The tide began to turn in February when a Prussian officer, Baron Friedrich von Steuben, arrived from France with a letter of introduction from Benjamin Franklin. A skilled officer, von Steuben began transforming the raw enlistees into an integrated army. He drilled them relentlessly, reorganizing troop structure, teaching musket volleys, and shoring up discipline.

In June, the British pulled out of Philadelphia, and Washington's newly spirited and confident army hurried to intercept them in New Jersey, staving off a British counterattack at the Battle of Monmouth. The war dragged on for another five years, but the triumph at Valley Forge over hunger, disease and hardship propelled the Continental Army to victory. "To see men without clothes to cover their nakedness," Washington wrote during the worst of the ordeal, "without blankets to lie on, without shoes... without a house or hut to cover them until those could be built, and submitting without a murmur, is a proof of patience and obedience which, in my opinion, can scarcely be paralleled."

Today, the site of Washington's fateful encampment is preserved at Valley Forge National Historical Park, 18 miles northwest of Philadelphia just off Highway 76 at the junction of North Gulph Road and Route 23. A number of original 18th-century buildings, including Washington's HQ, still stand on the 3,000-acre site, as do reconstructed huts, some occupied by costumed interpreters on weekends. ∎

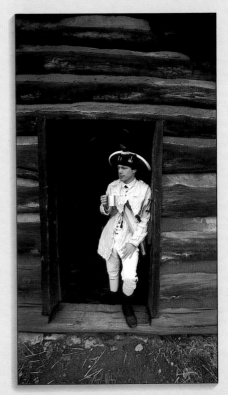

Costumed interpreter at Valley Forge.

BUCKS COUNTY

No sooner did William Penn design the layout of Philadelphia than he ran off to the suburbs. Pennsylvania's first suburbanite chose to make his home in the woods of Bucks County. And stressed-out city dwellers have been following in his trail ever since.

"The country life is to be preferred for there we see the works of God," Penn wrote. And 300 years later, travelers seeking a peaceful getaway are still finding the place heavenly. An hour north – and a world away – from center city, bucolic Bucks is graced with some of the most beautiful landscapes in the **Delaware Valley**. Despite suburban sprawl and a glut of weekend wanderers, the county – especially northern Bucks – remains a sanctuary of woods, farms and charming country inns. Back roads wind through forests ablaze with autumn color. Covered bridges span frigid creeks. Deer bound gracefully over fallen trees. Wildflowers blanket rolling meadows.

River mansions: Start your tour of Bucks County where William and Hannah Penn set up house, at **Pennsbury Manor**, off Route 9 in what is now the town of **Morrisville**. Pennsbury was an 8,400-acre estate situated on a bend in the Delaware River about 24 miles north of the city. Penn spent only two brief years at the plantation before returning to England in 1701.

"Let not poor Pennsbury be forgotten, or neglected," he wrote his servants, "keep the housen, the farme & the Gardens, till we come." But Penn never returned, his heirs had little interest, and the property fell into ruins.

That might have been the end of Pennsbury had it not been for a group of historians, architects and preservationists who quite literally brought the estate back to life. Meticulously reconstructed from archaeological studies and Penn's own detailed instructions, the property is now a working recreation of a colonial estate, fully furnished with one of the state's best collections of 17th-century antiques. Costumed guides are available to show visitors around the mansion, smokehouse, stable, kitchen, carpenter's shop, brew house and other outbuildings, and there is a packed schedule of special events, including workshops for children, garden tours, a 17th-century country fair, Christmas festivities, and demonstrations of open-hearth cooking, beer making, wood-working and other crafts.

Nearby, the colonial town of **Fallsington** (4 Yardley Avenue, off Route 1), where Penn came to worship while residing in the country, preserves several 18th-century buildings around a charming village square, including three Quaker meeting-houses and a log cabin.

Two other historic homes in the area are well worth a visit, too. The **Margaret R. Grundy Memorial Library and Museum** (610 Radcliffe Street, Bristol) is an elegant Victorian home, with a fine collection of period furnishings, that overlooks the Delaware River. Tours of the house and library, which is a modern structure built largely underground, are available by appointment.

Andalusia (State Road, Andalusia), one of the country's finest Greek Revival homes, is also on the Delaware. Originally a simple country house, Andalusia was purchased and fully redesigned by financier Nicholas Biddle, who hired Thomas U. Walter to handle the renovation. The 220-acre estate is still owned by the Biddle family; the house and its magnificent furnishings may be seen by reservation.

If you're traveling with children, you may want to set aside a day for nearby **Sesame Place** (just off Route 1 in Langhorne), a Sesame Street theme park with a wide range of rides, water slides, shows and other attractions like Rubber Duckie Rapids, Oscar's Obstacle Course, Mumford's Water Maze and the indoor Computer Gallery designed to engage young minds and bodies.

ceding
ies: fall
age
Bucks
inty.
t, Mercer
seum's
tral
rt.

Doylestown, the Bucks County seat, is directly north of center city. An important stagecoach station in the 1700s, Doylestown today is a Main Street town of charming gingerbread houses, interesting shops and first-rate inns and restaurants. Most tourists come to Doylestown to see the **Mercer Mile**, three fantastic structures built between 1908 and 1916 by Henry Chapman Mercer, a brilliant, if somewhat eccentric, archaeologist, artist and historian.

After years of studying ancient cultures in America and abroad, Mercer turned his attention to the tools and handicrafts of the Delaware Valley, searching the "bake-ovens, wagon-houses, cellars, hay lofts, smoke-houses, garrets and chimney-corners" scattered throughout the countryside for tools, utensils and other artifacts made obsolete by the Industrial Revolution. He called the collection "Tools of the Nation Maker," and with more than 40,000 objects, it remains the largest of its kind in the world. Mercer was also some-

thing of an artist. While researching local crafts, he became fascinated with a nearly forgotten style of Pennsylvania German pottery. He adapted the style to tile-making and eventually developed a commercial clay shop to produce tiles and other ceramics of his own design.

By 1905, Mercer's Moravian tiles had become a major exponent of America's own Arts and Crafts movement, and his work was being commissioned for such varied buildings as Grauman's Chinese Theater in Hollywood, the John D. Rockefeller estate at Pocantico Hills, the Harvard Lampoon building, the National Press Club in Washington, DC, the Pennsylvania Capitol in Harrisburg, and high-class hotels all over the world.

The first building Mercer designed was **Fonthill** (East Court Street and Swamp Road), a Tudor-style castle completed in 1910 and constructed entirely of reinforced concrete, a material that was just beginning to be used by professional architects. He built the castle from the inside out without benefit of detailed blueprints, improvising techniques as he went along, even pouring concrete over an existing farmhouse and incorporating it into the structure.

The rooms are irregular, the windows are unmatched, and stairways sometimes go nowhere, but the overall effect of the vaulted salons, maze-like floor plan, and the thousands of brilliantly colored tiles is really quite astonishing. It's probably safe to say that you have never seen anything like it. Guided tours of Fonthill are offered several times a day; it's advisable to make reservations at least several hours in advance.

Mercer started the neighboring **Moravian Pottery and Tile Works** even before Fonthill was completed. Modeled after several California missions, this second concrete fantasy served as a tile factory well into the 1950s. The Bucks County Parks Department reopened the Tile Works as a working museum in the 1970s, and it continues to turn out tiles using Mercer's original designs and techniques, although on a much smaller **American beauty.**

scale. Tours of the Tile Works leave every half hour.

Mercer followed the Tile Works with yet another medieval-style castle designed to house his massive collection of preindustrial tools and farm implements. Located at Pine and Ashland streets, the **Mercer Museum** is crammed with everything from stagecoaches to sausage-makers. And believe it or not, much of the collection is suspended by wires in the four-story central court. An iconoclast in almost everything he did, Mercer felt that the unusual display allowed visitors to see ordinary objects from a new perspective. Whatever his reasoning, the effect is likely to make your jaw drop.

The **James A. Michener Art Center**, named in honor of Doylestown's well-known author, is directly across the street. The museum is located on the grounds of the former Bucks County Jail. Prison walls surround part of the site, and the warden's house now serves as gallery space. Traveling exhibits change several times a year; the center's shows feature selections from the permanent collection in addition to work by regional artists.

You can also visit the homestead of another renowned Bucks County writer, Pearl S. Buck, author of *The Good Earth* and winner of both the Pulitzer and Nobel prizes. Located just north of Doylestown on Dublin Road in Perkasie, Buck's 60-acre spread, **Green Hills Farm**, is centered on an early 19th-century farmhouse, now headquarters of the Pearl S. Buck Foundation, an international children's-aid agency. Guided tours are offered daily.

Up the river: A 10-minute drive southeast of Doylestown on Route 202, **Peddlar's Village** is a complex of about 80 boutiques and restaurants specializing in antiques, folk art, fashions and handcrafted gifts. The shops are built around a landscaped "village green" with a pond, water wheel, gingerbread gazebo and award-winning gardens. Bargain hunters should try **Penn's Flea**

Market across Route 202 for that once-in-a-lifetime discovery, although serious antiquers may do better at more out-of-the-way dealers and flea markets.

It's a 5-mile drive on Route 202 south to the village of **New Hope**, a former ferry crossing on the Delaware River that now caters to the hordes of tourists who flock here every weekend. As a result, traffic can be horrendous, so be sure to give yourself plenty of time. A small mill town in the 1700s, New Hope boomed with the opening of the Delaware Canal in 1832. The railroad came along and put the waterway out of business in the early 1900s, but by then New Hope was attracting a newer, different sort of crowd.

The arrival of William Lathrop, Daniel Graber, Edward Redfield and other influential painters led to the growth of a lively artists' colony. And today, artists and collectors are still flocking to New Hope for the galleries and special exhibitions. The **Delaware Canal**, recently named a National Heritage Corridor, is also still in operation, although the mule-drawn barges now carry loads of tourists rather than coal and lumber. You can also catch a ride on the **New Hope & Ivyland Railroad**, which runs a Baldwin steam locomotive on a 9-mile, 50-minute round-trip between New Hope and Lahaska.

While you're milling through the crowds, look for some of the town's historic buildings. More than 200 are listed on the National Register of Historic Places. At South Main and Ferry streets, for example, the **Logan Inn** surrounds the shell of the original Ferry Tavern, which opened for business in the 1720s. Nearby, the **Coryell House**, old **Town Hall** and **Vansant House** all date to the latter half of the 18th century. Built in 1784, the **Parry Mansion** now serves as a museum of decorative arts.

New Hope is also home to the **Bucks County Playhouse**, which has been offering summer stock for more than 50 years from a renovated gristmill. And don't forget New Hope's sister city across the bridge in New Jersey. **Lambertville**, New Hope's less commercial alter-ego, is filled with homey restaurants, quirky shops and a more low-key attitude – in short, a perfect place to take shelter from New Hope's crowded sidewalks.

History buffs should make a point of visiting **Washington Crossing State Park**, where General George Washington launched his daring Christmas attack on the British and Hessian camp at Trenton, an event that is re-enacted every Christmas Day. The park is divided into two units. The first is about 2 miles south of New Hope; here you'll find the **Thompson-Neely House**, where the general and his officers met to plan the attack. A short drive away, the 110-foot **Bowman's Tower**, built in 1930 to commemorate a Revolutionary War lookout point, affords a spectacular view of the valley. A 100-acre **Wildflower Preserve** surrounds the tower; a naturalist is usually on hand to answer questions and suggest tours along the many trails.

Washington Crossing.

About 5 miles farther south, the second unit includes the **Washington Crossing Memorial Building**, where a replica of Emanuel Leutze's famous painting, *Washington Crossing the Delaware*, hangs, and the **Old Ferry Inn**, where Washington had his evening meal before crossing the river.

But the real flavor of Bucks County lies along the back roads and untrammeled spaces of its many farms and natural preserves. From New Hope, River Road winds along the Delaware River to the three charming towns of **Lumberville**, **Erwinna** and **Uhlerstown**. Along the way, at **Point Pleasant**, you can rent canoes and inner tubes for a float down the river. You'll find the area's loveliest parks in these northern reaches of the county, too, including the fascinating boulder field of **Ringing Rocks County Park**, the peace and isolation of **Bull's Island State Park**, the 1,450-acre **Lake Nockamixon**, which is the biggest body of water in the county, **Tohickon Valley County Park**

and **Ralph Stover State Park** in the stunning Tohickon Valley, **Peace Valley** just north of Doylestown, and the 19th-century **Erwin Stover House** and **Tinicum County Park** overlooking the Delaware River in Erwinna.

Northern Bucks is also home to most of the county's 11 **covered bridges**, most built in the 1870s. Contact the Bucks County Tourist Commission for a guide to the bridges.

A wine-tasting tour is a good way to see the countryside. Bucks County has four wineries that welcome visitors: **Buckingham Valley Vineyards** on Route 413 in Buckingham, **Bucks County Vineyards** on York Road outside New Hope, **Peace Valley Winery** on Old Limekiln Road in Chalfont, and **Sand Castle Winery** on River Road in Erwinna. And, of course, Bucks County is famous for its cozy bed-and-breakfast inns and classy restaurants, many in restored historic buildings.

● *Addresses of tour companies are listed in the Travel Tips section of this book.*

rging down e Delaware nal.

BY THE SEA

Since 1801, when the first newspaper advertisements pushed the New Jersey coast as a tourist attraction, it's been Philadelphia's favorite getaway spot. With traffic in your favor, you can make it "down the shore" in about 90 minutes. Traffic can be daunting on summer weekends, but, like an oasis shimmering on the horizon, the beach always seems within reach.

Of course, there's really more than one Jersey Shore. The colorful beach towns strung along the coast from the tip of Cape May to the shoals of Long Beach Island appeal to an amazing variety of tastes and interests. From the Victorian doll houses of Cape May to the hormone-charged revelries of Wildwood's bar scene, from the glitz and would-be glamour of Atlantic City to the family ambience of Ocean City, the coastal towns of southern New Jersey have little in common but the ocean lapping at their toes.

Solitude seekers: Before heading for the shore, however, be advised of some pitfalls. With the exception of Atlantic City and Wildwood, for example, visitors can't stroll the beaches without paying a fee. The amount is usually a trifle, but annoying all the same. In addition, because so many people summer at the shore, you're liable to run into the same exasperating crowds you thought you left behind in the city. Seekers of solitude should look elsewhere during the summer season.

And yet, for sheer nostalgia, sheer romance, sheer unadulterated fun, the Jersey Shore can't be beat. It's close, it's relaxing, and it's a tradition that Philadelphians will always hold close to their hearts.

Cape May, a narrow peninsula named after Dutch Captain Cornelius Jacobson Mey, who arrived at New Jersey's southernmost point in 1620, dips into the Atlantic Ocean like an elongated toe

testing the water. At the very tip of the peninsula is the town of **Cape May** itself, a laid-back resort of gingerbread homes, quaint shops and countless bed-and-breakfasts. Nearly razed by fire in 1878, the town reconstituted itself in the Victorian style, giving it an effete appeal that has kept the upper-crust crowd coming back season after season. For vacationers with more than a passing interest in architecture, walking and trolley tours of the historic district are offered daily during the summer.

For information, call or visit the **Mid-Atlantic Center for the Arts** at the **Emlen Physick House** (1048 Washington Street), a landmark Victorian home designed by well-known Philadelphia architect Frank Furness.

Nautical knick knacks: As for Cape May's beach, it is fairly small and, due to erosion, getting smaller every year. There are a few blocks of boardwalk, known locally as the **Promenade**, featuring a game room and the requisite fudge shop. More shopping is available at the **Washington Street Mall**, a quaint downtown walkway closed to traffic where you'll find handcrafted gifts, antiques, jewelry and a variety of nautical knick knacks. Another worthwhile strolling spot is **Cape May Point**, which has a lovely uncrowded beach, a working lighthouse dating to 1859, a 400-acre nature preserve that offers excellent birdwatching, and a half-submerged hulk known as the "concrete ship."

Cape May is the only South Jersey shore town that takes its cuisine seriously. For early risers, the Mad Batter (19 Jackson Street) dishes up great breakfasts on its comfy veranda. At lunchtime, you can treat yourself to belly-busting hoagies at Joe's. And for dinner, there are few places lovelier, or tastier, than the second-story veranda at Restaurant Maureen (429 Beach Drive), a romantic little eatery called Peaches (101 Sunset Boulevard) or the harbor-hugging Lobster House (Fisherman's Wharf). Afterwards, the locals usually meet for drinks at the Ugly Mug (426

ceding
ges: Lucy
elephant
National
toric
ndmark.
t,
pe May
torian
use.

Washington Street), gather around the piano for a sing-along at the Chalfonte Hotel (307 Howard Street), or catch a free concert at the Rotary Bandstand on Lafayette Street. If you prefer to skip the nightlife, you can indulge in one of Cape May's time-honored pastimes – setting your bones down in a rocking chair on the porch of your favorite bed-and-breakfast inn and listening to what the night sounded like a century ago.

Wild thing: It's a joke that Cape May and Wildwood are so close together, because no two towns could be more different. Once a family-oriented community, **Wildwood** began luring a younger and rowdier crowd during the 1970s, earning the nickname "Child-wood" in the process. When the drinking age was raised to 21, the kids could no longer drink legally at the island's many high-octane night spots. By that time, most of the family business was scared away, leaving the town with something of an identity crisis, not to mention an economic shortfall.

Wildwood is still a rite of passage for graduating students at Philadelphia high schools, and the two weeks in June known as "Senior Weeks" can get hectic. But during the rest of the summer, it isn't nearly as wild as it once was. And no matter what the critics say, it still has the best boardwalk in New Jersey, maybe even on the entire East Coast.

There's actually four towns here – Wildwood, **Wildwood Crest**, **North Wildwood** and the tiny island of **West Wildwood**, which even locals forget about. The boardwalk, which stretches from the Wildwood Crest border through Wildwood and into North Wildwood, has all the latest rides and water slides at the Jersey Shore's two best amusement piers – **Mariner's Landing** and **Morey's Pier**. Unlike the practice in most amusement parks, the rides here are pay-as-you-go, but day passes are available for both.

Don't worry about finding the right place to eat. The boardwalk is designed for grazing, with nonstop temptations like pizza (try Sam's), funnel cake, curly fries, ice cream (Kohr Brothers is tops), fudge (Laura's is outstanding), and salt-water taffy (kudos to James). Aside from some (mostly tacky) T-shirts and other souvenirs, shopping is negligible. For accommodations, there are hundreds of motels, most built during the 1950s, with limited amenities but colorful names like the Lollipop, the Suitcase and the Buccaneer.

An unassuming trio of towns – **Stone Harbor**, **Avalon** and **Sea Isle City** – occupy the island between Wildwood and Ocean City. Although they have a lower profile than their neighbors, their centralized location makes them an ideal place to stay during a week at the shore. Stone Harbor is noted primarily for its bird sanctuary, a 21-acre facility occupied by herons, ibises and egrets and a variety of migratory birds.

Both Sea Isle City and Avalon attract tourists to the bay side of the island with popular fishing and party boats. The island's best dining spots are also situ- **Atlantic City showgirl.**

228

ated on the bay. Locals and tourists alike line up for the seafood at Marie's, the Lobster Loft and Carmen's, all located a seashell's throw from 40th Street and Landis Avenue.

Pink elephants: Founded in 1881 by Methodists as a "proper Christian summer resort," **Ocean City** may be the best of all possible beach towns. It has a manageable boardwalk, civilized beaches and, best of all, Johnson's Popcorn. Johnson's is the reason why it seems that almost everyone on the boardwalk is chomping on caramel popcorn from giant plastic buckets. The town offers an impressive program of family activities ranging from sand-castle contests to a hugely popular baby parade. Ocean City is a dry town – the sale of alcohol is prohibited making this a decidedly family-oriented resort – but there's nightlife within an easy drive inland to **Somers Point**.

There's one day of the year when Ocean City shakes off its Methodist reticence and becomes an honest-to-goodness party town. That's when a regatta of elaborately decorated boats parade through the bay during the annual **Night in Venice** celebration. For one evening you would swear you were in, well, if not Venice, at least a mature version of Wildwood.

Continuing north, you can zip right through Longport – a residential community that generally keeps to itself – into **Margate**, where you'll find a 90-ton, six-story-high elephant named **Lucy**. Built as a real-estate promotion and later used as a tavern and hotel, this pachyderm has been a Margate treasure since 1881. Now she's a National Historic Landmark and the object of fierce loyalty among Margate residents. Collectors of kitschy memorabilia will have a field day at the Lucy gift shop.

Margate itself is an upper-income residential town. The best places to soak up the atmosphere are the deli counter at Casel's Supermarket (8008 Ventnor Avenue) and the rooftop bar at Ventura's Greenhouse (106 S. Benson Street).

Next door, summer houses and condominiums fill **Ventnor**, the town where the Atlantic City boardwalk actually begins. Here, though, there are no casinos, arcades or hot-dog stands. Instead, this is prime bicycle-riding boardwalk territory, where the only distractions are the crowds who come to gawk at the elegant oceanfront homes.

Monopoly city: The big draw on the Jersey Shore is **Atlantic City**, and the big draw in Atlantic City are the casinos. With the approval of gambling in 1976, this decaying seaside resort was granted a second lease on life. The first casino, Resorts International, opened in 1978. Donald Trump's Taj Mahal cut the ribbon in 1991.

Today, Atlantic City is one of the most popular tourist destinations in America, with more than 33 million visitors a year. Unfortunately, things haven't improved much in the real-life town beyond the showy, high-glitter facade. Once you leave the casinos, Atlantic City is still one of the most economically depressed towns on the East Coast.

Atlantic City isn't an oasis like Las Vegas. There are fewer casinos here, and the Atlantic City versions don't try as hard to get your attention. You can find big-name entertainers like Tony Bennett and Joan Rivers, but headliner shows aren't put on as often as they once were. Instead, comedy clubs, revues and condensed versions of Broadway musicals are the norm. But for those who have never seen a casino, or never put a few dollars down on a spin of the roulette wheel, comparisons with Vegas don't matter. Gambling is a fascinating process for both player and observer.

The games are essentially the same wherever you go – blackjack, baccarat, roulette, the money wheel, and those ubiquitous slot machines. The characteristics that distinguish Atlantic City's **casino hotels** from each other have to do with atmosphere. As the casinos are bunched in two locations – the boardwalk and the bay – you can stroll from one gaming hall to another (or, catch a ride on one of the boardwalk's famous **wicker rolling chairs**) until you find the place to try your luck.

There's **TropWorld** with its indoor **Tivoli Pier**, a 2-acre amusement park complete with Ferris wheel; the **Claridge**, which sells itself on intimate atmosphere; or the immense **Taj Mahal**, gussied up with neon baubles like an electrified pasha's palace. At the north end of the boardwalk is the **Showboat**, where great Dixieland jazz is played live in the lobby, and a large upstairs bowling alley provides extra-casino activity. These are, of course, only a few of the most interesting casinos.

For quintessential Atlantic City dining, steer away from the casino restaurants, where the prices are often jacked up to make the high-roller gamblers even more impressed with their "comp" meals. Instead, join the locals for legendary hoagies at the White House Sub Shop (2301 Arctic Avenue), Italian seafood at Angelo's Fairmont Tavern (2300

Atlantic City beach.

230

Fairmont Avenue), or, an Atlantic City institution, the Knife and Fork Inn (Atlantic and Pacific avenues). As you travel around the city, don't be surprised if the street names sound familiar. These are the same names used in the famous board game Monopoly, which was invented in Atlantic City in 1930. From Park Place to the Boardwalk, they're all here – although, much to the chagrin of unlucky gamblers, there's no "Pass 'Go' and Collect $200."

The streets are packed during the second week in September, the most exciting time of the year in Atlantic City, when the **Miss America Pageant** takes over the town. Say what you will about this long-running beauty contest – a sore point for feminists these days – but Miss America handicapping is one of the most popular diversions in the country. It's even more exciting when you've seen the Miss America Parade or sat through either the preliminary competition or the finals held at the **Atlantic City Convention Center**.

eft, Ocean
ity; sunset
ailers.

Just across the bridge from Atlantic City, **Brigantine**, a fairly quiet residential island, has uncrowded windswept beaches, especially at the northern tip, where there's a small nature preserve. Continuing north on the mainland brings you to aptly named **Long Beach Island**, a sliver of sand 18 miles long with a series of little towns strung along the main boulevard. Popular, crowded, friendly, and a bit removed from the party-town atmosphere of other shore spots, the island attracts a healthy mix of teenagers, families and well-off holidaymakers. Be sure to drive out to the scenic northern tip for a look at historic **Barnegat Lighthouse**. If you can make it to the top of the spiral staircase, the views are magnificent.

To the north, the Jersey Shore stretches all the way to Sandy Hook, passing the untrammeled sand dunes of **Island Beach State Park**, the boardwalk at **Seaside Heights**, the lovely old homes of **Spring Lake**, and many things of interest in between.

INSIGHT GUIDES
Travel Tips

Your vacation.

Your vacation after losing your wallet in the ocean.

 Lose your cash and it's lost forever. Lose American Express® Travelers Cheques and get them replaced. They can mean the difference between the vacation of your dreams and your worst nightmare. And, they are accepted like cash worldwide. Available at participating banks, credit unions, AAA offices and American Express Travel locations. *Don't take chances. Take American Express Travelers Cheques.*

do more

Travelers Cheques

For information, call 1-800-321-0882. ©1997 American Express Travel Related Services Company, Inc. All rights reserved.

Getting Acquainted

The Place 234
Climate 234
Culture and Customs 234
Fascinating Facts 234

Planning the Trip

What to Bring 234
Entry Regulations 234
Health 235
Money.............................. 235
Public Holidays 235
Getting There 236
Special Facilities.............. 236
Useful Addresses 237

Practical Tips

Business Hours 238
Tipping............................ 238
Media 238
Postal Services 238
Telecoms 239
Emergencies 239
Reservations 240

Getting Around

On Arrival 240
Public Transportation 240
Private Transportation 241

Where to Stay

Hotels.............................. 242
Bed & Breakfast/Inns 244
Seaside Lodgings 245
Youth Hostels 247
Campgrounds 247

Eating Out

What to Eat 247
Where to Eat 247

Attractions

Culture............................ 253
Historic Sites 257
Festivals 258

Shopping

Shopping Areas 261
What to Buy 262

Sports and Leisure

Participant Sports 263
Spectator Sports 264
Outdoor Activities 264

Further Reading

General 265
Other Insight Guides 265

Art/Photo Credits 266
Index 267

Getting Acquainted

*Telephone numbers preceded by 1-800 are toll free in the US. The prefix for all other numbers in the Philadelphia area is **215** unless otherwise noted. Do not use a prefix for calls within the same area code. The abbreviation for the state of Pennsylvania used in this book is PA.*

The Place

State: Pennsylvania.
Capital: Harrisburg.
Largest City: Philadelphia.
Population of Philadelphia: 3.8 million.
Time Zone: Eastern Time Zone or GMT minus 5 hours.
Weights and measures:
The US uses the Imperial system of weights and measures.
Metric is rarely used. Below is a conversion chart.
1 inch = 2.54 centimeters
1 foot = 30.48 centimeters
1 mile = 1.609 kilometers
1 quart = 1.136 liters
1 ounce = 28.4 grams
1 pound = .453 kilograms
1 yard = .9144 meters
Electricity: Standard is 110 volts.
International dialing code: (1).

Climate

Philadelphia's weather runs the gamut: hot and sticky in summer, biting cold in winter, pleasant but occasionally rainy in spring, cool and crisp in fall. Summer brings sudden rainstorms, winter has a few dustings of snow, although it doesn't usually last. Keep in mind that Philadelphia weather is unpredictable. Unseasonable cold or warm spells are not uncommon, Indian summer sometimes extends balmy weather well into October, and snow can fall as late as March.

Monthly Range:
Minimum–Maximum

January	26–40°F (-3.3–4.4°C)
February	26–41°F (-3.3–5°C)
March	33–50°F (0.5–10°C)
April	43–62°F (6–16.7°C)
May	53–73°F (11.7–22.8°C)
June	63–81°F (17.2–27.2°C)
July	68–95°F (20–35°C)
August	66–93°F (19–34°C)
September	60–80°F (15.6–26.7°C)
October	49–66°F (9.5–19°C)
November	39–54°F (4–12°C)
December	29–43°F (-1.7–6°C)

Culture and Customs

Philadelphia is in a cultural squeeze play. As the "high tide of the South," it shares much of Dixie's relaxed pace. In the shadow of New York City, it has adopted some of Gotham's raw energy and fast-paced lifestyle. This is still the Quaker City, however, and although it's heavily colonized by Southerners, New Yorkers and foreign immigrants, it maintains a distinct identity. It's a bit difficult to put one's finger on Philadelphia's Quaker ethic. Like William Penn, the city's Quaker founder, it has its share of incongruities. Generally speaking, Philadelphia's Quaker tradition respects wealth but eschews ostentation, values self-reliance but is generous to people in need, respects the law but tends to shy away from public service, welcomes outcasts but is clannish, values learning and culture but is notoriously provincial in taste and outlook, reveres the past but can be surprisingly progressive.

With rare exceptions, English is spoken everywhere in Philadelphia. Like all immigrant cities, there are ethnic pockets where other languages are spoken – Chinese in Chinatown, Vietnamese, Cambodian and Italian in a few South Philadelphia locations, Spanish in the Latino community of North Philadelphia – but even in these few areas English is spoken in nearly all stores and restaurants. If you travel to Pennsylvania Dutch country or meet Amish people in Philadelphia, you may notice that they speak a Pennsylvania German dialect, although they speak English to outsiders.

Fascinating Facts

Did you know that Philadelphia is a city of "firsts"? As well as being the United States' first capital, throughout its proud history it has given birth to the first:
• hospital
• fire company
• insurance company
• subscription library
• zoo

Planning the Trip

What to Bring

Philadelphia has four distinct seasons. Summer is hot and humid, with an occasional drenching cloudburst. Winter is bone-chilling. A significant accumulation of snow is unusual but not unheard of. The best plan for spring and fall is to dress in layers, so that you can put clothes on or take them off as the weather dictates. Although fancy restaurants and high-class hotels expect visitors to dress appropriately (some require jackets and ties for men), Philadelphians are, by and large, an informal lot. Most casual shops and restaurants don't mind if you wear neat shorts, a light shirt and tennis shoes during the summer, although it is always prudent to call ahead to check. In the hip parts of town, especially on South Street, just about anything goes. Most visitors prefer to walk around center city rather than drive or take a bus, so be sure to wear comfortable shoes or sneakers.

Entry Regulations

Visas and Passports

A passport, a visitor's visa and evidence of intent to leave the US after your visit are required for entry into the US by most foreign nationals. Visitors from the United Kingdom and several other countries (including but not limited to Japan, Germany, Italy, France, Switzerland, Sweden and the Netherlands) staying less than 90 days may not need a visa if they meet certain requirements. All other foreign nationals must obtain a visa from the US consulate or embassy in their country. An international vaccination certificate may also be required depending on your country of origin.

Exceptions are Canadians entering from the Western Hemisphere, Mexicans with border passes and British residents of Bermuda and Canada. Normally, these people do not need a visa or passport, although it's always best to confirm visa requirements before leaving your home country.

Once admitted to the US, you may visit Canada or Mexico for up to 30 days and re-enter the US without a new visa. If you happen to lose your visa or passport, arrange to get a new one at your country's nearest consulate or embassy.

Customs

All people entering the US must go through Customs. Be prepared to have your luggage inspected and keep the following guidelines in mind:

1. There is no limit to the amount of cash you can bring into the US. If the amount exceeds $10,000, however, you must file a special report.
2. Any objects brought for personal use may enter duty-free.
3. Adults may enter with a maximum of 200 cigarettes or 50 cigars or 2 kilograms of tobacco and/or 1 liter of alcohol duty-free.
4. Gifts valued at less than $400 can enter duty-free.
5. Agricultural products, meat and animals are subject to complex restrictions; to avoid delays, leave these items at home unless absolutely necessary.
6. Illicit drugs and drug paraphernalia are strictly prohibited. If you must bring narcotic or habit-forming medicines for health reasons, be sure that all products are properly identified, carry only the quantity you will need while traveling, and have either a prescription or a letter from your doctor.

In order to obtain additional information, contact US Customs, 1301 Constitution Ave NW, Washington, DC 20229. Tel: 202-927-6724. In Philadelphia: 2nd and Chestnut Sts. Tel: 597-4605).

Extensions of Stay

Visas are usually granted for six months. If you wish to remain in the country longer than six months, you must apply for an extension of stay at the Immigration and Naturalization Service, 2401 E St, Washington, DC 20520. Tel: 202-514-4330. In Philadelphia: 1600 Callowhill St. Tel: 656-7144.

Health

The bad news is that health care in the US is extremely expensive. If you don't already have insurance that is accepted in the US, ask your travel agent about a travel plan that, at the very least, covers emergency medical care. The good news is that Philadelphia boasts some of the country's most prestigious hospitals and medical schools. If you must become ill while traveling, Philadelphia is, all things considered, a good place to be. Bear in mind that many private practitioners expect payment upon delivery of services. If you are unable to pay at the time of your visit, or you don't have insurance, you may be turned away.

Money

American visitors: Major credit cards are widely accepted at shops, restaurants, hotels and gas stations, although not all cards are accepted by every vendor. To be safe, try to carry at least two kinds (American Express and Visa, for example).

Some credit cards may also be used to withdraw cash from automatic teller machines (ATMs) located throughout center city and the outlying areas. Out-of-town ATM cards may also work. Check with your bank or credit-card company for the names of the systems your cards will operate.

Money may be sent or received by wire at any Western Union Office (Tel: 1-800-325-6000) or American Express MoneyGram office (Tel: 1-800-543-4080).

Western Union
1618 N. Broad St. Tel: 232-2299.
1205 Walnut St. Tel: 351-4300.

American Express
16th and JFK Blvd. Tel: 587-2300.
615 Chestnut St. Tel: 592-9211.

Foreign visitors: American money is based on the decimal system. The basic unit, a dollar ($1), is equal to 100 cents. There are 4 basic coins, each worth less than a dollar. A penny is worth 1 cent (1¢). A nickel is worth 5 cents (5¢). A dime is worth 10 cents (10¢). And a quarter is worth 25 cents (25¢).

In addition there are several denominations of paper money. They are: $1, $5, $10, $20, $50, $100 and rarely, $2. Each bill is the same color, size and shape, so make sure you check the dollar amount on the face of the bill.

It's advisable to arrive with at least $100 in cash (in small bills) to pay for ground transportation and other incidentals. It's always a good idea to carry internationally recognized travelers' checks rather than cash. Travelers' checks are usually accepted by retailers in lieu of cash, or may be exchanged for limited amounts of cash at many banks. Bring your passport with you to the bank. Major credit cards are also a big help (American Express, Visa, MasterCard, Diners Club, Carte Blanche, Discover, etc.) and will be necessary if you want to rent a car.

In addition to select hotels and the airport, foreign currency may be exchanged at the following center city locations:
American Express Travel Service, 16th St and JFK Blvd. Tel: 587-2300.
Continental Bank, 1201 Chestnut St. Tel: 564-7188.
Thomas Cook Currency Services, 16 N. 17th St. Tel: 563-5544.
CoreStates First Pennsylvania Bank, 16th and Market Sts. Tel: 786-8880.
Fidelity Bank, 123 S. Broad St. Tel: 985-7068.
Mellon PSFS Bank, Broad and Chestnut Sts. Tel: 553-2145.
PNC Bank, Broad and Chestnut Sts. Tel: 585-5000.

Public Holidays

All government offices, banks and post offices are closed on public holidays, many of which are observed on the closest Monday, creating several three-day weekends. Public transportation does not run as frequently on these days. For a list of annual events, see "Festivals".

January 1: New Year's Day
January: Martin Luther King, Jr's
  Birthday
February : President's Day
March/April: Easter Sunday
May: Memorial Day
July 4: Independence Day
September: Labor Day
October: Columbus Day
November: Veterans' Day;
  Thanksgiving Day
December 25: Christmas Day

Getting There

By Air

Philadelphia has one major airport, servicing both domestic and international destinations. **Philadelphia International Airport** is in South Philadelphia about 25 minutes by car from center city. Major carriers that service the airport include:
Air Canada. Tel: 1-800-776-3000.
Air France. Tel: 1-800-237-2747.
Air Jamaica. Tel: 1-800-523-5585.
American Airlines. Tel: 1-800-433-7300.
American Eagle. Tel: 1-800-433-7300.
British Airways. Tel: 1-800-247-9297.
Continental Airlines. Tel: 1-800-525-0280.
Delta Airlines. Tel: 1-800-221-1212.
Lufthansa. Tel: 1-800-645-3880.
Mexicana Airlines. Tel: 1-800-531-7921.
Midwest Express. Tel: 1-800-452-2022.
Northwest Airlines. Tel: 1-800-225-2525.
Swissair. Tel: 1-800-221-4750.
TWA. Tel: 1-800-221-2000.
United Airlines. Tel: 1-800-241-6522.
USAir. Tel: 1-800-428-4322.

There is an information desk located at Terminal A, currency exchanges at Terminals A, D and Concourses B and E, and Travelers' Aid in Terminal E.

Baggage claim is located on the lower level, as are buses, taxis and rental car/hotel shuttles. A high-speed train line runs from the airport to 30th Street Station, Penn Center/Suburban Station and Market East Station in center city.

Atlantic City International Airport services most major East Coast cities. Carriers include Northwest Airlink, United Express, USAir and TW Ex-

press. It's about a 90-minute drive from Atlantic City to Philadelphia.

Newark International Airport in northern New Jersey and **Baltimore/Washington International Airport** in Maryland are within 2 hours by car.

Several airlines also operate ticket offices in center city. These include:
Alitalia, 2 Penn Center Plaza. Tel: 569-1245.
American Airlines, 1500 Market St. Tel: 1-800-433-7300.
British Airways, 1617 JFK Blvd. Tel: 1-800-247-9297.
Delta Airlines, Broad and Walnut Sts. One Penn Center Plaza. Tel: 928-1700.
Korean Air, 2 Penn Center Plaza. Tel: 665-9080.
Mexicana Airlines, 1600 Market St. Tel: 569-2080.
Olympic Airways, 3 Penn Center Plaza. Tel: 977-8601.
USAir, 123 S. Broad St. Tel: 563-8055.
United Airlines, 123 S. Broad St. Tel: 1-800-241-6522.
Varig Brazilian Airlines, 2000 Market St. Tel: 676-8311.

By Rail

Amtrak offers service from Philadelphia's majestic **30th Street Station** (originally built for the Pennsylvania Railroad) to hundreds of destinations across the country. Tel: 1-800-872-7245 for schedules, fares and other information.

Trains to New York City and Washington, DC, run hourly (if not more often). Travel time to New York is 2.5 hours. Travel time to Washington, DC is about 2 hours.

By Bus

Greyhound Bus Lines (Tel: 931-4000 or 931-4014), America's largest bus company with connections to cities and small towns throughout the country, is located at 1001 Filbert St, one block north of Market Street. The company routinely offers discounts such as a $99 go-anywhere fare and a $1 ticket for moms on Mother's Day. Call the Greyhound office nearest you for information regarding special rates and package tours.

Greyhound has a number of suburban stations just outside Philadelphia, including Bristol (Durham Road and Route 413. Tel: 785-3044), King of

Prussia (136 Town Center Road. Tel 768-7047) and Willow Grove (302 York Road. Tel: 659-3443).

By Car

Several highways lead to Philadelphia From New York City, the **New Jersey Turnpike** (exit 4) leaves you about 20 minutes from Philadelphia, near Camden, New Jersey. From Washington or Baltimore, **I-95** (also known as the Delaware Expressway) follows the Delaware River directly through the city. From the west, the **Pennsylvania Turnpike** intersects **I-76** (the Schuylkill Expressway); and from Atlantic City, the **Atlantic City Expressway** leads to the Walt Whitman Bridge and the Benjamin Franklin Bridge.

Bridges crossing the Delaware River connecting Philadelphia to New Jersey include: the Walt Whitman Bridge, Benjamin Franklin Bridge, Betsy Ross Bridge and Tacony-Palmyra Bridge.

Three major arteries cross Philadelphia. Although often slowed by rush-hour traffic, they make it easy to get from one end of the city to the other during off-hours. I-76, or the **Schuylkill Expressway** (known derisively as the Sure-Kill Crawlway), runs along the Schuylkill River from northwest Philadelphia to the Walt Whitman Bridge in South Philadelphia. **I-95** runs north-south through the city along the Delaware River. And 676, or the **Vine Street Expressway**, runs east-west across center city from I-95 to I-76.

If you plan to do a lot of driving during your visit, it's worth buying a membership to the **Automobile Association of America** (**AAA**), which, in addition to free maps and guidebooks, provides emergency road service, insurance and bail bond protection.
Keystone Automobile Club (Automobile Association of America), 2040 Market St. Tel: 864-5000.
Emergency Road Service. Tel: 569-4411

Special Facilities

Disabled and Elderly

SEPTA. For information on SEPTA's services for elderly and disabled riders, call 580-7365 or 580-7853 (TDD). SEPTA also operates **Paratransit**, a door-to-door van service for those who are unable to ride the bus or train. Riders must register with SEPTA in advance

nd make reservations. Tel: 580-7000
ır 580-7712 (TDD).

ibrary for the Blind and Physically **Handicapped**, 919 Walnut St. Tel: 925-3213. 9am–5pm weekdays. This branch of the Free Library carries audio books, Braille books, large-print books and other materials designed or handicapped readers.

Moss Rehabilitation Hospital, 1200 N. Tabor Road. Tel: 456-9600 or 456-9602 (TTY). 9am–5pm weekdays. Moss's **Travel Information Service** provides disabled travelers with all sorts of information on accessibility and other issues in the United States and abroad.

Mayor's Commission on the Disabled. Tel: 686-2798.

Philadelphia Corporation for Aging Seniors Helpline. Tel: 765-9040.

Travelers Aid

f you're stranded in the city, you may request assistance from any of these offices:

Greyhound Bus Terminal, 9th and Filbert Sts. Tel: 238-0999. Monday 10am–3pm, Tuesday 10am–4pm, Wednesday–Thursday 9am–4pm, Friday 10am–1pm.

Philadelphia International Airport, Terminal E. Tel: 365-6525. Sunday–Tuesday noon–8pm, Wednesday 11am–8pm, Thursday noon–8pm, Friday noon–9pm.

Social Services Building, 311 S. Juniper St. Tel: 546-0571. Monday–Friday 8.45am–4.45pm.

30th Street Station. Tel: 386-0845. Monday–Saturday 9am–5pm.

Useful Addresses

Tourist Offices

Philadelphia Visitors Center, 1525 John F. Kennedy Blvd. Tel: 636-1666.

Philadelphia Convention and Visitors Bureau, 1515 Market St. Tel: 636-3300 or 1-800-537-7676.

Independence National Historical Park Visitor Center, 3rd and Chestnut Sts. Tel: 597-8974 or 597-8975.

Bucks County Tourist Commission, PO Box 912, Doylestown, PA 18901-9999. Tel: 345-4552.

Pennsylvania Dutch Convention and Visitors Bureau, 501 Greenfield Road, Lancaster, PA 17601. Tel: 717-299-3901.

Valley Forge Convention and Visitors

Bureau, PO Box 311, Norristown, PA 19404. Tel: 610-834-1550.

Greater Atlantic City Convention and Visitors Bureau, 2314 Pacific Ave, Atlantic City, NJ 08401. Tel: 609-348-7100.

Chamber of Commerce of Greater Cape May, PO Box 556, Cape May, NJ 08204. Tel: 609-884-5508.

Cape May County Chamber of Commerce, PO Box 74, Cape May Court House, NJ 08210. Tel: 609-465-7181.

The Welcome Center, 405 Lafayette St, Cape May, NJ 08204. Tel: 609-884-9562.

Tour Companies

PHILADELPHIA

African-American Historical Tours, 4601 Market St, Suite 4000. Tel: 748-3222. Five tours focusing on the people and places of the city's African-American history.

At Your Service, PO Box 390, Devon, PA. Tel: 296-2828. Multilingual tours of historic district and environs for private and corporate groups.

AudioWalk & Tour, Norman Rockwell Museum, 6th and Sansom Sts. Tel: 925-1234. Audio tape and player rentals allow visitors to explore the historic district on their own.

Black History Strolls and Tours, 339 S. 2nd St. Tel: 923-4136. Walking and bus tours of historic district with emphasis on black history and culture; available in several languages.

Centipede Tours, 1315 Walnut St. Tel: 735-3123. Tours of historic district led by costumed guides; available in many languages.

Choo Choo Trolley, 4941 Longshore Ave. Tel: 333-2119. Popular group tours on a trolley-bus.

Gilboy Tours, 210 Locust St. Tel: 925-7868. Multilingual bus and walking tours of Philadelphia, Amish country, Brandywine country and Valley Forge with costumed guides.

Foundation for Architecture, One Penn Center, Suite 1165. Tel: 569-3187. Call the foundation for a schedule of over 20 walking tours focusing on the city's architectural history; one of the most informative tours and best values in the city.

Friends of Independence National Historical Park, 313 Walnut St. Tel: 597-7919. One-hour evening tours of Independence Park; summer only.

International Visitors Council, 34th St and Civic Center Blvd. Tel: 823-7264. A private nonprofit corporation offering multilingual bus and walking tours of Philadelphia's historic district and Amish country for groups.

NoTourious Philadelphia, PO Box 33143. Tel: 625-2680. A 2-hour bus tour featuring crime scenes, scandals, movie locations and other offbeat attractions. Available April–November.

Old Town Trolley Tours, 60 Laurel St. Tel: 928-8687. Two-hour narrated tours of historic areas and Fairmount Park.

BUCKS COUNTY

Executive Events, 4647 Point Pleasant Pike, Doylestown, PA 18901. Tel: 766-2211. Customized group and individual guided tours specializing in Bucks County.

PENNSYLVANIA DUTCH COUNTRY

Amish Country Tours, 3121 Old Philadelphia Pike, Bird-in-Hand. Tel: 717-392-8622. Bus tours of Lancaster County farmland and Amish communities.

Historic Lancaster Walking Tour, 100 S. Queen St, Lancaster, PA 17603. Tel: 717-392-1776. Walking tours of downtown Lancaster led by costumed guides.

Lancaster Bicycle Touring, 41 Greenfield Road, Lancaster, PA 17602. Tel: 717-396-0456. Guided bicycle tours for groups.

SOUTHERN NEW JERSEY SHORE

Mid-Atlantic Center for the Arts, 1048 Washington St, Cape May, NJ 08204. Tel: 609-884-5404. Walking and trolley-bus tours of Cape May's historic district and surrounding area.

Embassies and Consulates

Austria, 3 Benjamin Franklin Parkway. Tel: 665-7348.

Belgium, Curtis Center, Suite 1150, Independence Square West. Tel: 238-8729.

Canada, 1 Belmont Ave, Bala Cynwyd. Tel: 610-667-8210.

France, 1717 Arch St. Tel: 994-2175.

Germany, 5th and Market Sts. Tel: 922-7415.

Israel, 230 S. 15th St. Tel: 546-5556.

Italy, 421 Chestnut St. Tel: 592-7329.

Mexico, Bourse Building. Tel: 922-4262.

The Netherlands, 45 Brennan Drive, Bryn Mawr. Tel: 610-520-9591.
Norway, 112 Christian St. Tel: 462-2502.
Spain, 3410 Warden Drive. Tel: 848-6180.
Switzerland, Public Ledger Building. Tel: 922-2215.

Practical Tips

Business Hours

Standard business hours are 9am–5pm. Many banks open a little earlier, usually 8–8.30am, and nearly all close by 3pm. A few have Saturday morning hours. Major department stores are open 10am–7pm Monday–Saturday, until 8pm on Wednesday, and noon–5pm on Sunday. A few large supermarkets are open 24 hours.

The shops in downtown Philadelphia are famous for closing promptly at 5pm. A group of enterprising business people have joined together in an effort to keep shops open late on Wednesday evenings in the hope of attracting after-work shoppers.

Tipping

As elsewhere, service personnel in Philadelphia depend on tips for a large part of their income. With few exceptions, tipping is left up to your discretion; gratuities are not automatically added to the bill. In most cases 15–20 percent is the going rate for tipping waiters, taxi drivers, bartenders, barbers and hairdressers. Porters and bellmen usually get about 75¢–$1 per bag, but never less than $1 total.

Media

Newspapers and Magazines

Philadelphia has two major daily newspapers, *The Philadelphia Inquirer* and *The Daily News*, both owned by the same firm. The *Inquirer* is considered to be the thinking person's paper, with award-winning journalists and in-depth coverage. Look for the Friday "Week-

end" section for entertainment information. *The Daily News,* which calls itself the "People Paper," is published in a tabloid format, with good overviews of the news, a large sports section and popular special sections. Both papers list upcoming events.

There are a number of weekly newspapers, too, most available at corner boxes, delicatessens, laundromats and bookstores throughout center city, with listings or advertisements for local nightclubs, galleries, restaurants, museums and shops. *The City Paper* and *The Philadelphia Weekly* are the two most popular.

Philadelphia Magazine is a glossy magazine, published monthly, and contains feature articles covering culture, social life, politics and people in the Delaware Valley. The restaurant reviews are great for tips on the latest developments in the Philly food scene. "Datebook," the rundown of upcoming events, is also very helpful.

Many bookstores in center city carry a wide range of magazines. These include Tower Books, Borders Book Shop, Brentano's, Encore Books and Waldenbooks. A selection of major daily newspapers are also available at newstands throughout center city.

International magazines and journals can be purchased at Afterwords (218 S. 12th St), Avril 50 (3406 Sansom St) and Popi (526 S. 4th St and 116 S. 20th St).

Radio

There are more than 50 radio stations on the FM and AM dial in the Philadelphia area. These are some of the major ones:

	Radio Station	Dial Position
News/Talk	WKYW	1060 AM
	WHYY	90.9 FM
Country	WCZN	1590 AM
	WXTU	92.5 FM
Rock	WMMR	93.3 FM
	WYSP	94.1 FM
Pop	Eagle 106	106 FM
	Q 102	102.1 FM
	WYXR	104.5 FM
Classical	WFLN	95.7 FM
Oldies	WOGL	98.1 FM
	WFIL	560 AM
Urban	WUSL	98.9 FM
Contemporary	WIOQ	102.1 FM
	WDAS	1480 AM
Easy Listening	WEAZ	101 FM
Jazz	WRTI	90.1 FM

Gospel	WNAP	1110 AM
Spanish	WYIS	690 AM
Sports	WIP	610 AM
Alternative	WXPN	88.5 FM

Television

Philadelphia is served by more than 10 television stations. With cable service, the number can go over 30. There are three major commercial networks: ABC, NBC and CBS and a fairly new contender, Fox Broadcasting. The Public Broadcasting System (PBS) is viewer supported and commercial-free. Stations which are available without cable include:

Channel	Station	Network Affiliation
3	WKYW	NBC
6	WPVI	ABC
10	WCAU	CBS
12	WHYY	PBS
17	WPHL	
29	WTXF	
35	WYBE	
57	WGBS	
61	WTGI	

Postal Services

Standard postal hours are 8.30am–5pm Monday–Friday, 9am–12pm Saturday. A few post offices have extended hours, including the Main Post Office at 2970 Market St (24 hours Monday–Saturday) and the William Penn Annex at 9th and Chestnut Sts (8.30am–6pm Monday–Friday, 9am–4pm Saturday). There are also three self-service postal centers open 24 hours a day: Main Post Office (2970 Market St), Northeast Shopping Center (Welsh Road and Roosevelt Blvd) and Philadelphia Airport Concourse C. Stamps are sold at all post offices and self-service centers, and from vending machines at some convenience stores, filling stations, hotels and transportation terminals.

For overnight delivery try Express Mail. For expedited delivery, often within two days, ask for Priority Mail. For postal information, tel: 382-9201; for zip code information, tel: 895-9000.

Post offices in center city are:
B. Free Franklin Station, 316 Market St. Tel: 592-1289.
Commerce Station, 1301 Callowhill. Tel: 592-1294.
Continental Station, 325 Chestnut St. Tel: 627-1171.

Fairmount Station, 900 N. 19th St. Tel: 232-4600.

John Wanamaker Station, 1300 Market St. Tel: 557-9944.

Middle City, 2037 Chestnut St. Tel: 567-3772.

Middle City East, 2970 Market St. Tel: 895-8978.

Penn Center Station, Subway Concoure, 2 Penn Center. Tel: 496-9679.

William Penn Annex, 900 Market St. Tel: 592-9610.

Courier Service

For overnight or expedited delivery of letters and packages, contact Federal Express (Tel: 1-800-238-5355), DHL (Tel: 1-800-345-2727) or United Parcel Service (Tel: 1-800-272-4877) for the office or drop box nearest you.

There are **Federal Express** offices in center city at: 121 S. Broad St; 615 Chestnut St; 11th and Market Sts; 1617 JFK Blvd; 1500 Market St; 1900 Market St; 2 Penn Center; 820 Spring Garden St.

United Parcel Service, 15 E. Oregon Ave. Tel: 463-7300.

Telecoms

Western Union (Tel: 351-4300) can arrange telegram, telex and facsimile transmissions. MCI International (Tel: 496-3200) handles business telexes and facsimiles. Check the phone directory or call for the nearest office.

Fax machines are available at most hotels. Printers, copy shops, stationers and office supply shops may also have them, as well as a number of convenience stores.

Pay phones can be found throughout the city: at restaurants, bars, hotels, gas stations, public buildings and many street corners. To operate, drop in at least 25¢ and dial your number. If you need to deposit more change, a recorded voice will tell you the amount. The prefix, or area code, in the Philadelphia area is 215. Do not dial the prefix if you are calling within the same area code. The prefix for areas immediately west and north of this calling region is 610. The prefix for the Lancaster area is 717. The prefix for southern New Jersey is 609. You must dial 1 before the prefix.

If you need assistance, dial 0 and wait for the operator to answer. For directory information, dial 555-1212.

Take advantage of toll-free 800 numbers whenever possible. Long-distance rates tend to be lower on weekends and after 5pm.

To dial other countries (Canada follows the US system), first dial the international access code 011, then the country code: Australia (61); France (33); Germany (49); Italy (39); Japan (81); Mexico (52); Spain (34); United Kingdom (44). If using a US phone credit card, dial the company's access number below, then 01, then the country code. Sprint, tel: 10333; AT & T, tel: 10288.

Emergencies

Security and Crime

As with other big cities, crime is a concern in Philadelphia, but with a few precautions you shouldn't run into any trouble. For starters, use common sense. Don't carry large sums of cash or wear flashy or expensive jewelry. Hang on to your purse or shoulder bag and keep your wallet in your front pocket. Women should not travel alone at night, and no one should go into a strange or deserted area alone at night. Your best asset is knowing where you are and where you're going. Always walk purposefully, with confidence, even if you're lost. With a little forward planning, you should be able to avoid dangerous areas.

If you need to take the subway at night, be sure to stand near other people, or, if possible, a SEPTA police officer. Avoid riding in a car with just a few people in it. If you get on an empty bus, sit near the driver.

If you are mugged, or run into some other trouble, call or go to the nearest police station and report the crime. The police may not be much help finding your assailant, but they can do the proper paperwork for insurance claims. There is no good response to a mugging. Your safest bet is to give the mugger your money and then run away as quickly as possible, making as much noise as possible. Report the crime immediately to the police.

For police, medical or fire emergencies, dial **911** anywhere in the city.

Loss of Belongings

If any of your possessions are lost or stolen in Philadelphia, report it to the police at once. It is unlikely that your property will be returned, but they will have you file reports necessary to make an insurance claim. Auto theft and break-ins are a real problem in Philadelphia. Make sure you keep your car doors locked (even when you're inside the car), and lock all belongings firmly inside the trunk. If you have anything particularly valuable, you may want to ask your concierge to lock it in the hotel safe.

Lost or stolen credit cards or traveler's checks:

American Express. Tel: 1-800-528-4800.

Visa. Tel: 1-800-336-8472.

Carte Blanche/Diners Club. Tel: 1-800-234-6377.

MasterCard. Tel: 1-800-826-2181.

Lost Luggage

If your luggage is lost or delayed en route to Philadelphia by air, many airlines will deliver it to your hotel when, and if, it is found. If you don't already have insurance for lost or stolen luggage, ask your airline or travel agent for a travel policy. Before you check in, make sure each piece of luggage has an identification tag.

Medical Services

For a medical emergency, call **911** for an ambulance or go to the nearest hospital emergency room. There are over 50 hospitals in the Philadelphia area. These are only a few of the largest:

The Children's Hospital of Philadelphia, 34th St and Civic Center Blvd. Tel: 590-1000.

Albert Einstein Medical Center, York and Tabor Road. Tel: 456-7890.

Presbyterian Medical Center, 39th and Market Sts. Tel: 662-8000.

Hahnemann University Hospital, Broad and Vine Sts. Tel: 762-7000.

Hospital of the University of Pennsylvania, 3400 Spruce St. Tel: 662-4000.

Thomas Jefferson University Hospital, 11th and Walnut Sts. Tel: 955-6000.

Temple University Hospital, Broad and Ontario Sts. Tel: 221-2000.

Pennsylvania Hospital, 8th and Spruce Sts. Tel: 829-3000.

Friends Hospital, 4641 Roosevelt Blvd. Tel: 831-4600.

Northeastern Hospital, 2301 E. Allegheny Ave. Tel: 291-3000.

Methodist Hospital, 2301 S. Broad St. Tel: 952-9000.

Medical College of Pennsylvania Hospital, 3300 Henry Ave. Tel: 842-6000.
Hospital of Philadelphia College of Osteopathic Medicine, 4150 City Ave. Tel: 871-1000.
Graduate Hospital, 1800 Lombard St. Tel: 893-2000.
Misericordia Hospital, 5301 Cedar Ave. Tel: 748-9000.

A number of hospitals offer physician referral services for non-emergency visits:
Children's Hospital of Philadelphia. Tel: 1-800-879-2467.
Hahnemann University. Tel: 448-3627.
Medical College Hospitals. Tel: 1-800-776-4325.
Philadelphia County Medical Society. Tel: 563-5343.
Prologue. Tel: 1-800-362-8677.
Thomas Jefferson University Health Services. Tel: 1-800-533-3669.
Temple University Medical Practices. Tel: 1-800-836-7536.
University of Pennsylvania Medical Center. Tel: 662-7366.

Pharmacies sell over-the-counter drugs without a doctor's prescription. For controlled drugs, including narcotics and most antibiotics, you must obtain a written doctor's prescription or, in some cases, you can ask the doctor to call the pharmacy directly. There are 24-hour CVS Pharmacies at 6501 Harbison Ave at Roosevelt Blvd in Northeast Philadelphia and Passyunk Ave and Reed St in South Philadelphia.

Reservations

It is advisable to make reservations well in advance at all hotels, especially during the warm-weather tourist season. Reservations are essential at finer restaurants, and always a good idea at more casual places. If a restaurant doesn't take reservations, you can call ahead and ask how long the wait will be, if any. Overbooking is not a big problem in Philadelphia. Most restaurants make a genuine effort to seat you promptly.

Getting Around

Thanks to William Penn, getting around center city is fairly easy. The streets are laid out in an orderly grid. Traffic isn't too bad, although rush hours tend to be congested. There is plenty of public transportation. But the best way to get around center city is on foot. From City Hall, you can walk just about anywhere in center city within about 45 minutes.

Outside of center city, Philadelphia seems to spawl interminably. Public transportation is necessary to visit surrounding areas. Driving is usually convenient, too, although finding a parking spot may be difficult in some neighborhoods.

SEPTA (Southeastern Pennsylvania Transportation Authority) operates an extensive public transit system with buses, trolleys, subways, and surface-subway cars able to take you anywhere in the city, and commuter rail lines (like the famous Main Line) linking the city with the suburbs. Tel: 580-7800.

On Arrival

The least expensive way to travel between the airport and center city is SEPTA's Airport Rail Line (R1), which operates daily 6am–midnight, every half hour. The train departs from Market East, Suburban Station and 30th Street Station and services terminals A, B, C, D and E. The trip takes less than 30 minutes. Purchase tickets before boarding.

Taxis and shuttle vans are also available. A taxi from center city to the airport will cost about $25–35 without tip. A shuttle van costs much less.

Some hotels offer complimentary shuttle service, too. Ask your hotel when you make reservations.

Public Transportation

Bus

SEPTA offers bus service throughou the city. For details on routes an schedules, contact SEPTA, tel: 580 7800. Exact change is necessary.

The most useful bus route for vis tors is the **Route 76 Ben Frankline** which makes a round-trip from the In dependence National Historical Par Visitor Center at 3rd and Chestnut runs along Market Street to City Ha and then up the Benjamin Frankli Parkway to the Museum of Art. **Rout 42** is also convenient. It runs cross town along the Chestnut Stree Transitway between 2nd and 17t streets and then crosses into Wes Philadelphia on Walnut Street.

Maps, timetables and tokens ar available at the SEPTA customer serv ice center at 841 Chestnut St (8am– 4.30pm Monday–Friday). If you plan o using public transit often, a weekly o monthly **Transpass**, or daily **DayPas** may be worthwhile. Passes may b purchased at sales offices at Marke East Station, Suburban Station, 30t Street Station and 16th and JFK Blvd

The new **Philly Phlash** is also con venient. The purple shuttle bus make a loop from Logan Circle throug Center City to South Street and th waterfront.

New Jersey Transit offers bus serv ice from the Greyhound terminal a 10th and Filbert streets to Atlanti City, New York and other destinations For further information, tel: 569-3752

Subway, Train and Trolley

Four subway lines run through th heart of Philadelphia:
The Market-Frankford Line run along Market Street from 69th Stree to 2nd Street and then north to th Frankford Terminal.
The Subway-Surface Line run along Market Street from 13th Stree to 33rd Street and then branches off into West Philadelphia.
The Broad Street Line runs alon Broad Street from Fern Rock (in Nort Philadelphia) to Pattison Avenue (a the South Philadelphia Sports Com plex), with a spur from Girard Street t 8th and Market.
Patco operates a rail link acros the Delaware River between Philadel phia and Camden terminating a

indenwold, New Jersey. Patco has our underground stations in center city: Locust Street at 16th, 13th and 10th streets, and 8th and Market streets. Trains depart every 11 minutes weekdays 9am–midnight, every 20 minutes at other times. For further information, tel: 922-4600.

An extensive network of **Regional Rail Lines** link the city with suburbs in Bucks, Montgomery, Delaware and Chester counties. Board regional lines at 30th Street Station, Suburban Station or Market East Station.

Philadelphia once had one of the country's most extensive trolley systems. Today, only one trolley line remains. The **Penn's Landing Trolley** is an antique trolley that runs on Delaware Avenue (this stretch was recently renamed Columbus Avenue) along the waterfront. Saturday and Sunday, 11am–dusk. Board at Race, Market, Walnut, Dock, Spruce, Lombard or Fitzwater streets.

Taxis

Taxis are usually available at center city tourist spots. Rates are fairly reasonable. A 15 percent tip is customary. Call at least 30 minutes ahead for door-to-door service to take you anywhere in the city.

These are a few of the largest taxi companies:
United Cab. Tel: 625-9170.
Yellow Cab. Tel: 922-8400.
Quaker City Cab. Tel: 728-8000.
Academy Cab. Tel: 333-8294.
Olde City Taxi. Tel: 338-0838.

Private Transportation

Limousine

Luxurious but expensive, most limousine companies charge a minimum fee plus an hourly and/or mileage rate.
Limelight Limousine. Tel: 342-5557.
Dave's Best Limousine. Tel: 288-8000.
Knights Limousine. Tel: 333-1333.
Liberty Limousine. Tel: 1-800-654-8614.
Carey Limousine. Tel: 492-8402.
RV Limousine. Tel: 743-2700.

Car Rental

Cars may be rented at the airport, many hotels and rental agencies throughout the city and suburbs. You must be at least 21 years old, have a valid driver's license and at least one major credit card to rent a car. Be sure that you are properly insured for both collision and liability. Insurance is usually not included in the base rental fee. You may already be insured by your own insurance or credit-card company. It is also a good idea to inquire about an unlimited mileage package. If not, you may be charged extra per mile over a given limit.

Rental fees vary depending on the time of year, how far in advance you book your rental, and if you travel on weekdays or weekends. Inquire about any discounts or benefits you may be eligible for, including corporate, credit card or frequent flyer programs.

Alamo
US   (800) 327-9633
International   +1-305-522 0000
Avis
US   (800) 331-1212
International   +1-918-664 4600
Budget
US   (800) 527-0700
International   +1-214-404 7600
Dollar
US   (800) 800-4000
International   +1-813-877 5507
Enterprise
US   (800) 325-8007
International   +1-314-781 8232
Hertz
US   (800) 654-3131
International   +1-405-749 4424
National
US   (800) 227-7368
International   +1-612-830 2345
Thrifty
US   (800) 331-4200
International   +1-918-669 2499

Parking: Two words strike fear in the heart of every Philadelphia motorist: meter maid! The Parking Violations Bureau is extremely efficient. If you park illegally, you will get a ticket. And if you don't pay the fine within the allotted time, you will get slapped with a hefty penalty.

Street parking in center city can be frustrating. Spaces are often scarce, and most parking meters accept quarters only. If you can't find a space, it is almost always cheaper to leave the car in a parking lot or garage than to pay a parking ticket. There are garages and parking lots throughout center city; rates tend to be lower in Chinatown.

For information on locations and rates, check the telephone directory.

Carriages

Horse-drawn carriages are a romantic (although expensive) way to see the historic district of Philadelphia. Drivers, many in costume, act as guides. You can almost always catch a carriage at Head House Square or Independence Hall. For more information or reservations, contact:
Society Hill Carriage. Tel: 627-6128.
Philadelphia Carriage. Tel: 922-6840.
'76 Carriage. Tel: 923-8516.

Ferry

A private company runs a ferry between Penn's Landing (Delaware and Walnut Sts) and the New Jersey Aquarium in Camden every 30 minutes on the quarter hour, 7.15am–6.30pm Monday–Friday, 9.15am–8.30pm Saturday, 8.30am–5.30pm Sunday. Tel: 1-800-634-4027.

Where to Stay

The opening of several high-quality hotels in recent years has encouraged competitive prices, making Philadelphia hotels especially good value. Reservations are essential at nearly all center city hotels, especially during the May to September season. If you reserve by telephone, you will need a credit card to guarantee the room. If you do not have a credit card, you may be asked to send a deposit by mail. Be sure to ask about weekend specials. Many hotels rely on the business trade and are willing to offer discounts in order to boost occupancy rates over the weekend. For a less expensive alternative, try the chain motels outside the city, most of which are clean, simple and reasonably priced.

The price guide below indicates approximate rates for a standard double room.

$	under $100
$$	$100 to $150
$$$	$150 to $200
$$$$	over $200

Top Hotels

The Barclay, 237 S. 18th St, Philadelphia, PA 19103. Tel: 545-0300 or toll free 1-800-411-3434. A classic on Rittenhouse Square, with fine old-world furnishings; a traditional favorite of the Social Register crowd. Amenities: canopy and four-poster beds, antiques and reproductions, Le Beau Lieu restaurant, concierge, gift shop, air conditioning, TV. Credit cards: all major. $$–$$$

Doubletree Hotel, Broad and Locust Sts, Philadelphia, PA 19107. Tel: 893-1600 or toll free 1-800-222-8733. Formerly the Hilton, a 25-story establishment with modern amenities near City Hall and Academy of Music. Amenities: restaurant, indoor swimming pool, sun deck, health club, sauna, air conditioning, minibar, TV, valet parking. Credit cards: all major. $$

The Four Seasons Hotel, 18th St and Franklin Parkway, Philadelphia, PA 19103, Tel: 963-1500 or toll free 1-800-332-3442. Elegant, newer hotel on Logan Square near Franklin Institute and Museum of Art. Amenities: first-class Fountain Restaurant and Swann Café, concierge, indoor pool, spa, massage, air conditioning, minibar, TV, valet parking. Credit cards: all major. $$$$

Guest Quarters, 4101 Island Ave, Philadelphia, PA 19153. Tel: 365-6600 or toll free 1-800-424-2900. Plush accommodation popular with business travelers near airport about 15–20 minutes south of center city. Amenities: restaurant, lounge, health club, indoor pool, complimentary breakfast, air conditioning, TV, free parking, airport shuttle. Credit cards: all major. $$–$$$

Hotel Atop the Bellevue, Broad and Walnut Sts, Philadelphia, PA 19102. Tel: 893-1776 or toll free 1-800-221-0833. Elegant but unpretentious, the revamped Bellevue is comfortable and stylish with an airy central atrium and many rooms with lovely city views; near City Hall and Academy of Music. Amenities: Founders, a gourmet restaurant with breathtaking views, health club with indoor pool, swank shops on lower level, valet parking, concierge, air conditioning, TV, VCR, minibar. Credit cards: all major. $$$–$$$$

Korman Suites Hotel, 20th and Hamilton Sts, Philadelphia, PA 19130. Tel: 569-7200. Luxury hotel and conference center especially designed for business travelers and long-term visitors, located near Benjamin Franklin Parkway. Amenities: restaurant, health club, outdoor pool, kitchenettes and washer-dryers, meeting facilities, shuttle service to center city, air conditioning, TV, free parking. Credit cards: American Express, Diners Club, MasterCard, Visa. $$$

Latham, 17th and Walnut Sts, Philadelphia, PA 19103. Tel: 563-7474 or toll free 1-800-528-4261. Renovated old-world style hotel near Rittenhouse Square. Amenities: restaurant, lounge, concierge, laundry service, nearby health club, air conditioning, minibar, TV. Credit cards: all major. $$$

Omni Hotel at Independence Park, 401 Chestnut St, Philadelphia, PA 19106. Tel: 925-0000 or toll free 1-800-843-6664. Plush, sleek, new hotel located in Old City adjacent to Independence National Park. Amenities: Azalea, a gourmet restaurant, and lounge; indoor pool, health club, sauna, concierge, air conditioning, TV. Credit cards: all major. $$$$

Penn's View Inn, 14 N. Front St, Philadelphia, PA 19106. Tel: 922-7600 or toll free 1-800-331-7634. A converted 19th-century warehouse in Old City, now on the National Register of Historic Places, with 28 tastefully and comfortably furnished rooms overlooking the Delaware River. Amenities: fine dining at Ristorante Panorama, some rooms with Jacuzzi and fireplace, complimentary Continental breakfast, air conditioning, TV, parking. Credit cards: all major. $$

Rittenhouse Hotel, 210 W. Rittenhouse Square, Philadelphia, PA 19103. Tel: 546-9000 or toll free 1-800-635-1042. The city's highest level of luxury, convenience, comfort and decor in a modern concrete-and-glass tower on Rittenhouse Square. Amenities: fine dining at Restaurant 210 and Treetops overlooking the park, Boathouse Row Bar, and afternoon tea at the cozy Cassatt Tea Room (the hotel stands on the site of the former Cassatt mansion), fitness club, indoor pool, fully staffed business center, bank branch, minibar, air conditioning, TV. Credit cards: all major. $$$$

Ritz-Carlton, 17th and Chestnut Sts Liberty Place, Philadelphia, PA 1910 Tel: 563-1600 or toll free 1-800-24 3333. Part of the new Liberty Plac complex in business/financial distric tasteful decor evokes Federal Philade phia. Amenities: two restaurants ar bar, several restaurants elsewhere Liberty Place complex, fitness cente currency exchange, gift shop, co cierge, valet, air conditioning, miniba TV, valet parking. Credit cards: all m jor. $$$$

Sheraton Society Hill, 1 Dock S Philadelphia, PA 19106. Tel: 23 6000 or toll free 1-800-325-353 Understated Society Hill hotel wit Colonial style furnishings, convenie to Independence Park, historic distric South Street and riverfront. Amenitie restaurant, lounge, indoor pool, heal club, concierge, laundry service, val parking, air conditioning, minibar, T Credit cards: all major. $$$–$$$$

The Warwick, 17th and Locust St Philadelphia, PA 19103. Tel: 73 6000 or toll free 1-800-523-421 Luxurious, European-style form apartment building located ne Rittenhouse Square and Liberty Plac lavishly decorated with painstaking a tention to detail. Amenities: fine dinir at 1701 Café, Capriccio Café, bar an grill, concierge, free use of nearl health club, air conditioning, TV. Cred cards: all major. $$$

Wyndham Franklin Plaza, 17th an Race Sts, Philadelphia, PA 19103. Te 448-2000 or toll free 1-800-82 4200. Modern hotel with thoughtf contemporary details located ne Logan Square. Amenities: two resta rants, indoor pool, fitness center, te nis courts, concierge, air conditionin TV, valet parking. Credit cards: all m jor. $$$

Good Value

Adam's Mark Philadelphia, City Lir Ave and Monument Road, Philade phia, PA 19131. Tel: 581-5000 or t free 1-800-231-5858. Large conter porary hotel in western flank of ci 15-minute drive from center ci Amenities: two restaurants, nightclu sports bar, extensive meeting faci ties, indoor and outdoor pools, heal club, air conditioning, TV, free parkin Credit cards: all major. $$

Embassy Suites Hotel, 9000 Bartra Ave, Philadelphia, PA 19153. Tel: 36

500 or toll free 1-800-362-2779. Well-appointed business hotel with two-room suites, located close to the airport and 15–20 minutes from center city. Amenities: restaurant, indoor pool, health club, airport shuttle, complimentary breakfast, air conditioning, TV, free parking. Credit cards: all major. $$

Holiday Inn-Center City, 18th and Market Sts, Philadelphia, PA 19103. Tel: 561-7500. A comfortable chain hotel located within walking distance of Rittenhouse Square, City Hall, Liberty Place, Logan Square. Amenities: restaurant, lounge, pool, gift shop, small fitness room, air conditioner, TV, parking. Credit cards: all major. $$

Holiday Inn-City Line, 4100 Presidential Blvd, Philadelphia, PA 19131. Tel: 477-0200 or toll free 1-800-465-4329. Eight-story modern hotel located at the western edge of the city about 15 minutes from downtown. Amenities: restaurant, lounge, meeting rooms, ballroom, gift shop, indoor pool, exercise facilities, air conditioning, TV, free parking. Credit cards: all major. $$

Holiday Inn-Independence Mall, 4th and Arch Sts, Philadelphia, PA 19106. Tel: 923-8660 or toll free 1-800-465-4329. Old City hotel with Early American-style decor; within walking distance of Independence Hall and Liberty Bell. Amenities: restaurant, lounge, café, outdoor pool, air conditioning, TV, parking. Credit cards: all major. $$

Holiday Inn-Midtown, 1305 Walnut St, Philadelphia, PA 19107. Tel: 735-9300 or toll free 1-800-465-4329. Mid-range accommodation two blocks from City Hall. Amenities: restaurant, lounge, outdoor pool, air conditioning, TV, parking. Credit cards: all major. $$

Holiday Inn–Philadelphia Stadium, 10th St and Packer Ave, Philadelphia, PA 19148. Tel: 755-9500 or toll free 1-800-465-4329. Formerly a Hilton, contemporary establishment with 238 rooms located near airport and sports complex. Amenities: restaurant, bar, outdoor pool, airport shuttle, air conditioning, TV, free parking. Credit cards: all major. $–$$

Independence Park Inn, 235 Chestnut St, Philadelphia, PA 19106. Tel: 922-4443 or toll free 1-800-624-2988. Smaller five-story Victorian hotel, newly renovated, with homey Colonial-style

decor. Amenities: morning paper, afternoon tea, concierge, air conditioning, TV, free Continental breakfast. Credit cards: all major. $$

Marriot Hotel-Convention Center, 1201 Market St, Philadelphia, PA 19106. Tel: 625-2900 or toll-free 800-228-9290. Comfortable new chain hotel next to Convention Center designed for business travelers, Amenities: three restaurants, coffee house, health club, indoor pool, air conditioning, TV, airport shuttle. Credit cards: all major. $$

Penn Tower Hotel, Civic Center Blvd and 34th St, Philadelphia, PA 19104. Tel: 387-8333 or toll free 1-800-356-7366. A pleasant modern hotel owned by the University of Pennsylvania. Close to the Civic Center, University Museum, Franklin Field and other campus sites. Amenities: restaurant, lounge, concierge, meeting facilities, gift shop, air conditioning, TV, parking. Credit cards: all major. $$

Radisson Hotel at the Airport, 500 Stevens Drive, Philadelphia, PA 19113. Tel: 610-521-5900 or toll free 1-800-333-3333. Business hotel with fine appointments about 15–20 minutes south of center city. Amenities: restaurant, sports bar, lounge, indoor pool, fitness facilities, air conditioning, TV, free parking, airport shuttle. Credit cards: all major. $$

Sheraton University City, 36th and Chestnut Sts, Philadelphia, PA 19104. Tel: 387-8000 or toll free 1-800-325-3535. Comfortably appointed with surprisingly pleasant decorative touches, popular with business people and tourists, and within walking distance to University of Pennsylvania campus and Civic Center. Amenities: restaurant, gift shop, outdoor pool, shuttle to airport and 30th Street Station, air conditioning, TV, parking. Credit cards: all major. $$

Thomas Bond House, 129 S. 2nd St, Philadelphia, PA 19106. Tel: 923-8523 or toll free 1-800-845-2663. A charming Federal-style bed and breakfast maintained by the National Park Service with 10 rooms and two suites in the heart of historic district. Amenities: private and shared bath, some rooms with fireplace, whirlpool, sofa bed, free Continental breakfast. Credit cards: all major. $$

Budget

Airport Ramada, 76 Industrial Highway, Essington, PA 19029. Tel: 610-521-9600 or toll free 1-800-228-2828. Comfortable lodging near stadiums and airport, popular with business travelers, about 15 minutes from center city. Amenities: restaurant, lounge, coffee shop, gift shop, fitness room, outdoor pool, airport shuttle, air conditioning, TV, free parking. Credit cards: all major. $

Best Western, 11580 Roosevelt Blvd, Philadelphia, PA 19116. Tel: 464-9500 or toll free 1-800-528-1234. Good, clean, motel lodging at a decent price, about 25–30 minutes north of center city by car. Amenities: restaurant, lounge, fitness center, outdoor pool, game room, air conditioning, TV, free parking. Credit cards: all major. $

Comfort Inn at Penn's Landing, 100 N. Columbus Blvd, Philadelphia, PA 19106. Tel: 627-7900. Comfortable lodging near Penn's Landing between busy riverfront street and I-95. Amenities: lounge, shuttle to historic district, air conditioning, TV, free parking, free Continental breakfast. Credit cards: all major. $–$$

The International House, 3701 Chestnut St, Philadelphia, PA 19104. Tel: 387-5125. Clean but minimal dormitory-style lodging near University of Pennsylvania campus; popular with students. Amenities: Eden II, a surprisingly good cafeteria; shared bath, gift shop; bring your own soap and toiletries. Credit cards: Visa, MasterCard. $

Quality Inn-Downtown Suites, 1010 Race St, Philadelphia, PA 19107. 922-1730 or toll free 1-800-228-5151. Located in the heart of Chinatown, with 96 suites decked out in interesting Chinese-style decor. Amenities: conference facilities, free Continental breakfast, air conditioning, TV, free parking (on first-come-first-served basis). Credit cards: all major. $

The Sheraton Inn, 9461 Roosevelt Blvd, Philadelphia, PA 19114. Tel: 671-9600 or toll free 1-800-325-3535. Chain hotel located in Northeast Philadelphia about 30 minutes from center city. Amenities: restaurant, lounge, gift shop, fitness facilities, indoor pool, air conditioning, TV, free parking. Credit cards: all major. $

Bed & Breakfast/Inns

Philadelphia

Scores of people in the city, suburbs and countryside open their homes to guests. Situations and rates vary widely, from inexpensive and rather modest accommodations to the truly elegant and unique. If you are interested in an inside look at Philadelphia living, contact these bed-and-breakfast agents for more information:

All About Town-Bed and Breakfast in Philadelphia, PO Box 562, Valley Forge, PA 19481. Tel: 610-783-7838.
Bed and Breakfast-Center City, 1804 Pine St, Philadelphia, PA 19103. Tel: 735-1137.
Bed and Breakfast Connections, PO Box 21, Devon, PA 19333. Tel: 687-3565 or toll free 1-800-448-3619.
Bed and Breakfast of Philadelphia, 1530 Locust St, Suite K, Philadelphia, PA 19102. Tel: 735-1917 or toll free 1-800-220-1917.

Bucks County Lodging

Aaron Burr House, 80 W. Bridge St, New Hope, PA 18938. Tel: 862-2343. A lovely Victorian bed and breakfast in town with six rooms. Amenities: some rooms with canopy beds and/or fireplaces, air conditioning, parking. Complimentary breakfast. Credit cards: American Express. $–$$$
Barley Sheaf Farm, Route 202, Holicong, PA 18928. Tel: 794-5104. Ivy-covered stone house dating to 1740 on a 30-acre farm 5 miles west of New Hope. Amenities: private bath, antiques, garden, pool, some rooms with fireplaces, complimentary country breakfast. Credit cards: American Express, MasterCard, Visa. $$
Black Bass Hotel, River Road, Lumberville, PA 18933. Tel: 297-5770. Historic inn on the Delaware River with seven rooms and three suites. Amenities: shared bath, river views, restaurant open for lunch and dinner, bar, small corporate meetings, parking. Credit cards: all major. $–$$$
Centre Bridge Inn, Route 32, New Hope, PA 18938. Tel: 862-2048. Modern inn less than 4 miles from town with views of river. Amenities: dining room, canopy, brass or four-poster beds, deck, private bath, some rooms with TV and air conditioning, parking. Credit cards: American Express, Visa, MasterCard. $–$$

Evermay on the Delaware, River Road, Erwinna, PA 18920. Tel: 610-294-9100. Sixteen rooms on 25-acre garden spot on Delaware River. Amenities: private bath, meeting facilities, dinner served Friday–Sunday, free breakfast and afternoon tea. Credit cards: MasterCard, Visa. $–$$
Golden Plough Inn, Route 202 and Street Road, Lahaska, PA 19831. Tel: 794-4004. American country inn located in the Peddler's Village shopping complex. Amenities: charming decor featuring four-poster and canopy beds, private bath, refrigerator, TV, air conditioning, some rooms with fireplace and/or whirlpool, VCR and balcony, parking. Several restaurants within complex, free Continental breakfast. Credit cards: all major. $$
Hacienda Inn, 36 W. Mechanic St, New Hope, PA 18938. Tel: 862-2078. Unique modern lodging in center of town with 30 guest rooms, studios and suites. Amenities: antiques, some rooms with Jacuzzi or fireplaces, decks, pool, restaurant, air conditioning, TV, parking, credit vouchers for dinner at restaurant. Credit cards: all major. $–$$
Isaac Stover House Bed and Breakfast, Route 32, Erwinna, PA 18920. Tel: 610-294-8044. A Victorian mansion with five rooms situated on 13 acres overlooking the Delaware River. Amenities: private and shared bath, antiques, free three-course breakfast, parking. Credit cards: American Express, MasterCard, Visa. $–$$
Logan Inn, 10 W. Ferry St, New Hope, PA 18938. Tel: 862-2300. Renovated inn dating to 1727 with 16 rooms decorated in Colonial style. Amenities: four-poster beds, antiques, private bath, restaurant, tavern, air conditioning, TV, parking, free full breakfast. Credit cards: all major. $$
New Hope Motel in the Woods, 400 W. Bridge St, New Hope, PA 18938. Tel: 862-2800. Comfortable but modest lodging on five wooded acres less than a mile from town center. Amenities: heated pool, air conditioning, color cable TV, parking. Credit cards: MasterCard, Visa, Carte Blanche, Diners Club, Discover. $
Pine Tree Farm, 2155 Lower State Road, Doylestown, PA 18901. Tel: 348-0632. Stone farmhouse dating to 1730 on 16 acres with four guest rooms located just outside of town.

Amenities: fireplaces in living roo[m] and library, antiques, pool, tenn[is] courts, air conditioning and parkin[g,] free full breakfast. Credit cards: a[ll] major. $$
Tattersall Inn, River and Caffer[ty] Roads, Point Pleasant, PA 18950. Te[l:] 297-8233. Bed and breakfast in hi[s]toric Stover Mansion set on Delawa[re] River. Amenities: breakfast in yo[ur] room, on the veranda or in the dinin[g] room, private bath, common room wit[h] walk-in fireplace, air conditioning, par[k]ing. Credit cards: American Expres[s,] MasterCard, Visa, Discover. $
The Wedgewood Inn of New Hop[e,] 111 W. Bridge St, New Hope, P[A] 18938. Tel: 862-2570. Lovely bed an[d] breakfast on 2-acre landscape[d] grounds with 12 rooms and suite[s] near village center. Amenities: air co[n]ditioning, some rooms with fireplace[s,] carriage rides, croquet, turndown ser[v]ice and parking. Credit cards: Ame[ri]can Express. $–$$$

Lancaster County Lodging

Brunswick Hotel, Chestnut and Quee[n] Sts, Lancaster, PA 17608. Tel: 71[7-]397-4801. Modern 10-story hotel, fo[r]merly a Hilton, located in downtow[n] Lancaster. Amenities: restaurant, c[of]fee shop, gift shop, fitness facilitie[s,] indoor pool, air conditioning, TV, fre[e] parking. Credit cards: all major. $
Cameron Estate Inn, 1895 Doneg[al] Springs Road, Mount Joy, PA 1755[2.] Tel: 717-653-1773. Historic countr[y] manor house on 15 acres located i[n] peaceful rural area 15 miles from Lan[-]caster. Amenities: restaurant, compl[i]mentary Continental breakfast, Amis[h] quilts, brass, four-poster and canop[y] beds, some rooms with fireplace, pr[i]vate and shared bath, outdoor poo[l,] tennis court, air conditioning, fre[e] parking. Credit cards: all major. $–$[$]
Comfort Inn Sherwood Knoll, 50[0] Centerville Road, Lancaster, P[A] 17601. Tel: 717-898-2431 or toll fre[e] 1-800-228-5151. Large chain hote[l] with 166 rooms located about 5 mile[s] from downtown Lancaster. Amenitie[s:] restaurant, lounge, outdoor pool, a[ir] conditioning, TV, free parking. Cred[it] cards: all major. $
Fulton Steamboat Inn, PO Box 333[,] Rt. 30, Strasburg, PA 17602. Tel: 71[7-]299-9999. Named after steamboat in[-]ventor Robert Fulton, this country in[n] recreates steamboat decor in 96 com[-]

rtable rooms. Amenities: restaurant, rivate bath, microwave, refrigerator, many rooms with deck and whirlpool, xercise room, pool, gift shop, laundry, ir conditioning, TV, free parking. Credit cards: Visa, MasterCard, American Express. $

The Gardens of Eden, 1894 Eden Road, Lancaster, PA 17601. Tel: 717-293-5179. 19th-century Victorian bed and breakfast with three rooms in main house and private guest cottage n 3-acre garden spot overlooking the Conestoga River. Amenities: antiques, shared and private bath, complimentary full breakfast, air conditioning, free parking, tour guides available. Credit cards: Visa, MasterCard may be used for holding reservations only. $

Greystone Manor Bed and Breakfast, 2658 Old Philadelphia Pike, Bird-in-Hand, PA 17505. Tel: 717-393-4233. A handsome 19th-century mansion and carriage house decorated in Victorian style. Amenities: antiques, quilts, private bath, complimentary Continental breakfast, air conditioning, TV, free parking. Credit cards: Visa, MasterCard. $

Guesthouse at Doneckers, 318-24 N. State St, Ephrata, PA 17522. Tel: 717-738-9502. Three historic houses with 15 rooms and four suites all tastefully and comfortably furnished. Amenities: complimentary Continental breakfast, antiques, some rooms with Jacuzzi, fireplace, balcony or kitchenette, air conditioning, free parking. Credit cards: all major. $–$$

Harvest Drive Farm Motel, 3370 Harvest Drive, Intercourse, PA 17534. Tel: 717-768-7186. Basic lodging in rural setting just outside of Intercourse. Amenities: restaurant, gift shop, bicycle rental, air conditioning, TV, free parking. Credit cards: American Express, Visa, MasterCard, Discovery. $

Historic General Sutter Inn, 14 E. Main St, Lititz, PA 17543. 717-626-2115. Cozy inn with 12 rooms with Victorian, country-style furnishings located in center of town. Amenities: restaurant, lounge, private bath, TV, free parking. Credit cards: American Express, MasterCard, Visa, Discovery. $

Quality Inn, 2363 Oregon Pike, Lancaster, PA 17601. Tel: 717-569-0477 or toll free 1-800-228-5151. Large modern inn on more than 100 acres in farm area outside Lancaster. Amenities: restaurant, lounge, outdoor pool,

tennis courts, exercise facilities, sauna, nine-hole golf course, shops nearby, air conditioning, TV, free parking. Credit cards: all major. $

Red Caboose Motel, Paradise Lane, Strasburg, PA 17572. Tel: 717-687-6646. Always wanted to be a train engineer? This is the place for you. Built of converted railroad cabooses, the 39 rooms offer quirky, comfortable lodging in a country setting near the Pennsylvania Railroad Museum. A unique experience. Amenities: restaurant, ice-cream parlor, game room, steam train rides, Amish buggy rides, private bath, air conditioning, TV, free parking. Credit cards: all major. $

Strasburg Village Inn, 1 W. Main St, Strasburg, PA 17579. Tel: 717-687-0900. Fully renovated 18th-century buildings, now a bed-and-breakfast inn with Colonial decor in the center of town. Amenities: private bath, some rooms with Jacuzzi, complimentary full breakfast (Continental breakfast on Sunday), air conditioning, TV, free parking. Credit cards: American Express, Visa, MasterCard, Discover. $–$$

Your Place Country Inn, 2133 Lincoln Highway, Lancaster, PA 17602. Tel: 717-393-3413. Cheerful country inn with 79 comfy rooms featuring locally made furnishings. Amenities: private bath, adjacent restaurant, lounge, outdoor pool, air conditioning, TV, free parking. Credit cards: all major. $

Seaside Lodgings
Atlantic City

Bally's Grand Hotel Casino, Boston and Pacific aves, Atlantic City, NJ 08404. Tel: 609-347-7111 or toll free 1-800-257-8677. A glitzy contemporary hotel with ocean views located at the southern end of the Boardwalk. Amenities: five restaurants (Continental, Italian, Chinese, steak, café), desert café, cabaret theater, entertainment, health club, indoor pool, air conditioning, TV, valet and free parking. Credit cards: all major. $$–$$$

Bally's Park Place Casino Hotel and Tower, Park Place and Boardwalk, Atlantic City, NJ 08401. Tel: 609-340-2000 or toll free 1-800-225-5977. A complex of three handsome turn-of-the-century hotels with a modern 30-story addition on a beachfront site at a central Boardwalk location. Amenities: two fine restaurants (seafood and

steak), snack bar, oyster bar, deli, ice-cream parlor, cabaret theater, entertainment, fitness facilities, indoor and outdoor pools, game rooms, air conditioning, TV, free parking. Credit cards: all major. $$

Caesars Atlantic City Hotel Casino, Arkansas Ave and Boardwalk, Atlantic City, NJ 08401. Tel: 609-348-4411 or toll free 1-800-232-7277. Enormous, modern 19-story hotel with elaborate Roman theme located centrally on Boardwalk next to Ocean One shopping complex. Amenities: nine restaurants (Chinese, steak, Italian, Japanese, cafés), Appian Way shopping mall, pools, health spa, game room, volleyball, tennis courts, air conditioning, TV, valet and free parking. Credit cards: all major. $$

Claridge Casino Hotel, Indiana Ave, Atlantic City, NJ 08401. Tel: 609-340-3400 or toll free 1-800-257-8585. Sleek 24-story hotel in renovated structure dating to 1930s, centrally located near Boardwalk casinos. Amenities: several restaurants (including fine Italian, grill, deli, coffee shop), cabaret theater, comedy club, fitness facilities, indoor pool, spas, air conditioning, TV, free valet parking. Credit cards: all major. $$

Comfort Inn, 539 E. Absecon Blvd, Absecon, NJ 08201. Tel: 609-641-7272 or toll free 1-800-228-5150. Comfortable, contemporary chain hotel 3 miles from Boardwalk on Absecon Bay. Amenities: coffee shop, casino shuttle, outdoor pool, air conditioning, TV, free parking. Credit cards: all major. $–$$

Harrah's Marina Hotel Casino, 777 Harah's Blvd, Atlantic City, NJ 08401. Tel: 609-441-5000 or toll free 1-800-427-7247. Contemporary hotel towers located 3 miles from Boardwalk on Absecon Bay. Amenities: several restaurants (fine Italian, French, Chinese, steak, coffee shop, deli), cabaret theater, indoor pool, fitness room, marina, air conditioning, TV, free parking. Credit cards: all major. $$

Merv Griffin's Resorts Casino Hotel, Boardwalk and North Carolina Ave, Atlantic City, NJ 08401. Tel: 609-344-6000 or toll free 1-800-438-7424. Modern structure with facade of old Victorian hotel, located at north end of Boardwalk near Steeplechase Pier. Amenities: several restaurants (which include fine French, Italian, deli, oyster bar, coffee shop), medieval theme restaurant, ice-cream parlor, cabaret theater, health club, pool, saunas, game room, air conditioning, TV, free parking. Credit cards: all major. $$–$$$

Quality Inn, South Carolina and Pacific aves, Atlantic City, NJ 08401. Tel: 609-345-7070 or toll free 1-800-228-5151. A 200-room chain hotel near Boardwalk and casinos incorporating parts of a 1920s Quaker meetinghouse. Amenities: restaurant, lounge, air conditioning, TV, free parking. Credit cards: all major. $–$$

Sands Hotel Casino, Indiana Ave and Brighton Park, Atlantic City, NJ 08401. Tel: 609-441-4457 or toll free 1-800-257-8580. Plush contemporary accommodations decorated in a medley of styles. Amenities: several restaurants (including French, Italian, steak, coffee shop), food court, cabaret theater, pool, tennis, fitness facilities, shops, free use of nearby golf course, air conditioning, TV, valet parking. Credit cards: all major. $$

Showboat Hotel and Casino, 801 Boardwalk and Delaware Ave, Atlantic City, NJ 08401. Tel: 609-343-4000 or toll free 1-800-621-0200. 25-story oceanfront hotel decorated in Victorian riverboat theme. Amenities: restaurants (including steak, Italian, Chinese, seafood), pizzeria, deli, coffee shop, ice-cream parlor, cabaret theater, pool, whirlpool, game room, bowling alley, air conditioning, free parking. Credit cards: all major. $$

TropWorld Casino and Entertainment Resort, Brighton Ave and Boardwalk, Atlantic City, NJ 08401. Tel: 609-340-4000 or toll free 1-800-843-8767. An enormous, rambling hotel which has over 700 rooms and 300 suites and Tivoli Pier, a 2-acre indoor amusement park. Amenities: more than 15 restaurants (including Italian, Chinese, steak, seafood, coffee shop, deli), comedy club, theater, food court, fitness club, massage, tanning salon, tennis courts, indoor and outdoor pools, shopping arcades, air conditioning, TV, free parking. Credit cards: all major. $$–$$$$

Trump Castle Casino Resort by the Bay, Huron Ave and Brigantine Blvd, Atlantic City, NJ 08401. Tel: 609-441-2000 or toll free 1-800-441-5551. Nearly 1,000 rooms and suites in plush Art-Deco-style hotel overlooking

Absecon Bay and city. Amenities: several expensive restaurants (Italian, seafood, steak), deli, coffee shop, ice-cream parlor, two ballroom/theaters, fitness facilities, tennis courts, pro shop, air conditioning, TV, free parking. Credit cards: all major. $$$

Trump Plaza Hotel and Casino, Boardwalk and Mississippi Ave, Atlantic City, NJ 08401. Tel: 609-441-6000 or toll free 1-800-677-7378. 600-room tower hotel in central Boardwalk location. Amenities: several expensive restaurants (Continental, Italian, Asian, steak), theater with top-name acts, deli, café, tennis courts, indoor pool, spa, game room, shops, air conditioning, TV, free parking. Credit cards: all major. $$$

Trump Taj Mahal Casino Resort, 1000 Boardwalk and Virginia Ave, Atlantic City, NJ 08401. Tel: 609-449-1000 or toll free 1-800-825-8786. Said to be the largest casino hotel in America, and the tallest building in New Jersey, this overblown 1,200-unit pleasure dome is decked out like a neon pasha's palace. This is Trump at his most garish. Amenities: Several first-class restaurants (International, Italian, Asian, seafood, steak), deli, ice-cream parlor, café, 5,500-seat arena, ballroom and nightclub, health club, tennis courts, game room, air conditioning, TV, free parking. Credit cards: all major. $$–$$$$

Cape May Lodging

Abbey, 34 Gurney St at Columbia Ave, Cape May, NJ 08204. Tel: 609-884-4506. Among the most popular bed-and-breakfast inns in town; a beautiful Victorian gingerbread house and cottage with 14 rooms. Amenities: private bath, beach passes, complimentary full breakfast, air conditioning, limited free parking. Credit cards: Visa, MasterCard. $–$$

Angel of the Sea, 5 Trenton Ave, Cape May, NJ 08204. Tel: 609-884-3369 or toll free 1-800-848-3369. Handsome 19th-century houses with 26 rooms lavishly furnished in Victorian style; located on ocean about 20 minutes by foot from downtown. Amenities: private bath, complimentary full breakfast, afternoon tea, evening wine and cheese, many original furnishings, free parking, beach passes, bicycles. Credit cards: American Express, Visa, MasterCard. $–$$$$

Blue Amber Motel, 605 Madison Ave, Cape May, NJ 08204. Tel: 609-884-8266. Comfortable contemporary lodging in historic district and about a 10-minute walk to beach. Amenities: private bath, some rooms with kitchenettes, outdoor pool, beach passes, children's play area, air conditioning, TV, free parking. Credit cards: American Express, Visa, MasterCard. $

Captain Mey's Inn, 202 Ocean St, Cape May, NJ 08204. Tel: 609-884-7793. Lovingly decorated 19th-century Victorian bed and breakfast with nine guest rooms. Amenities: antiques, European furnishings, private and shared bath, hearty complimentary breakfast, afternoon tea, beach passes, free parking. Credit cards: Visa, MasterCard. $–$$

Chalfonte, 301 Howard St, Cape May, NJ 08204. Tel: 609-884-8409. A grand three-story Victorian hotel dating to 1876 with 77 tastefully and comfortably decorated rooms. Amenities: shared and private bath, complimentary breakfast and dinner for two, restaurant, entertainment, various arts and crafts workshops, babysitting. Credit cards: Visa, MasterCard. $–$$$

Gingerbread House, 28 Gurney St, Cape May, NJ 08204. Tel: 609-884-0211. Charming Victorian house with six rooms just a half-block from beach. Amenities: shared and private bath, complimentary full breakfast, afternoon tea, antique furnishings, beach passes. Credit cards: MasterCard, Visa. $–$$

Mainstay Inn, 635 Columbia Ave, Cape May, NJ 08204. Tel: 609-884-8690. Extremely popular and beautifully preserved, this elaborate 12-bedroom Victorian mansion is an architectural landmark. Amenities: private bath, antique furnishings, quilts, garden, complimentary country breakfast, afternoon tea, beach passes. No credit cards accepted. $–$$$

Montreal Inn, Beach Drive and Madison Ave, Cape May, NJ 08204. Tel: 609-884-7011 or toll free 1-800-525-7011. Simple but comfortable oceanfront lodging near historic district. Amenities: private bath, restaurant, lounge, outdoor pool, miniature golf, a few units with kitchenette, air conditioning, TV, free parking. Credit cards: American Express, Visa, MasterCard. $

Queen Victoria, 102 Ocean St, Cape May, NJ 08204. Tel: 609-884-8702. Grand, sprawling Victorian B&B with 17 rooms and seven suites one block from beach. Amenities: private bath, library, complimentary full breakfast, some rooms or suites with gas fireplace, whirlpool and/or TV, air conditioning. Credit cards: Visa, MasterCard. $–$$$

Sea Breeze Motel, Pittsburgh and New York aves, Cape May, NJ 08204. Tel: 609-884-3352. Modest motel lodging two blocks from beach. Amenities: private bath, refrigerator, beach passes, air conditioning, TV, free parking. Credit cards: Visa, MasterCard, Discover. $

Virginia Hotel, 25 Jackson St, Cape May, NJ 08204. Tel: 609-884-5700. A 19th-century 24-room hotel with contemporary furnishings, located in historic district. Amenities: restaurant, entertainment, garden, free morning paper, free Continental breakfast, private bath, fireplace in lounge, room service, air conditioning, TV, VCR, free valet parking. Credit cards: American Express, Visa, MasterCard, Diners Club. $–$$

Youth Hostels

Chaminoux Mansion, an early-19th-century country estate in western Fairmount Park, serves as Philadelphia's link in the international chain of youth hostels. Both accommodations (dormitory-style) and fees are minimal. An American or International Youth Hostel card is required. Closed: December 16–January 16. Tel: 878-3676.

Campgrounds

Campsites are available at state parks throughout the Philadelphia area. For detailed information, contact:

Department of Environmental Resources, Bureau of State Parks, P.O. Box 8551, Harrisburg, PA 17105. Tel: 717-772-0239 or toll free 1-800-637-2757.

Eating Out

What to Eat

Visitors are often surprised at the variety and quality of Philadelphia dining. Fact is, Philly is a great restaurant town, with a wide range of ethnic eateries, truly fine cuisine, casual spots and hotel dining. Dining here is a good value, too, especially at the high end. With the exception of the fancier places, casual but neat dress is suitable for just about any occasion. Reservations at the fancier restaurants are usually necessary (and may be required), and are strongly recommended elsewhere.

For those who have never experienced Philly foods there are a few local specialties that you may not be familiar with, many of which come from the city's rich Pennsylvania Dutch heritage. Often served with breakfast, *scrapple* is a spicy mixture of ground meat and cornmeal fried up and served hot as a side dish. Philadelphia's favorite snack – *soft pretzels* with mustard – is another Pennsylvania Dutch treat and is sold by street vendors throughout center city (*see Pretzel Logic for details*). If a waiter asks you whether you like your bottom wet or dry, don't be offended. He's probably talking about *shoofly pie*, a rich molasses pie which may be served with a sticky wet bottom or a dry crumbly bottom.

Philadelphia is also home to the *cheesesteak*, a hot sandwich made with paper-thin strips of grilled beef smothered in gooey orange cheese, garnished with fried onions, hot peppers, mushrooms (optional, of course) and served on a hoagie roll. What's a *hoagie*? In other towns, they're called submarine sandwiches or grinders. In Philly, these long overstuffed sandwiches are called hoagies, a name which some Philadelphians believe is a reference to the preferred repast at the old Hog Island Shipyard, the largest of its day. If you're prowling South Philly for good eats, you may also see

signs for *water ice*, a refreshing combo of crushed ice and pulpy juice known elsewhere as Italian ice.

Liquor Laws

Thanks to the city's Quaker heritage, Philadelphia's liquor laws are arcane and restrictive. Hard liquor and a limited selection of wines (but not chilled wine) are sold at state liquor stores. Cold beer can be purchased at licensed convenience stores, delicatessens, taverns or restaurants but tends to be expensive. For large quantities of beer at a decent price, you have to go to a beer distributor. Wine, beer and mixed drinks are available by the bottle or by the glass at restaurants with a liquor license. Restaurants that do not serve alcohol often permit customers to bring their own. The legal drinking age is 21. You may be asked to show picture identification proving your age at bars, restaurants or liquor stores. Alcohol may not be served at bars or restaurants after 2am, 3am at private clubs.

Where to Eat

The price guide indicates approximate cost of dinner excluding beverages, tax and tip. Standard tip is 15%, more for exceptional service or a large party. In some cases, the gratuity may be included in the bill.

$ under $15
$$ $15 to $25
$$$ $25 to $40
$$$$ over $40

Philadelphia

AMERICAN

American Diner, 4201 Chestnut St. Tel: 387-1451. Terrific diner fare in a 1950s "retro" atmosphere in University City. Fun for burgers, meat loaf, hearty breakfasts and late-night crowd. Breakfast, lunch and dinner daily. No credit cards accepted. $

Astral Plane, 1708 Lombard St. Tel: 546-6230. A romantic, artsy hideaway with an inventive American menu. Lunch weekdays, dinner daily, Sunday brunch. Credit cards: all major. $$$

Café Einstein, 208 Race St. Tel: 625-0904. Snazzy, cheerful restaurant and bar in Old City's art-gallery territory. Dinner daily, Sunday brunch. Credit cards: all major. $$

City Tavern, 2nd and Walnut Sts. Tel: 413-1443. This reconstructed 18th-century tavern serving Colonial-style cuisine makes a great stop for history buffs trying to round out the Old City experience. Lunch and dinner daily. Credit cards: American Express, MasterCard, Visa. $$

Copabanana, 4th and South Sts. Tel: 923-6180.

Copa, Too, 263 S. 15th St. Tel: 735-0848. Boisterous bar-and-burger places with Tex-Mex dishes. The Spanish fries are a greasy treat. South Street and Rittenhouse locations. Lunch and dinner served daily, Sunday brunch at Copabanana. Credit cards: all major. $

Dock Street Brewing Company Brewery and Restaurant, 18th and Cherry Sts. Tel: 496-0413. A contemporary tavern/restaurant/brewery serving hearty eclectic fare and a variety of ales and lagers brewed on the premises. Located off the Parkway near museum district and popular with singles, business people and families. Lunch and dinner daily. Credit cards: all major. $$.

Jack's Firehouse, 2130 Fairmount Ave. Tel: 232-9000. Innovative (occasionally unusual) American regional country cooking presented in a nifty converted firehouse near Museum of Art. Lunch Monday–Friday, dinner daily, Sunday brunch. Credit cards: American Express, MasterCard, Visa, Carte Blanche. $$$

Jake's Restaurant, 4365 Main St. Tel: 483-0444. A Manayunk favorite featuring tasty American cooking, an outstanding wine list and a lively social scene. Lunch Monday–Friday, dinner daily. Credit cards: American Express, MasterCard, Visa, Diners Club, Discover. $$$

Judy's Café, 3rd and Bainbridge Sts. Tel: 928-1968. A friendly Queen Village spot known for hearty American specialties and warm, neighborhood atmosphere. Dinner daily. Credit cards: all major. $$

Melrose Diner, 1501 Snyder Ave. Tel: 467-6644. South Philadelphia's monument to the gum-chewing waitress. Solid diner fare. Usually fun for a late-night stop, although the service is occasionally too gruff for some people's liking. Daily 24 hours. No credit cards accepted. $

Momi, 526 S. 4th St. Tel: 625-0370. Great fun at a 1950s-style diner near South Street. Lunch Monday–Saturday, dinner daily, Sunday brunch. No credit cards accepted. $

Ron's Ribs, 1627 South St. Tel: 545-9160. Stripped-down rib joint that does one thing and does it right. Takeout, too. Lunch and dinner Monday–Saturday, Sunday brunch. Credit cards: American Express, MasterCard, Visa. $

Valley Green Inn, Springfield Ave and Wissahickon Creek. Tel: 247-1730. A converted 19th-century road house serving hearty American food, set on a wooded trail in Fairmount Park near Wissahickon Creek. Dining on the porch in warm weather. Lunch and dinner daily, Sunday brunch. Credit cards: MasterCard, Visa, Discover. $$–$$$

White Dog Café, 3420 Sansom St. Tel: 386-9224. A perfect fit in University City's casual, politically correct, artsy atmosphere, with imaginative American cuisine, great desserts and a lively bar. Lunch Monday–Friday, dinner daily, Saturday and Sunday brunch. Credit cards: all major. $$–$$$

ASIAN

Imperial Inn, 142-6 N. 10th St. Tel: 627-2299. Well-known Chinatown restaurant with reasonably priced and consistently good, if not dazzling, food and service. Hours: Lunch and dinner daily. Credit cards: all major. $$

Joe's Peking Duck House, 925 Race St. Tel: 922-3277. The decor is non-existent, the ambience loud and crowded, but many think this Chinatown standard serves the best Chinese food in town. Lunch Monday–Friday, dinner daily. No credit cards accepted. $$

Meiji-En, Pier 19, Delaware Ave and Callowhill St. Tel: 592-7100. A large Japanese restaurant on the Delaware River with great views and a wide-ranging menu. Dinner daily, Sunday brunch. Credit cards: all major. $$–$$$

Ray's Coffee Shop, 141 N. 9th St. Tel: 922-5122. A favorite Chinatown meeting place serving well-prepared food and gourmet coffee. Breakfast, lunch and dinner daily. Credit cards: American Express, MasterCard, Visa. $–$$

Sala Thai, 700 S. 5th St. Tel: 922-4990. A relaxing contemporary ambience for authentic, carefully prepared Thai cuisine located near South Street.

Lunch Tuesday–Sunday, dinner Monday–Sunday. No credit cards accepted. $–$$

Susanna Foo, 1512 Walnut St. Tel: 545-2666. Regarded by critics as one of the finest Chinese restaurants in the country. Rather expensive, especially compared to other Chinese restaurants, but truly in a class by itself. Lunch Monday–Friday, dinner Monday–Saturday. Credit cards: American Express, MasterCard, Visa. $$$–$$$$

Thai Garden, 349 S. 47th St. Tel: 471-3663.

Thai Garden East, 101 N. 11th St. Tel: 629-9939. Both locations offer a relaxing setting for excellent Thai cuisine served by an attentive staff. Lunch and dinner daily. Credit cards: MasterCard, Visa. $$

Vinh Hoa Vietnamese, 746 Christian St. Tel: 925-0307. A simple setting near the Italian Market for delectable, carefully prepared, and reasonably priced Vietnamese cuisine. Lunch Monday and Wednesday–Saturday, dinner Wednesday–Monday. Credit cards: all major. $$

CAJUN/NEW ORLEANS

Café Nola, 328 South St. Tel: 627-2590. A South Street favorite offering tantalizing, carefully prepared Cajun fare in a spirited and comfortable setting. Lunch Tuesday–Saturday, dinner daily, Sunday brunch. Credit cards: all major. $$–$$$

The Magnolia Café, 1602 Locust St. Tel: 546-4180. Informal and fun Cajun restaurant housed in a beautiful old mansion close to Rittenhouse Square. Lunch and dinner daily, Saturday and Sunday brunch. Credit cards: American Express, MasterCard, Visa, Diners Club. $$

CONTINENTAL/INTERNATIONAL

Saloon, 750 S. 7th St. Tel: 627-1811. Highly regarded gathering spot of local movers and shakers, known for excellent steaks and Italian dishes. Reservations required. Lunch Tuesday–Friday, dinner Monday–Saturday. Credit cards: American Express. $$$–$$$$

Cutter's Grand Café, 2005 Market St. Tel: 851-6262. Smart and swanky newer establishment winning kudos for wide-ranging menu, terrific bar and high-profile atmosphere. Lunch Monday–Friday, dinner daily. Credit cards: all major. $$$

Dickens Inn, 421 S. 2nd St. Tel: 928-9307. A cheerful English pub on Head House Square, featuring authentic English dishes and a great selection of draft beer. Lunch and dinner daily. Credit cards: all major. $$

Friday Saturday Sunday, 261 S. 21st St. Tel: 546-4232. A friendly standby near Rittenhouse Square with pleasing, creative International fare and a lovely romantic atmosphere. Lunch Monday–Friday, dinner daily. Credit cards: all major. $$–$$$

The Garden, 1617 Spruce St. Tel: 546-4455. An elegant, sophisticated center city town house with outdoor dining in warm weather known for superior Continental cuisine. Lunch Monday–Friday (closed for lunch on Monday in January, February and March), dinner Monday–Saturday. Closed weekends in summer. Credit cards: all major. $$$$

Knave of Hearts, 230 South St. Tel: 922-3956. A romantic, funky South Street pioneer that still pleases with creative Continental fare and a cozy setting. Lunch and dinner daily, Sunday brunch. Credit cards: all major. $$–$$$

Lickety Split, 401 South St. Tel: 922-1173. A colorful South Street favorite known for creative food and lively atmosphere. Lunch and dinner daily, Sunday brunch. Credit cards: all major. $$–$$$

16th Street Bar and Grill, 264 S. 16th St. Tel: 735-3316. Tasty Mediterranean dishes served in a cozy neighborhood bistro. Lunch Monday–Saturday, dinner daily, Sunday brunch. Credit cards: all major. $$

FRENCH

Alouette Restaurant, 334 Bainbridge St. Tel: 629-1126. A romantic Queen Village spot specializing in imaginative French cuisine with an Asian touch; outdoor dining in warm weather. Lunch Monday–Friday, dinner daily, Sunday brunch, closed Tuesday. Credit cards: all major. $$$

Ciboulette, 200 S. Broad St at the Bellevue. Tel: 790-1210. Exquisite Provencal French cuisine in a well-appointed dining room convenient to the Academy of Music. Lunch Monday–Friday, dinner Monday–Sunday, Sunday brunch. Credit cards: American Express, MasterCard, Visa, Diners Club. $$$

Deux Cheminees, 1221 Locust St. Tel: 790-0200. Traditional French dishes in an elegant building designed by Frank Furness. Dinner Tuesday–Saturday. Reservations recommended. Credit cards: all major. $$$$

La Truffe, 10 S. Front St. Tel: 925-5062. Superb and pricey French dining in an elegant Old City setting. Lunch Tuesday–Friday, dinner Monday–Saturday. Credit cards: American Express, MasterCard, Visa. $$$$

Le Bec-Fin, 1523 Walnut St. Tel: 567-1000. Regarded as one of the finest restaurants in the country, this very expensive French favorite near Rittenhouse Square garners rave reviews from critics and clients alike. Lunch Monday–Friday, seatings at 11.30am and 1.30pm; dinner Monday–Saturday, seatings at 6pm and 9pm. Reservations required. A la carte menu served at the downstairs bistro; no reservations required. Credit cards: all major. $$$$

ITALIAN

Dante's and Luigi's, 762 S. 10th St. Tel: 922-9501. Stripped-down, inexpensive South Philly dining; decent Italian food, no atmosphere to speak of, but a recent Mafia hit adds mystique. Lunch and dinner daily. Credit cards: MasterCard, Visa. $-$$

Dilullo Centro, 1407 Locust St. Tel: 546-2000. A sumptuous, romantic dining room – one of the loveliest in the city – featuring fine Northern Italian cuisine. Located next to the Academy of Music and convenient to Rittenhouse Square and City Hall. Lunch Monday–Friday, dinner Monday–Saturday. Credit cards: all major. $$$$

La Famiglia, 8 S. Front St. Tel: 922-2803. An Old City favorite for high-class Italian food in a lovely formal setting. Lunch Tuesday–Friday, dinner Tuesday–Sunday. Credit cards: all major. $$$–$$$$

Frankie's Seafood Restaurant, 1100 Tasker St. Tel: 468-9989. Great Italian seafood at a lively South Philly establishment with hokey but charming nautical decor. Lunch Tuesday–Friday, dinner Tuesday–Sunday. Credit cards: Carte Blanche, MasterCard, Visa. $$–$$$

Girasole, 1305 Locust St. Tel: 985-4659. A lovely ristorante serving light but tasty dishes in a relaxing contemporary setting. Lunch Monday–Friday,

dinner Monday–Saturday. Credit cards: American Express, MasterCard, Visa, Diners Club. $$

Marabella's, 1700 Benjamin Franklin Pkwy. Tel: 981-5555. Upbeat and casual quasi-Italian eatery. Lunch and dinner daily. Credit cards: all major. $$

Marra's, 1700 E. Passyunk Ave. Tel: 463-9249. A friendly, home-style South Philly eatery with tasty pizza, pastas and other specialties (try the mussels) located in South Philly shopping district. Lunch Tuesday–Saturday, dinner Tuesday–Sunday. No credit cards accepted. $$

Mezzanotte, 1701 Green St. Tel: 765-2777. A trendy neighborhood trattoria near the Art Museum. Lunch and dinner daily. Credit cards: all major. $

Monte Carlo Living Room, 2nd and South Sts. Tel: 925-2220. Sophisticated European-style restaurant offering fresh pasta, seafood, veal and beef and excellent service. Dinner daily. Credit cards: American Express, MasterCard, Visa, Diners Club. $$$–$$$$

Osteria Romana, 935 Ellsworth St. Tel: 271-9191. A bastion of fine Roman cuisine near the Italian Market in a lovely old-fashioned setting; a cut above its other competitors, but expensive. Dinner Tuesday–Sunday. Credit cards: American Express, MasterCard, Visa. $$$$

Sfuzzi, 1650 Market St. Tel: 851-8888. Snazzy contemporary restaurant and bar at Liberty Place with a tantalizing Italian menu. Serves lunch Monday–Saturday, dinner daily, Sunday brunch. Credit cards: all major. $-$$$

Sonoma, 4411 Main St. Tel: 483-9400. A lovely Manayunk location serving a light combination of Italian and California cuisine. Lunch and dinner daily. Credit cards: American Express, Diners Club, MasterCard, Visa. $-$$

Victor Café, 1303 Dickinson St. Tel: 468-3040. Opera is the big attraction at this South Philly Italian restaurant where the waiters are as likely to serve up arias as antipasto. Dinner daily. Credit cards: all major. $$$

MEXICAN

Tequila's, 1511 Locust St. Tel: 546-0181. A high-class Mexican restaurant, more expensive than most but a cut above the average cantina. Lunch

Monday–Friday, dinner Monday–Saturday. Credit cards: all major. $$–$$$

Zocalo, 3600 Lancaster Ave. Tel: 895-0139. A creative, colorful Mexican restaurant in University City with spicy, well-prepared food, grilled dishes and a bar. Lunch Monday–Friday, dinner daily. Credit cards: American Express, MasterCard, Visa. $$–$$$

SEAFOOD

Bookbinder's Seafood House, 215 S. 15th St. Tel: 545-1137. An old-time Philadelphia establishment located near Academy of Music specializing in seafood and steaks, popular with businessmen and the older crowd. Lunch Monday–Friday, dinner daily. Credit cards: all major. $$$

Catfish Café, 4007 Ridge Ave. Tel: 229-9999. Friendly, tavern-like setting for a tasty variety of catfish and other dishes; located in East Falls, near Manayunk. Lunch Monday–Friday, dinner Monday–Saturday. Credit cards: American Express, MasterCard, Visa. $$

Chart House, 555 S. Columbus Ave. Tel: 625-8383. Large, modern establishment overlooking the Delaware River at the south end of Penn's Landing, a favorite for those who love fresh seafood, juicy steaks and bountiful salads and deserts. Dinner daily, Sunday brunch. Credit cards: all major. $$$–$$$$

DiNardo's Famous Crabs, 312 Race St. Tel: 925-5115. A well-known Old City seafood eatery that lures hordes of crab-lovers with spicy hard-shell crabs and casual atmosphere. Lunch Monday–Saturday, dinner daily. Credit cards: all major. $$

Hardshell Café, 9th and Market Sts. Tel: 592-9110. Casual center city spot specializing in crabs and other seafood. Lunch and dinner daily. Credit cards: all major. $$

Old Original Bookbinders, 125 Walnut St. Tel: 925-7027. Located in Old City, this well-known seafood spot is a favorite with out-of-towners, although locals tend to shy away from the crowds and pricey menu. Lunch Monday–Friday, dinner daily. Credit cards: all major. $$$

Philadelphia Fish & Co., 207 Chestnut St. Tel: 625-8605. Friendly Old City seafood restaurant popular with both tourists and locals and known for fresh, consistently pleasing fare; outdoor dining in warm weather. Lunch

Monday–Saturday (no lunch on Saturday in winter), dinner daily. Credit cards: American Express, MasterCard, Visa. $$–$$$

Samuel Adams Brew House, 1516 Sansom St. Tel: 563-2326.

Sansom Street Oyster House, 1516 Sansom St. Tel: 567-7683. A fun, informal seafood place with no pretensions and solid food. The Samuel Adams Brew House, serving bar food and beer brewed on the premises, is located upstairs. Lunch and dinner Monday–Saturday. Credit cards: all major. $$

Striped Bass, 1500 Walnut St. Tel: 732-4444. Savory fish and shellfish carefully prepared in full view of customers. Lunch Monday–Friday, dinner daily, Saturday brunch. Credit cards: all major. $$$$

Walt's King of Crabs, 806 S. 2nd St. Tel: 339-9124. There's no decor to speak of at this Queen Village favorite, but it's the perfect place for simple, unpretentious crustacean cuisine. Sunday–Thursday 11am–11pm, Friday–Saturday 11am–midnight. Credit cards: MasterCard, Visa. $$

STEAK HOUSES

Kansas City Prime, 4417 Main St. Tel: 482-3700. A lively Manayunk eatery featuring hefty servings of char-grilled steaks. Fish and chicken dishes are also choices on the menu. Lunch Monday–Friday, dinner daily. Credit cards: all major. $$–$$$

Morton's of Chicago, 19th and Cherry Sts. Tel: 557-0724. A favorite among carnivores, this classy, convivial steak house features aged beef, lobster, veal and attentive service. Lunch Monday–Friday, dinner daily. Credit cards: all major. $$$–$$$$

The Palm, 200 S. Broad St. Tel: 546-7256. A clubby steak house located at the Bellevue known for its giant slabs of beef and high-powered clientele (including the late Frank Rizzo). Lunch Monday–Friday, dinner daily. Reservations necessary. Credit cards: all major. $$$–$$$$

Ruth's Chris Steak House, 260 S. Broad St. Tel: 790-1515. Humongous slabs of beef are the specialty here; a favorite among businessmen and other power-munchers; convenient to the Academy of Music and City Hall. Lunch Monday–Friday, dinner daily. Credit cards: all major. $$$$

CAFE/DELI/PASTRY SHOP/CHEESESTEAKS

Essene Cafe, 719 S. 4th St. Tel: 928-3722. Organic vegetarian and seafood dishes are featured at this informal Queen Village cafe. Lunch (except Tuesday) and dinner daily, Sunday brunch. Credit cards: MasterCard, Visa. $

Famous 4th Street Delicatessen, 700 S. 4th St. Tel: 922-3274. A busy Jewish deli one block from South Street famous for its overstuffed sandwiches and scrumptious chocolate-chip cookies. Daily 7am–6pm, Sunday to 4pm. Credit cards: American Express $

Geno's Steaks, 1219 S. 9th St. Tel: 389-1455. The challenger in the "great South Philly cheesesteak war" has won its place at the highest tier of the cheesesteak hierarchy; located at the southern end of the Italian Market, outdoor tables only. Open 24 hours. No credit cards accepted. $

Jim's Steaks, 400 South St. Tel: 928-1911. Many cheesesteak connoisseurs consider this funky little place the tastiest in town. Open daily. No credit cards accepted. $

More Than Just Ice Cream, 1141-43 Pine St. Tel: 574-0586. Famous for its gargantuan helpings of ice cream and mountainous slices of apple pie, this fun, often crowded little place on Antique Row also offers burgers, sandwiches and other light fare. Serves lunch and dinner daily. No credit cards accepted. $

Old City Coffee, 221 Church St. Tel: 629-9292. A comfy café located on a narrow alley near Christ Church with freshly baked goods, wonderful coffees and a lively clientele. 7.30am–5.30pm Monday–Friday, 8.30am–5pm Saturday, 9.30am–3.30pm Sunday. Credit cards: MasterCard, Visa. $

Pat's King of Steaks, 1237 E. Passyunk Ave. Tel: 468-1546. The original cheesesteak king is still holding its own against all comers at the southern end of the Italian Market. Open 24 hours. No credit cards accepted. $

Pink Rose Pastry Shop, 630 S. 4th St. Tel: 592-0565. A pretty little pastry shop/café in Queen Village; a great place to decompress after cruising South Street. Tuesday–Thursday 10.30am–10.30pm, Friday 10.30am–11.30pm, Saturday 9am–11.30pm, Sunday 9am–8.30pm. No credit cards accepted. $

Reading Terminal Market, 12th and Arch Sts. Tel: 922-2317. A carnival of good food with everything from sushi to soul food in a cavernous train shed recently engulfed by the new Philadelphia Convention Center; an essential Philadelphia experience. Open 8am–6pm Monday–Saturday, but hours at some places vary. $–$$

HOTEL DINING

Azalea, Omni Hotel, 401 Chestnut St. Tel: 931-4260. Elegant, comfortable hotel dining room featuring regional American cuisine in the heart of the historic district. Breakfast, lunch and dinner daily, Sunday brunch. Credit cards: all major. $$$

Capriccio, Warwick Hotel, 1701 Locust St. Tel: 735-6000. Classy café near Rittenhouse Square with tasty baked goods, sandwiches, ice cream, cappuccino and other light fare. Breakfast, lunch and dinner daily. No credit cards accepted. $–$$

Cassatt Tea Room, Rittenhouse Hotel, 210 W. Rittenhouse Square. Tel: 546-9000. Afternoon tea is a recent tradition at this lovely, upscale room in a modern hotel with a garden view. Open daily for tea 2–5pm, for cocktails 5–11pm. Credit cards: all major. $$

The Dining Room, Ritz-Carlton Hotel, 17th and Chestnut Sts. Tel: 563-1600. This luxurious dining room in the new Ritz-Carlton Hotel at Liberty Place has been roundly praised for its contemporary French cuisine and sumptuous setting. Breakfast and lunch Monday–Saturday, dinner Tuesday–Saturday, Sunday brunch. Credit cards: all major. $$$$

Founders Restaurant, Hotel Atop the Bellevue, 200 S. Broad St. Tel: 893-1776. Breathtaking views from this formal, sky-high dining room compliment fine French and Continental cuisine. Breakfast, lunch and dinner daily, Sunday brunch. Credit cards: all major. $$$$

The Fountain, Four Seasons Hotel, 18th St and Ben Franklin Parkway. Tel: 963-1500. Highly praised International cuisine offered in a sumptuous hotel dining room overlooking Logan Square. Breakfast daily, lunch Monday–Saturday, dinner daily, Sunday brunch. Credit cards: all major. $$$$

Restaurant 210, The Rittenhouse Hotel, 210 W. Rittenhouse Square. Tel: 790-2534. Masterfully created Conti-

nental cuisine served at a gracious dining room with wonderful views of Rittenhouse Square. Lunch Monday–Friday, Dinner Monday–Saturday. Credit cards: all major. $$$$

Mia's, Warwick Hotel, 1701 Locust St. Tel: 545-4655. Mediterranean cuisine served in the high-class lobby of this handsome old hotel. Breakfast, lunch and dinner served daily. Credit cards: all major. $$$

Swann Café, Four Seasons Hotel, 18th St and Ben Franklin Parkway. Tel: 963-1500. An elegant setting in Museum District for inventive American cuisine, especially good for lighter fare. Lunch and dinner daily, Sunday brunch. Credit cards: all major. $$$.

TreeTops, The Rittenhouse Hotel, 210 W. Rittenhouse Square. Tel: 790-2533. Plush dining room specializing in imaginative American dishes; less formal than Restaurant 210, which is also at the Rittenhouse. Breakfast and dinner daily, lunch Monday–Saturday, Sunday brunch. Credit cards: all major. $$$

Main Line

Bravo Bistro and Bar, 175 King of Prussia Road, Radnor, PA. Tel: 610-293-9521. A popular spot for fine International dishes and friendly service in an informal café-style setting. Credit cards: American Express, Diners Club, MasterCard, Visa. $$

Central Bar & Grill, 39 Morris Ave, Bryn Mawr, PA. Tel: 610-527-1400. A trendy bar and restaurant housed in a converted train station offering a wide range of American dishes with a few Asian and European touches. Lunch Monday–Saturday, dinner daily, Sunday brunch. Credit cards: all major. $$

La Fourchette, 110 N. Wayne Ave, Wayne, PA. Tel: 610-687-8333. Consistently pleasing French cuisine offered in an elegant and comfortable establishment prepared and served by an attentive staff. Lunch Monday–Friday, dinner daily, Sunday brunch. Credit cards: all major. $$$$

Passerelle, 175 King of Prussia Road, Radnor, PA. Tel: 610-293-9411. Elegant French cuisine in a relaxing country setting. Lunch Tuesday–Friday, dinner Tuesday–Saturday. Credit cards: all major. $$$$.

Restaurant Taquet, Wayne Hotel, 139 E. Lancaster Ave, Wayne, PA. Tel: 610-687-5005. Popular French restaurant

with a casual but elegant ambience and an excellent bar. Lunch Monday–Saturday, dinner daily, Sunday brunch. Credit cards: American Express, MasterCard Visa. $$$$

San Marco, 27 City Ave, Bala Cynwyd, PA. Tel: 610-664-7844. Creative, first-class regional Italian cuisine served in a romantic 19th-century mansion. Lunch Monday–Friday, dinner Monday–Saturday. Credit cards: all major. $$$

Toscana-Cucina Rustica, 24 N. Merion Ave, Bryn Mawr, PA. Tel: 610-527-7700. A popular Italian restaurant featuring grilled fish, beef and poultry as well as breads and pizza baked in a wood-burning oven. Lunch Monday–Friday, dinner daily. Credit cards: American Express. $$$

Yangming, 1051 Conestoga Road, Bryn Mawr, PA. Tel: 610-527-3200. Creative and traditional Chinese dishes are the specialty of this Main Line favorite housed in a lovely historic building. Lunch Monday–Saturday, dinner daily. Credit cards: American Express, MasterCard, Visa. $$–$$$

Bucks County

Black Bass Inn, River Road, Lumberville, PA. Tel: 297-5770. Fine country fare with European touches presented at a lovely inn dating to 1745 perched on the banks of the Delaware River. Lunch Monday–Saturday, dinner daily, Sunday brunch. Credit cards: American Express, Visa, MasterCard, Diners Club, Discover. $$$

Carversville Inn, Aquetong and Carversville roads, Carversville, PA. Tel: 297-0900. A charming country inn located in a quiet village, serving solid American dishes. Lunch Wednesday–Sunday, dinner Tuesday–Sunday. Credit cards: American Express, Visa, MasterCard. $$$

Cuttalossa Inn, River and Cuttalossa roads, Lumberville, PA. Tel: 297-5082. Imaginative International cuisine in a peaceful, creatively furnished 18th-century building. Lunch, dinner Monday–Saturday. Credit cards: American Express, Visa, MasterCard. $$$–$$$$

Doylestown Inn, 18 W. State St, Doylestown, PA. Tel: 345-6610. Serving consistently pleasing, hearty, mostly American dishes this historic Victorian inn is situated in central Doylestown. Breakfast daily, lunch Monday–Saturday, dinner daily. Credit cards: all major. $$

Evermay on the Delaware, River Road, Erwinna, PA. Tel: 294-9100. A gorgeous Victorian mansion set on lovely grounds offering a menu of consistently pleasing French-influenced cuisine. One seating at 7.30pm Friday–Sunday only. Credit cards: Visa, MasterCard. $$$$

Havana, 105 S. Main St, New Hope, PA. Tel: 862-9897. Eclectic menu for adventurous eaters at a fun-loving bar/restaurant, great for watching the carnival on Main Street. Lunch and dinner daily (closed Tuesday–Wednesday from January-March). Credit cards: all major. $$

Odette's, River Road near Route 232, New Hope, PA. Tel: 862-2432. Imaginative Continental dishes at a historic and cheerful riverside place, often with live entertainment. Lunch Monday–Saturday, dinner daily, Sunday brunch. Credit cards: all major. $$–$$$

Sign of the Sorrel Horse, Old Easton Rd, Doylestown, PA. Tel: 215-230-9999. French cuisine lovingly prepared and served in a romantic dining room. Dinner Wednesday–Saturday. Reservations required. Credit cards: Visa, MasterCard. $$$

Lancaster County

Catacombs Restaurant at Bube's Brewery, 102 N. Market St, Mount Joy, PA. Tel: 717-653-2056. Snug in the underground chamber of a 19th-century brewery, this unusual eatery serves up hearty steak, seafood, veal and poultry. Ask about the Sunday Medieval Feast. Bar upstairs. Dinner daily. Credit cards: all major. $$–$$$

Groff's Farm, Pinkerton Road, Mount Joy, PA. Tel: 717-653-2048. A bounty of Pennsylvania Dutch hospitality and heaping plates of hearty specialties greet you at this charming 18th-century farmhouse; family-style or a la carte. Dinner Tuesday–Saturday, lunch Tuesday–Saturday. Credit cards: Visa, MasterCard, Discover, Diners Club. $$

The Log Cabin, 11 Lehoy Forest Drive, Leola. Tel: 717-626-1181. Savory steaks, seafood, lamb and poultry are served in a former speakeasy; a peaceful, out-of-the-way location, but worth the trip. Dinner daily. Credit cards: all major. $$–$$$

Market Fare, 25 W. King St, Lancaster, PA. Tel: 717-299-7090. Classic American cuisine served in a relaxing establishment with 19th-century art,

cushy armchairs, and upper level café. Lunch Monday–Saturday, dinner daily, Sunday brunch. Credit cards: American Express, MasterCard, Visa, Diners Club. $$–$$$

Olde Greenfield Inn, 595 Greenfield Road, Lancaster, PA. Tel: 717-393-0668. Interesting, carefully prepared International seafood, poultry, steak and pasta in a historic farmhouse just outside of town. Breakfast Saturday–Sunday, lunch Tuesday–Friday, dinner Tuesday–Saturday, Sunday brunch. Credit cards: all major. $$

The Press Room, 26–28 W. King St. Tel: 717-399-5400. An upscale bistro serving a variety of pastas, salads, hearth-baked pizzas and hamburgers. Lunch Monday–Saturday, dinner Monday–Sunday. Credit cards: American Express, MasterCard, Visa. $–$$

Restaurant at Doneckers, 333 N. State St, Ephrata, PA. Tel: 717-738-9501. Fine French cuisine and a large wine list in a welcoming country atmosphere; located at the Doneckers complex of shops and accommodations. Lunch Monday–Tuesday Thursday–Saturday, dinner Monday–Tuesday Thursday–Sunday, Sunday brunch. Credit cards: all major. $$$

Revere Tavern, 3063 Lincoln Highway, Paradise, PA. Tel: 717-687-8601. An 18th-century tavern, later a house owned by President James Buchanan, now a fine restaurant serving exceptional American fare in a colonial atmosphere. Dinner daily. Credit cards: all major. $$$

Stoltzfus Farm Restaurant, Route 772, Intercourse, PA. Tel: 717-768-8156. Homemade Pennsylvania Dutch treats like sausage, smoked ham, chow chow and shoofly pie in a homey country setting. Lunch and dinner Monday–Saturday. Credit cards: Visa, MasterCard. $

Zinn's Diner, Route 272, Denver, PA. Tel: 717-336-2210. Although part of a tourist-oriented complex near the Pennsylvania Turnpike, the Pennsylvania Dutch specialties are generally quite good and always abundant; a winner with kids. Breakfast, lunch, dinner daily. No credit cards accepted. $

Atlantic City and Jersey Shore

Angelo's Fairmount Tavern, 2300 Fairmount Ave, Atlantic City, NJ. Tel: 609-344-2439. Family-run Italian restaurant with heaping portions and spir-

ited atmosphere. Lunch Monday–Friday, dinner daily. No credit cards accepted. $$

Capriccio, Merv Griffin's Resort Hotel, North Carolina Ave and the Boardwalk, Atlantic City, NJ. Tel: 609-340-7836. Well-prepared Italian fare at Boardwalk location overlooking the ocean. Dinner Friday–Tuesday. Credit cards: all major. $$$–$$$$

Dock's Oyster House, 2405 Atlantic Ave, Atlantic City, NJ. Tel 609-345-0092. One of the oldest restaurants in Atlantic City is still a ship-shape operation offering delectable seafood and charbroiled steaks in a warm, friendly setting. Dinner Wednesday–Sunday. Closed December-mid-February. Credit Cards: all major. $$$

Knife and Fork Inn, Atlantic and Pacific aves, Atlantic City, NJ. Tel: 609-344-1133. A landmark restaurant with outstanding seafood, lobster, soft-shelled crab, beef, lamb in a comfortable, nautical atmosphere. Dinner Monday–Saturday. Credit cards: all major. Jackets required. $$$–$$$$

Mad Batter, 19 Jackson St, Cape May, NJ. Tel: 609-884-5970. Popular restaurant in a charming house serving an imaginative combination of International dishes in lovely dining room; outdoor dining in warm weather. Breakfast, lunch, dinner daily May-September; call for off-season hours. Credit cards: Visa, MasterCard. $$–$$$

Peking Duck House, 2801 Atlantic Ave, Atlantic City, NJ. Tel: 609-344-9090. Among the most popular Chinese restaurants in Atlantic City with consistent, high-quality service and fine cuisine. Lunch Monday–Saturday, dinner daily. Credit cards: all major. $$$

Restaurant Atop the Winery, Renault Winery, 72 N. Bremen Ave, Egg Harbor City. Tel: 609-965-2111. Unique establishment set in a working winery featuring full International six-course dinners and wine-tasting in charming historic surroundings. Lunch Monday–Saturday, dinner Friday–Sunday only, Sunday brunch. Credit cards: American Express, Visa, MasterCard, Diners Club. $$$

Restaurant Maureen, 429 Beach Drive, Cape May, NJ. Tel: 609-884-3774. Exquisite Continental cuisine at an intimate oceanfront establishment perfect for couples. Dinner daily in summer season; call for hours in off-season. Credit cards: American Express, Visa, MasterCard. $$$

Washington Inn, 801 Washington St, Cape May, NJ. Tel: 609-884-5697. Light but filling International cuisine in a handsome 19th-century manor house with cheerful Victorian decor. Dinner daily in season. Limited hours off-season, call ahead. Credit cards: all major. $$$

The White House, 2301 Arctic St, Atlantic City, NJ. Tel: 609-345-1564. This beloved Atlantic City standby is legendary for its king-sized, belly-busting submarine sandwiches; mostly takeout. Monday–Saturday 10am–midnight, Sunday 11am–midnight. No credit cards accepted. $

Attractions

Culture

Museums

Academy of Natural Sciences, 19th St and Benjamin Franklin Parkway. Tel: 299-1000. Monday–Friday 10am–4.30pm, Saturday–Sunday 10am–5pm. Admission charge.

Afro-American Historical and Cultural Museum, 7th and Arch Sts. Tel: 574-0380. Tuesday–Saturday 9am–5pm. Admission charge.

American Swedish Historical Museum, 1900 Pattison Ave. Tel: 389-1776. Tuesday–Friday 10am–4pm, Saturday–Sunday noon–4pm. Admission charge.

Army-Navy Museum, Independence National Historical Park. Daily 9am–5pm. Admission free.

Atwater Kent Museum, 15 S. 7th St. Tel: 922-3031. Tuesday–Saturday 9.30am–4.30pm. Admission charge.

Balch Institute, 18 S. 7th St. Tel: 925-8090. Monday–Saturday 10am–4pm. Admission charge.

Barnes Foundation, 300 N. Latchs Lane, Merion, PA. Tel: 667-0290. Friday–Saturday 9.30am–4.30pm, Sunday 1–4.30pm, closed July and August. Admission charge.

Cigna Corporation Museum, 17th and Arch Sts. Tel: 761-1000. Monday–Fri-

day 9am–5pm. Admission free.

Civil War Library and Museum, 1805 Pine St. Tel: 735-8196. Monday–Saturday 10am–4pm. Admission charge.

Dental Museum, Temple University, 323 N. Broad St. Tel: 221-2816. Call ahead for hours.

Drexel University Museum, Main Building, 32nd and Chestnut Sts. Tel: 895-2424. Monday–Wednesday 1–7pm, Thursday–Friday 1–4pm. Admission free.

Fireman's Hall, 2nd and Quarry Sts. Tel: 923-1438. Tuesday–Saturday 9am–5pm. Admission free.

Fonthill Museum, E. Court St at Swamp Road, Doylestown, PA. Tel: 348-9461. Monday–Saturday 10am–5pm, Sunday noon–5pm, call ahead for tour reservations. Admission charge.

Franklin Institute, 20th St and Benjamin Franklin Parkway. Tel: 448-1200. Daily 9.30am–5pm, Tuttleman Omniverse Theater and Mandell Futures Center are open until 9pm Thursday–Sunday. Admission charge.

Girard Collection, Founder's Hall, Girard College, Girard and Corinthian aves. Tel: 787-2600. Thursday 2–4pm, and by appointment. Admission free.

Grand Army of the Republic Civil War Museum, 4278 Griscom St. Tel: 289-6484. First Sunday of every month, every Sunday in January noon–5pm. Admission free.

Heritage Center of Lancaster County, 13 W. King St, Lancaster, PA. Tel: 717-299-6440. April–November Tuesday–Saturday 10am–4pm. Admission free.

Historical Society of Pennsylvania, 1300 Locust St. Tel: 732-6201. Tuesday, Thursday–Saturday 10am–5pm, Wednesday 1–9pm. Admission charge.

Independence Seaport Museum, Columbus Ave and Walnut St at Penn's Landing. Tel: 925-5439. Daily 10am–5pm. Admission charge.

Institute of Contemporary Art, University of Pennsylvania, 36th and Sansom Sts. Tel: 898-7108. Wednesday 10am–7pm, Thursday–Sunday 10am–5pm. Admission charge.

James A. Michener Art Center, 138 S. Pine St, Doylestown, PA. Tel: 340-9800. Tuesday–Friday 10am–4.30pm, Saturday–Sunday 10am–5pm. Admission charge.

Landis Valley Museum, 2451 Kissel Hill Road, Lancaster, PA. Tel: 717-569-0401. Tuesday–Saturday 9am–5pm, Sunday noon–5pm. Admission charge.

Marine Corps Memorial Museum, Independence National Historical Park. Daily 9am–5pm. Admission free.

Mercer Museum, Pine St at Ashland St, Doylestown, PA. Tel: 345-0210. Monday–Saturday 10am–5pm, Sunday noon–5pm, Tuesday evening 6–9pm. Admission charge.

Moravian Pottery and Tile Works, Swamp Road, Doylestown, PA. Tel: 345-6722. Daily 10am–4.45pm. Admission charge.

Morris Arboretum, 100 Northwestern Ave. Tel: 247-5882. Daily 10am–5pm April–October, 10am–4pm November–March. Admission charge.

Mummers Museum, 2nd St and Washington Ave. Tel: 336-3050. Tuesday–Saturday 9.30am–5pm, Sunday noon–5pm; closed Sunday in July and August. Admission charge.

Mutter Museum, 19 S. 22nd St. Tel: 563-3737. Tuesday–Friday 10am–4pm. Admission charge.

Norman Rockwell Museum, 601 Walnut St. Tel: 922-4345. Monday–Saturday 10am–4pm, Sunday 11am–4pm. Admission charge.

National Museum of American Jewish History, 55 N. 5th St. Tel: 923-3811. Monday–Thursday 10am–5pm, Friday 10am–3pm, Sunday noon–5pm. Admission charge.

New Jersey State Aquarium, 1 Riverside Drive, Camden, NJ. Tel: 609-365-3300. Daily 10am–5pm. Admission charge.

Parry Mansion, Main and Ferry Sts, New Hope, PA. Tel: 862-5652. May–October Friday–Sunday 1–5pm. Admission charge.

Pennsylvania Academy of the Fine Arts, Broad and Cherry Sts. Tel: 972-7600. Tuesday–Saturday 10am–5pm, Sunday 11am–5pm. Admission charge.

Philadelphia Museum of Art, 26th St and Benjamin Franklin Parkway. Tel: 763-8100. Tuesday–Sunday 10am–5pm, Wednesday til 8.45pm. Admission charge.

Philadelphia Zoological Gardens, 34th St and Girard Ave. Tel: 243-1100. Daily 9.30am–5pm. Admission charge.

Please Touch Museum, 210 N. 21st St. Tel: 963-0667. Daily 9am–4.30pm. Admission charge.

Polish-American Cultural Center, 308 Walnut St. Tel: 922-1700. January–April Monday–Friday 10am–4pm, May–December Monday–Saturday 10am–4pm. Admission free.

Port of History Museum, Penn's Landing at Walnut St. Tel: 925-3802. Wednesday–Sunday 10am–4.30pm. Admission charge.

Railroad Museum of Pennsylvania, Route 741, Strasburg, PA. Tel: 717-687-8628. Tuesday–Saturday 9am–5pm, Sunday noon-5pm. Admission charge.

Rodin Museum, 22nd St and Benjamin Franklin Parkway. Tel: 763-8100. Tuesday–Sunday 10am–5pm. Free.

Rosenbach Museum, 2010 Delancey Place. Tel: 732-1600. Tuesday–Sunday 11am–4pm, last tour at 2.45pm. Admission charge.

Shoe Museum, Pennsylvania College of Podiatric Medicine, 8th and Race Sts. Tel: 629-0300; call in advance for tour. Admission free.

University Museum, University of Pennsylvania, 33rd and Spruce Sts. Tel: 898-4000. Tuesday–Saturday 10am–4.30pm, Sunday 1–5pm. Admission charge.

Wagner Free Institute of Science, 17th St and Montgomery Ave. Tel: 763-6529. Tuesday–Friday 9am–4pm. Admission free.

Woodmere Museum, 9201 Germantown Ave. Tel: 247-0476. Tuesday–Saturday 10am–5pm, Sunday 1–5pm. Admission free.

Art Galleries

Many art galleries in the Old City area coordinate their openings for **First Friday**, the first Friday of every month except July and August. Galleries in the Rittenhouse Square area have followed suit with **Second Saturday**, held on the second Saturday of every month between December and June. Here are a few:

I. Brewster & Co, 1628 Walnut St. Tel: 731-9200. Monday–Saturday 11am–5.30pm. A wide range of styles and media.

Calderwood Gallery, 1427 Walnut St. Tel: 568-7475. Tuesday–Friday 11am–5pm, Saturday noon–5pm. 20th-century decorative arts.

The Clay Studio, 139 N. 2nd St. Tel: 925-3453. Tuesday–Friday noon–6pm, Saturday–Sunday noon–5pm. Work in clay.

deVecchis, 404-1/2 South St. Tel: 922-5708. Tuesday, Wednesday, Thursday 10am–6pm, Friday–Saturday 10am–8pm, Sunday noon–5pm. Contemporary graphics.

Eyes Gallery, 402 South St. Tel: 925-0193. Monday–Thursday 11am–7pm, Friday–Saturday 11am–8pm, Sunday noon–6pm. Latin American folk art, ethnic jewelry and exotic clothing.

Helen Drutt Gallery, 1721 Walnut St. Tel: 735-1625. Wednesday–Friday 10am–5pm, Saturday 10am–4pm. Ceramics.

F.A.N. Gallery, 311 Cherry St. Tel: 922-5155. Tuesday–Sunday 11am–6pm. Contemporary work.

Fleisher Art Memorial, 709-721 Catharine St. Tel: 922-3456. Monday–Friday 11am–5pm and Monday–Thursday 6.30–9.30pm, Saturday 1–3pm, closed August. Work by faculty, students, local artists.

Janet Fleisher Gallery, 211 S. 17th St. Tel: 545-7562. Monday–Friday 10.30am–5.30pm, Saturday 11am–5.30pm. Contemporary American art.

Jeffrey Fuller Fine Art Ltd, 132 S. 17th St. Tel: 564-9977. Monday–Friday 9.30am–5.30pm. 19th- and 20th-century American and European masters.

Hahn Gallery, 8439 Germantown Ave. Tel: 247-8439. Monday–Saturday 10am–5.30pm, Wednesday until 8pm. A wide range of styles and media.

Highwire Gallery, 137 N. 2nd St. Tel: 829-1255. Monday–Friday noon–6pm, Saturday–Sunday noon–5pm. Cooperative gallery with group and individual shows.

Indigo, 1102 Pine St. Tel: 440-0202. Monday–Saturday 11.30am–6.30pm, Sunday noon–6pm. Art and artifacts from Asia, Africa and the Americas.

Jaipaul Galleries, 1610 Locust St. Tel: 735-7303. Monday–Friday 10.30am–5pm, Saturday 11am–4pm. Ancient Indian art.

Esther M. Klein Art Gallery, University City Science Center, 3600 Market St. Tel: 387-2255. Monday–Friday 9am–5pm. Wide range of styles and media.

Gilbert Luber, 1220 Walnut St. Tel: 732-2996. Open Monday–Saturday 11.30am–5.30pm. Asian art.

Lucien Crump Art Gallery, 6380 Germantown Ave. Tel: 843-8788. Monday–Saturday 11am–7pm, Sunday 1–5pm. African-American art.

Newman, 1625 Walnut St. Tel: 563-1779. Monday–Friday 9am–5.30pm, Saturday 10am–4.30pm, Wednesday til 7pm. 19th- and 20th-century art.

Nexus Foundation for Today's Art, 137 N. 2nd St. Tel: 629-1103. Mon-

day–Friday noon–6pm, Saturday–Sunday noon–5pm. Contemporary work.

October Gallery, 3805 Lancaster Ave. Tel: 387-7177. Monday–Friday 10am–6pm, Saturday noon–6pm. African American art.

Philadelphia Art Alliance, 251 S. 18th St. Tel: 545-4302. Monday–Friday 11.30am–5.30pm, Saturday noon–5pm, Sunday noon–4pm, closed August. A mixed-media gallery featuring visual, performance and literary arts.

The Print Club, 1614 Latimer St. Tel: 735-6090. Tuesday–Saturday 11am–5.30pm, call ahead to confirm hours. Contemporary prints and photographs.

Prints in Progress Gallery, 54 N. 3rd St. Tel: 928-0206. Monday–Friday 9am–5pm. Children's art.

Vera Redmond Gallery, 4223 Main St. Tel: 482-7514. Friday–Sunday 1–5pm, Friday and Saturday evenings 6–9pm. Abstract painting and sculpture.

Rosenfeld Gallery, 113 Arch St. Tel: 922-1376. Wednesday–Saturday 10am–5pm, Sunday noon–5pm. Emerging American artists in all media.

Arthur Ross Gallery, University of Pennsylvania, 220 S. 34th St. Tel: 898-4401. Tuesday–Friday 10am–5pm, Saturday–Sunday noon–5pm. Eclectic work, all media.

Sande Webster Gallery, 2018 Locust St. Tel: 732-8850. Monday–Friday 10am–6pm, Saturday 11am–4pm. Contemporary work in a variety of media and styles.

Snyderman Gallery, 303 Cherry St. Tel: 238-9576. Tuesday–Saturday 10am–6pm. One-of-a-kind furniture, glass works and sculpture.

Taller Puertorriqueno, 2721 N. 5th St. Tel: 426-3311. Tuesday–Saturday 10am–6pm. Minority artists.

University of the Arts, Haviland Hall Gallery, Mednick Gallery, Rosenwald-Wolf Gallery, Broad and Pine Sts. Tel: 875-1116 or 875-1020. Monday–Friday 10am–5pm, Wednesday til 9pm, Saturday–Sunday noon–5pm. Contemporary work.

Vox Populi, 17 N. 2nd St. Tel: 925-4249. Wednesday–Thursday 4–8pm, Friday–Sunday noon–8pm. Contemporary work by local artists.

Works Gallery, 319 South St. Tel: 922-7775. Tuesday–Saturday 11am–7pm, Sunday noon–6pm. Contemporary crafts in clay, fiber, glass and metal.

Ruth Zafir Gallery, 13 S. 2nd St. Tel: 627-7098. Monday–Friday noon–6pm;

call ahead to confirm hours. Sculpture by local artists.

Film

For information on films currently playing in Philadelphia and theater locations, call **MovieFone** at 222-3456.

Annenberg Center, 3680 Walnut St. Tel: 898-6701. Documentary films.

Eric's Place Theatre, 1519 Chestnut St. Tel: 563-3086.

Franklin Mills Cinema, 903 Franklin Mills Circle, Tel: 281-2750. 10 screens.

Free Library of Philadelphia, 19th and Vine Sts. Tel: 686-5322. Free film series.

International House Film and Folklife Center, 3701 Chestnut St. Tel: 895-6542. Independent and foreign films.

Ritz 5, 214 Walnut St, Tel: 925-7900. Independent, limited-run, foreign films.

Ritz at the Bourse, 4th and Chestnut Sts. Tel: 925-7900. Independent, limited-run and foreign films.

United Artists Theatres, Columbus Blvd and Washington Ave. Tel: 963-0620. First-run films shown on multiple screens.

Music

Academy of Music, Broad and Locust Sts. Tel: 893-1930. Home of the Philadelphia Orchestra.

All-Star Forum, 1521 Locust St. Tel: 735-7506. A series of concerts between October and May by outstanding international orchestras, soloists and ensembles at the Academy of Music.

Choral Arts Society, 1420 Locust St. Tel: 545-8634. 150-member symphonic chorus; performances are held at the Academy of Music and other sites throughout the city.

Concerto Soloists. Tel: 574-3550. Classical chamber music featuring many members of the Philadelphia Orchestra; performances at the Walnut Street Theater and the Church of the Holy Trinity on Rittenhouse Square.

Cultural Affairs Council/Department of Recreation, 1450 Municipal Services Building, Kennedy Blvd and 15th St. Tel: 686-8685. The City of Philadelphia sponsors outdoor jazz, classical and pop concerts at locations throughout the city, including JFK Plaza adjacent to City Hall, Penn's Landing, Rittenhouse Square, Robin Hood Dell East in Fairmount Park and Independence Mall.

Curtis Institute of Music, 1726 Locust St. Tel: 893-5252. Over 80 free concerts, opera and recitals are held at the Institute's small concert hall.

Electric Factory Concerts. Tel: 568-3222. Sponsors most of the big rock shows that come through Philadelphia.

International House, 3701 Chestnut St. Tel: 387-5125. International folk music, dance and film.

Mann Music Center, 52nd St and Parkside Ave, West Fairmount Park. Tel: 567-0707. Summer home of the Philadelphia Orchestra; free tickets (limit 2 per concert) are available on a first-come-first-served basis. Look for coupons in local papers and send them to the Mann Music Center Concerts, Department of Recreation, P.O. Box 1000, Philadelphia, PA 19105.

Mendelssohn Club of Philadelphia. Tel: 735-9922. 35-member chorus; performances at the Academy of Music and venues throughout the city.

Merriam Theater, 250 S. Broad St. Tel: 732-5446. Classical, jazz and pop music as well as dance and theater.

Opera Company of Philadelphia, 30 S. 15th St. Tel: 928-2110. The city's premier opera company presents 4 operas a year at the Academy of Music.

Penn's Landing. Tel: 923-9129. Summer series of jazz and pop concerts, many free, at the outdoor riverfront stage.

Pennsylvania Opera Theater, 1217 Sansom St. Tel: 440-9797. Three performances each year presented in English at the Merriam Theater.

Philadelphia Boys Choir. Tel: 222-3500. An acclaimed ensemble of 90 boys and 30 men which performs at venues throughout the city and the world.

Philadelphia Folksong Society, 7113 Emlen St. Tel: 247-1300. American and international folk music presented at the Commodore Barry Club; the Society also sponsors the annual Philadelphia Folk Festival at the Old Poole Farm in Schwenksville, PA.

Philadelphia Orchestra, Academy of Music, 1420 Locust Sts. Tel: 893-1930. World-famous ensemble formerly conducted by Leopold Stokowski, Eugene Ormandy and Riccardo Muti, now under the baton of Wolfgang Sawallisch, performs at the Academy of Music, summer concerts at the outdoor Mann Music Center in Fairmount Park.

Philly Pops. Tel: 735-7506. Performances at the Academy of Music October–May.

Relache. Tel: 574-8246. Contemporary experimental music presented at Drexel University's Mandell Theater and the Philadelphia Ethical Society on Rittenhouse Square.

Savoy Company. Tel: 735-7161. Gilbert and Sullivan troupe; performances at the Academy of Music.

Corestates Spectrum, Broad St and Pattison Ave. Tel: 336-3600. 17,000-seat arena, used for giant rock shows.

Theater of the Living Arts, 334 South St. Tel: 922-1011. Pop, jazz, rock and folk at this South Street institution; general admission for 800 people.

Tower Theater, 69th and Ludlow Sts, Upper Darby, PA. Tel: 610-352-0313. 3,000-seat rock music venue.

Dance

For information about local dance companies and performances, contact the **Philadelphia Dance Alliance,** 135 S. 23rd St. Tel: 564-5270.

Pennsylvania Ballet, Broad St and Washington Ave. Tel: 551-7014. Philadelphia's premier ballet company performs at the Academy of Music and Merriam Theater; the annual *Nutcracker* is a tradition.

Philadanco, 9 N. Preston St. Tel: 387-8200. A contemporary company which performs at the Zellerbach Theater at the Annenberg Center, the Walnut Street Theater and the Mandell Theater.

Theater and Cabaret

American Music Theater Festival, 123 S. Broad St. Tel: 893-1570. Stage four productions each year, many world premieres; most performances are held at the Plays and Players Theater.

Annenberg Center, 3680 Walnut St. Tel: 898-6791. A complex of theaters at the University of Pennsylvania that hosts the Annenberg Center Theater for Children and the International Theater Festival for Children as well as its own subscription series.

Arden Theatre Company, 2nd and Market Sts. Tel: 922-8900. Several productions each year including original literary adaptations, musicals, modern dramas and classics.

Arts Bank, 601 S. Broad St. Tel: 545-0630. A new rehearsal and performance space on the Avenue of the Arts used by a variety of theater and music organizations.

Bucks County Playhouse, 70 S. Main St, New Hope, PA. Tel: 862-2041. Musicals, comedies and dramas often featuring well-known actors.

Forrest Theater, 1114 Walnut St. Tel: 923-1515. Several big-time Broadway road shows each year.

Freedom Theater, 1346 N. Broad St. Tel: 765-2793. A black theater company that stages six or seven productions each year.

Mask & Wig Theatre, 310 S. Quince St. Tel: 923-4229. This charming theater tucked away in an alley in Washington Square West is home to the University of Pennsylvania's theater troupe and the Philadelphia Area Repertory Theatre.

McCarter Theater, 91 University Place, Princeton, NJ. Tel: 609-683-8000. A wide range of performances, including musicals, classical dramas, comedies and new works.

Painted Bride Art Center, 230 Vine St. Tel: 925-9914. Cutting-edge dance, performance art, music, mime, puppetry and more.

People's Light and Theater Company, 39 Conestoga Road, Malvern, PA. Tel: 610-644-3500. Exciting adaptations, contemporary and classical dramas presented on a stage in a 200-year-old converted barn, about 45 minutes outside center city.

Philadelphia Festival for New Plays, 3900 Chestnut St. Tel: 898-3900. Several new works presented each year at the Annenberg Center's Harold Prince Theater, often by well-known playwrights.

Philadelphia Theater Company, The Bourse, 111 S. Independence Mall East. Tel: 592-8333. A polished presenter of new American plays; several productions are staged each year.

Play and Players Theater, 1714 Delancey St. Tel: 735-0630. The oldest community theater in the country presents four light dramas or comedies each year and hosts other theater companies.

Society Hill Playhouse, 507 S. 8th St. Tel: 923-0210. Historic venue for a variety of off-Broadway fare.

Walnut Street Theater, 9th and Walnut Sts. Tel: 574-3550. The oldest continuously operated theater in the country presents musicals, dramas,

classics and Broadway road shows as well as four new plays each year at adjacent smaller theaters.

Wilma Theatre, 2030 Sansom St. Tel: 963-0249. Cutting-edge drama and comedy; planning to move into a new theater on Broad Street (the Avenue of the Arts) in early 1997.

Nightlife

NIGHTCLUBS, DANCE CLUBS AND BARS

Artful Dodger, 400-402 S. 2nd St. Tel: 922-7880. A traditional English pub on Head House Square with full menu and live entertainment Thursday, Friday and Saturday nights. Credit cards: all major.

The Bank, 600 Spring Garden St. Tel: 351-9404. A hip, contemporary dance club in a historic Frank Furness bank building that attracts a young and stylish crowd. Credit cards: all major.

Blue Moon Jazz Club and Restaurant, 4th St between Market and Chestnut Sts. Tel: 413-2272. Live jazz every night at this bar/cafe/restaurant featuring California cuisine. Credit cards: all major.

Boathouse Row Bar, The Rittenhouse Hotel, 220 W. Rittenhouse Square. Tel: 546-9000. A classy spot filled with rowing memorabilia in the plush, modern Rittenhouse Hotel. Credit cards: all major.

Chestnut Cabaret, 38th and Chestnut Sts. Tel: 386-8555. A popular rock club in University City which features local and touring bands with seating for several thousand people. Credit cards not accepted.

Comedy Cabaret, 126 Chestnut St. Tel: 625-5653. Top local and national talent at this Old City location upstairs from the Middle East restaurant, where tourists flock for Middle Eastern cuisine and belly dancing. Credit cards: all major.

Egypt, Christopher Columbus Blvd at Spring Garden St. Tel: 922-6500. Concert-quality sound and light system on a two-level dance floor. One of several popular night spots on the Delaware River. Credit cards: all major.

J.C. Dobbs, 304 South St. Tel: 925-4053. This down and dirty rock club with live local talent has been a South Street institution for years. Credit cards: Visa, MasterCard.

The Irish Pub, 2007 Walnut St. Tel: 568-5603. A spirited party bar popular

with the younger crowd. Credit cards: American Express, MasterCard, Visa.

Katmandu, Pier 25 at Delaware Ave and Willow St. Tel: 629-1101. Open May–October only. A popular outdoor bar on the riverfront in the shadow of the Ben Franklin Bridge with live world music, reggae, rock, dance space and outdoor dining. Credit cards: all major.

Khyber Pass Pub, 56 S. 2nd St. Tel: 440-9683. Rock club in Old City with live local bands nightly; a little rough around the edges but much beloved by regulars and visitors alike. No credit cards accepted.

Liberties, 705 N. 2nd St. Tel: 238-0660. A classy, comfortable, convivial spot north of Old City with interesting antique decor and live jazz on weekends. Credit cards: all major.

The Library Lounge, Hotel Atop the Bellevue, Broad and Walnut Sts. Tel: 893-1776. A plush, comfortably appointed bar perfect for having a relaxing drink and conversation. Credit cards: all major.

North Star Bar, 27th and Poplar Sts. Tel: 235-7827. Artsy and a little shaggy, with a lively crowd of regulars and live music several nights a week. Credit cards: all major.

Ortlieb's Jazzhaus, 847 N. 3rd St. Tel: 922-1035. The city's jazz favorite for years, a casual old-time nightclub and restaurant in the Northern Liberties with local and national jazz talent and jam sessions. Credit cards: American Express, Diners Club.

The River Deck Café & Dance Club, Main St and Shurs Lane. Tel: 483-4100. A large and usually crowded disco and restaurant with a raw bar, game room and outdoor deck. Credit cards: all major.

Rock Lobster, Columbus Blvd at Vine St. Tel: 627-7625. Riverfront bar and restaurant with outdoor dining and live music. Credit cards: all major.

Tin Angel, 20 2nd St. Tel: 928-0978. Cozy cafe with coffees, liqueurs, beer and wine and popular acoustic music. Credit cards: all major.

Zanzibar Blue, 301-305 S. 11th St. Tel: 829-0300. An upscale and exciting nightclub and restaurant with live jazz nightly, Sunday jazz brunch and food as electrifying as the music. Credit cards: all major.

US Hotel Bar & Grill, 4439 Main St. Tel: 483-9222. A well-mannered, welcoming neighborhood bar dating to the early 1900s, once part of Manayunk's best hotel during this mill town's boom years. Credit cards: all major.

Cruises

Spirit of Philadelphia, Penn's Landing between Market and Chestnut Sts. Tel: 923-1419. Brunch, lunch and dinner cruises on the Delaware River with live entertainment. Lunch Monday–Saturday, dinner daily, Sunday brunch.
Liberty Belle Charters, 337A N. Front St. Tel: 629-1131. Lunch, dinner and sightseeing cruises on the Delaware River. Lunch and dinner daily, Sunday brunch.

Historic Sites

Independence National Historical Park Visitor Center, 3rd and Chestnut Sts. Tel: 597-8974 or 597-8975. Daily 9am–5pm, until 6pm in summer. Known as the "most historic square mile" in the country, Independence Park takes in more than 25 historic sites, buildings and museums, most between Market and Walnut, 2nd and 6th streets, including:
Bishop White House, 309 Walnut St. Daily 9am–5pm; free tickets available at visitor center.
Carpenters' Hall, 320 Chestnut St. Tel: 925-0167. Tuesday–Sunday 10am–4pm. Admission free.
City Tavern, 2nd and Walnut Sts. Tel: 923-6059. Lunch and dinner daily.
Congress Hall, 6th and Chestnut Sts. Daily 9am–5pm, until 8pm in summer. By tour only. Admission free.
First Bank of the United States, 116 S. 3rd St. Closed to the public.
Franklin Court, 314-322 Market St. Tel: 597-2761. Daily 9am–5pm. Admission free.
Graff House, 7th and Market Sts. Daily 9am–5pm. Admission free.
Independence Hall, Chestnut St between 5th and 6th. Tel: 627-1776. Daily 9am–5pm, until 8pm in summer. By tour only. Admission free.
Liberty Bell Pavilion, Independence Mall. Daily 9am–5pm, until 8pm in summer. Admission free.

Library Hall, 105 S. 5th St. Tel: 440-3400. Closed to public.
Old City Hall, 5th and Chestnut Sts. Daily 9am–5pm, until 8pm in summer. By tour only. Admission free.
Philadelphia Exchange, 3rd and Walnut Sts. Closed to public.
Philosophical Hall, 5th and Chestnut Sts. Tel: 440-3400. Monday–Friday 9am–5pm. Admission free.
Second Bank of the United States, 420 Chestnut St. Daily 9am–5pm.
Todd House, 4th and Walnut Sts. Daily 9am–5pm; free tickets available at visitor center.

Other Historic Sites

Andalusia, State Rd, Andalusia, PA. Tel: 848-1777. By appointment only, seven-person group minimum. Admission charge.
Athenaeum of Philadelphia, 219 S. 6th St. Tel: 925-2688. Monday–Friday 9am–5pm. Admission free.
Belmont Mansion, Belmont Mansion Drive near Belmont Ave in Fairmount Park. Tel: 878-8844. Tuesday–Friday 10am–5pm, call ahead to confirm hours. Admission charge.
Betsy Ross House, 239 Arch St. Tel: 627-5343. Tuesday–Sunday 10am–5pm. Admission free.
Cedar Grove, West Fairmount Park. Tel: 763-8100. Tuesday–Sunday, 10am–4pm, call ahead to confirm hours. Admission charge.
Christ Church Burial Ground, 5th and Arch Sts. Contact Christ Church, tel: 922-1695 for admission. Admission free.
City Hall, Market and Broad Sts. Tel: 686-1776. Monday–Friday 9am–5pm. Admission free.
Cliveden, 6401 Germantown Ave. Tel: 848-1777. Tuesday–Saturday 10am–4pm, Sunday 1–4pm; closed January–March. Admission charge.
Deshler-Morris House, 5442 Germantown Ave, 5442 Germantown Ave. Tel: 596-1748. Tuesday–Sunday 1–4pm; closed mid-December to March. Admission charge.
Ebenezer Maxwell Mansion, 200 W. Tulpehocken St. Tel: 438-1861. Wednesday–Sunday 1–4pm; closed January–March. Admission charge.
Edgar Allan Poe House, 532 N. 7th St. Tel: 597-8780. Daily 9am–5pm. Admission free.
Ephrata Cloister, 632 W. Main St, Ephrata, PA. Tel: 717-733-6600. Mon-

day–Saturday 9am–5pm, Sunday noon–5pm. Admission free.
Fort Mifflin, Fort Mifflin Road. 492-3395. Wednesday–Sunday 10am–4pm; closed December–March. Admission charge.
Green Hills Farm (Pearl S. Buck House), 520 Dublin Road, Perkasie, PA. Tel: 249-0100. Tours offered March–December Tuesday–Saturday 10.30am, 1.30pm, 2.30pm; Sunday 1.30pm and 2.30pm; telephone ahead to confirm opening times. Admission charge.
Grumblethorpe, 5267 Germantown Ave. Tel: 843-4820. Saturday 1–4pm; closed mid-December to March. Call ahead to confirm hours. Admission charge.
Henry George School, 413 S. 10th St. Tel: 922-4278. Monday, Wednesday-Friday 1–4pm. Call ahead to confirm hours. Admission free.
Hill-Physick-Keith House, 321 S. 4th St. Tel: 925-7866. Tuesday–Saturday 10am–4pm, Sunday 1–4pm. Admission charge.
Hopewell Furnace National Historic Site, Route 345, Elverson, PA. Tel: 610-582-8773. Daily 9am–5pm. Admission charge.
Japanese House, Lansdowne Drive, West Fairmount Park. Tel: 878-5097. Wednesday–Sunday 10am–4pm, May-October, call ahead to confirm hours. Admission charge.
Laurel Hill, E. Edgely Drive, Fairmount Park. Tel: 235-1776. Wednesday–Sunday 10am–4pm, call ahead to confirm hours. Admission charge.
Laurel Hill Cemetery, 3200 block of Ridge Ave, Fairmount Park. Tel: 228-8817 or 228-8200. Call ahead for tour information. Admission charge.
Lemon Hill, Lemon Hill Drive, Fairmount Park. Tel: 232-4337. By appointment only. Admission charge.
Loudon, 4650 Germantown Ave. Tel: 685-2067. Tuesday, Saturday, Sunday 1–4pm; call ahead to confirm hours. Admission charge.
Masonic Hall, 1 N. Broad St. Tel: 988-1917. Tours Monday–Friday at 10am, 11am, 1pm, 2pm and 3pm, Saturday at 10am and 11am. Admission free.
Memorial Hall, N. Concourse Drive. Tel: 685-0000. Great hall open Monday–Friday 9am–5pm; call ahead for tour. Admission free.
Mikveh Israel Cemetery, Spruce St between 8th and 9th Sts.

Mount Pleasant, Mount Pleasant Drive, Fairmount Park. Tel: 763-8100. Tuesday–Sunday 10am–4pm, call to confirm hours. Admission charge.

Ormiston, Reservoir Drive, Fairmount Park. Tel: 763-2222. Under renovation, closed to the public, call for date of opening. Admission charge.

Pennsbury Manor, Pennsbury Memorial Road, Morrisville, PA. Tel: 946-0400. Tuesday–Saturday 9am–5pm, Sunday noon–5pm. Admission charge.

Pennsylvania Hospital, 800 Spruce St. Tel: 829-3971. Monday–Friday 9am–5pm; call in advance for tour. Admission free.

Philadelphia Contributionship, 212 S. 4th St. Tel: 627-1752. Monday–Friday 9am–4.30pm; call in advance for tour. Admission free.

Powel House, 244 S. 3rd St. Tel: 627-0364. Tuesday–Saturday 10am–4pm, Sunday 1–4pm. Admission charge.

Rittenhouse Town, 207 Lincoln Drive. Tel: 438-5711. Saturday and Sunday noon–4pm April–October and by appointment. Admission charge.

Stenton Mansion, 18th and Windrim Sts. Tel: 329-7312. Tuesday–Saturday 1–4pm; closed January–March. Admission charge.

Strawberry Mansion, Strawberry Mansion Drive, Fairmount Park. Tel: 228-8364. Tuesday–Sunday 10am–4pm, call ahead to confirm hours. Admission charge.

Sweetbriar, West Fairmount Park. Tel: 222-1333. By appointment only. Admission charge.

Thaddeus Kosciuszko National Memorial, 301 Pine St. Daily 9am–5pm. Admission free.

US Mint, 5th and Arch Sts. Tel: 597-7350. Monday–Friday 9am–4.30pm. Admission free.

Valley Forge National Historical Park, Route 23 and N. Gulph Road, Valley Forge, PA. Tel: 610-783-1076 or 610-783-1077. Daily 8.30am–5pm. Admission charge for Washington's Headquarters only.

Washington Crossing Historic Park, Routes 32 and 532, PO Box 103, Washington Crossing, PA. Tel: 493-4076. Monday–Saturday 9am–5pm, Sunday noon–5pm. Admission charge for guided tour.

Wheatland, 1120 Marietta Ave, Lancaster, PA. Tel: 717-392-8721. April–November daily 10am–4pm. Admission charge.

Woodford, Woodford Drive, Fairmount Park. Tel: 229-6115. Tuesday–Sunday 10am–4pm, call ahead to confirm hours. Admission charge.

Wyck, 6026 Germantown Ave. Tel: 848-1690. Tuesday, Thursday, Saturday 1–4pm, by appointment mid-December to March. Admission charge.

Historic Churches and Synagogues

Arch Street Presbyterian Church, 1724 Arch St. Tel: 563-3763. Services Sunday 10.45am; visits by appointment.

Cathedral of Saints Peter and Paul, 18th and Race Sts. Tel: 561-1313. Daily 9am–3.30pm.

Christ Church, 2nd and Market Sts. Tel: 922-1695. Monday–Saturday 9am–5pm, Sunday noon–4pm.

Church of the Holy Trinity, 1904 Walnut St. Tel: 567-1267. Call for times of services.

Free Quaker Meeting House, 5th and Arch Sts. Tel: 923-6777. Summer months, Tuesday–Saturday 10am–4pm, Sunday noon–4pm.

Gloria Dei Church (Old Swede's), Christian St and Delaware Ave. Tel: 389-1513. Daily 9am–5pm.

Holy Trinity Roman Catholic Church, 6th and Spruce Sts. Tel: 923-7930. Mass at Sunday noon, other visits by appointment.

Mother Bethel African Methodist Episcopal Church, 419 Richard Allen Ave (S. 6th St). Tel: 925-0616. Services at 10.45am Sunday; other visits by appointment.

Old First Reformed Church, 4th and Race Sts. Tel: 922-4566. Monday–Friday 9am–3pm, Sunday 11am–1pm.

Old Pine Street Presbyterian Church, 4th and Pine Sts. Tel: 925-8051. Monday–Friday 9am–5pm, Sunday service at 10.30am.

St Augustine's Roman Catholic Church, 243 N. Lawrence St. Tel: 627-1838. Monday–Friday Mass 7.30am and noon, Saturday 5.15pm and 11.30pm, Sunday 8am and 11am.

St Clement's Episcopal Church, 2000 Cherry St. 563-1876. Daily services, tours by appointment.

St George's Greek Orthodox Church, 256 S. 8th St. 627-4389. Daily 9am–4pm.

St George's United Methodist Church, 235 N. 4th St. Tel: 925-7788. Daily 10am–4pm.

St Joseph's Church, Willings Alley between 3rd and 4th Sts. Tel: 923-1733 Daily noon–4pm.

St Luke and the Epiphany Episcopal Church, 330 S. 13th St. Tel: 732-1918. Sunday services at 9am and 11am.

St Mark's Episcopal Church, 1625 Locust St. Tel: 735-1416. Daily services; call ahead for other visits.

St Mary's Church, 252 S. 4th St. Tel: 923-7930. Daily 9am–5pm.

St Peter's Episcopal Church, 3rd and Pine Sts. Tel: 925-5968. Tuesday–Saturday 9am–3.30pm.

Society Hill Synagogue, 418 Spruce St. Tel: 922-6590. Friday evening and Saturday morning services.

Temple Beth Zion-Beth Israel, 18th and Spruce Sts. Tel: 735-5148. Daily morning and evening services.

Tenth Presbyterian Church, 1700 Spruce St. Tel: 735-7688. Services Sunday 9.15am, 11am and 7pm.

Festivals

Listings and advertisements for upcoming special events can be found in *The Daily News*, *Philadelphia Inquirer*, *Philadelphia Magazine*, and weekly newspapers like *The City Paper* and *Philadelphia Weekly*.

January

Mummers Parade. 30,000 high-struttin' Mummers march all the way up Broad Street to City Hall on New Year's Day.

Philadelphia International Auto Show. Scores of new models and spiffy foreign imports exhibited at the Philadelphia Civic Center in West Philadelphia.

Benjamin Franklin's Birthday. The Franklin Institute celebrates the birth of its namesake and inspiration. Look for the kite-flying festival at Independence Mall in honor of Franklin's famous experiments with electricity.

Edgar Allan Poe Birthday. Special

tours, programs and exhibits are presented at the Poe National Historic Site.

Martin Luther King, Jr, Birthday. Ceremonies, special performances, lectures and other observances in honor of Dr King.

Philadelphia Boat Show. The latest in yachts, sailboats and motorboats, with more than 500 vessels on display at the Civic Center.

Philadelphia Sportsmen's and Recreational Vehicle Show. Another Civic Center exhibit with everything you'll need for your next camping trip.

February

Black History Month. A series of special exhibits, performances and presentations at venues throughout the city. Call the Afro-American Historical and Cultural Museum for information (574-0380).

Philadelphia Home Show. Products and plans for remodeling, renovating, furnishing and decorating your home exhibited at the Civic Center.

Presidents' Day. Look for special tours and events at Independence Park and Valley Forge National Historical Park, and other historic sites throughout the area in celebration of Washington's and Lincoln's birthday.

Chinese New Year. Chinatown celebrates the new year with traditional processions and festivities, and banquets at the Chinese Cultural Center.

Presidential Jazz Weekend. Four days of jazz at venues throughout the city featuring local talent and international jazz legends.

US Pro Indoor Tennis Championship. The world's top tennis players compete for a $1 million crown at the Spectrum.

March

Philadelphia Flower Show. The Civic Center is transformed into a many-colored sea of petals and pollen at the largest flower show in the country. The show is sponsored by the Pennsylvania Horticultural Society.

St Patrick's Day Parade. A celebration of Philadelphia's Irish heritage along Benjamin Franklin Parkway and Chestnut Street to Independence Hall.

Mummers String Band Show of Shows. Outlandishly costumed Mummers bring their fun-loving brand of music to the Civic Center.

The Book and the Cook. The city's finest and most innovative chefs hitch up with well-known cookbook authors and food critics for a celebration of food and drink.

Women's History Month. Look for the Women's Festival at the Bourse plus other events throughout the city.

Poetry Week. The American Poetry Center honors the muse with readings, lectures, exhibits and other events for local literati.

April

American Music Theater Festival. Premieres of original works, some mainstream, others cutting-edge, at a variety of venues. Some of the season's most exciting shows start right here in Philadelphia.

Easter Parade. An age-old tradition on Rittenhouse Square, showcasing imaginative fashions and music.

Penn Relays. The country's oldest and largest amateur track meet is held at Franklin Field on the University of Pennsylvania campus.

Valborgsmassoafton. A traditional Swedish rite of spring with folk music, dance and food at the American Swedish Historical Museum in South Philadelphia's Franklin Park.

Philadelphia Open House. Bus and walking tours through the homes, churches, gardens and other notable sites in the city's many historic neighborhoods.

Philadelphia Antiques Show and Sale. A tradition among the metropolitan area's dealers and collectors and one of the finest shows in the country; 103rd Engineers Armory, 33rd and Market Sts.

Philadelphia Folk Fair. Held at the Civic Center every other year (even-numbered years only), the fair features arts, crafts, song, dance and food from the city's many ethnic communities and visitors from around the world.

Virginia Slims Tennis Classic. The finest women tennis players compete at the Palestra on the University of Pennsylvania campus.

May

Africamericas Festival. A 12-day celebration of African-American culture with music, parades, films, theater and dance at sites throughout the city.

Philadelphia Festival of World Cinema. A two-week series featuring a selection of the finest new films from around the world screened at theaters throughout the city.

Dad Vail Regatta. With more than 3,000 rowers, the largest collegiate regatta in the country floats down the Schuylkill River near Strawberry Mansion and Boathouse Row.

Armed Forces Weekend. Philadelphia honors the men and women of America's military at Penn's Landing with entertainment, exhibits and tours of a naval vessel.

Israel's Independence Day. A celebration with a parade down Chestnut Street, culminating with entertainment and an Israeli bazaar at Independence Mall.

Italian Market Festival. A day of music and outdoor food stands at the 9th Street Market.

International Theater Festival for Children. Five days of theater, folktales, puppet shows and dance at the Annenberg Center (University of Pennsylvania), Walnut Street Theater and other venues.

Devon Horse Show and Country Fair. One of the country's largest outdoor horse shows, and a great old Main Line tradition, is held at the Devon Fairground about 45 minutes from center city.

Jambalaya Jam. A three-day Mardi Gras-like blast at Penn's Landing celebrating the music, cuisine and culture of New Orleans.

Memorial Day Observance. A formal observance is held aboard the 19th-century *USS Olympia* at Penn's Landing.

Rittenhouse Square Flower Market. An annual tradition for more than 75 years, featuring thousands of flowering plants and food stands.

Manayunk Canal Day. A parade and day-long festival showcase the colorful shops and restaurants along this old mill town's gentrified Main Street.

Mozart on the Square. Two weeks of performances at venues around Rittenhouse Square honor the genius of Wolfgang Amadeus Mozart.

Penn's Landing Summer Season. Dozens of free concerts and ethnic festivals are offered at this waterfront venue. It is one of the best entertainment values in the city; weekends through September.

June

Elfreth's Alley Day. The residents of the oldest residential street in the country, many in colonial dress, open their charming homes to visitors. Colonial crafts and baked goods are sold at the Museum House.

Italian National Day. A tribute to the people, history and culture of Italy at Penn's Landing on the occasion of Italy's national holiday.

Midsommerfest. A traditional celebration of summer with folk dancing, music and food at the American Swedish Historical Museum situated in South Philadelphia.

Rittenhouse Square Fine Arts Annual. Many of the area's most talented artists exhibit thousands of works at this five-day open-air "clothesline" exhibit.

Flag Day. Old Glory is celebrated with a parade and ceremonies at the Betsy Ross House.

Phillyfest. A series of free lunchtime performances featuring jazz, pop and ethnic musicians as well as sports competitions and other entertainment at JFK Plaza adjacent to City Hall; weekdays through August.

Mellon Jazz Festival. Some of the biggest names in jazz converge on Philly for concerts, master classes and jam sessions at venues in center city.

Head House Square Crafts Fair. Local crafts people and artists exhibit their work under the historic market shed; noon-midnight Saturday, noon-6pm Sunday, mid-June-August.

Mann Music Center Summer Concerts. A set of open-air performances by the world-renowned Philadelphia Orchestra in beautiful Fairmount Park. Free tickets are available on the day of the concert at the JFK Visitors Center.

CoreStates Pro Cycling Championship. A grueling 156-mile international bicycle race including the punishing climb up the Manayunk Wall. The race begins and ends in front of the Museum of Art on the Benjamin Franklin Parkway.

Harbor Festival. A fleet of tall ships, including Philadelphia's own *Gazela*, visits Penn's Landing.

Rock 'A' Rama. A nostalgic trip back to the sounds and styles of the 1950s, with a special emphasis on the heyday of the Philly Sound; features food, dancing and special performances; Penn's Landing.

Kutztown Folk Festival. Perhaps the area's best opportunity to experience Pennsylvania Dutch and Amish culture, crafts, food and people at this nine-day festival at the Kutztown Fairgrounds, approximately 15 miles northeast of Reading, PA.

July

Freedom Festival. Independence Day is a big event in Philadelphia. In addition to the traditional parade and fireworks, there are Mummers bands, a hot-air balloon race, a restaurant festival, sporting events and more. Most of the week's action is centered around Independence Hall, but events are held at Rittenhouse Square, the Museum of Art, JFK Plaza and other venues. Check the papers for a detailed list of events.

Singer-Songwriter Festival. A three-day series of performances by contemporary singer-songwriters at Penn's Landing.

RiverBlues Festival. A fantastic opportunity to hear some of the country's best blues musicians at a three-day celebration of American music, food and fun around Penn's Landing's outdoor stage.

International Folk Dancing. Folk dancing exhibitions are offered Tuesday evenings at the Philadelphia Museum of Art terrace.

Pennsylvania Renaissance Faire. A recreation of 16th-century life at a 38-acre English village complete with hundreds of costumed performers, jousting knights, ladies, lords, minstrels, dramas, jugglers, crafts people and food merchants; weekends through early October; Mount Hope Estate and Winery, 16 miles outside Lancaster.

August

Philadelphia Folk Festival. A weekend of international folk music performed outside Philadelphia at Old Poole Farm in Schwenksville, PA.

Pennsylvania Dutch Festival. Demonstrations of arts, crafts and food from Pennsylvania Dutch country; Reading Terminal Market.

Polish Festival. A two-day celebration of Polish dance, music, food and culture at Penn's Landing.

Pennsylvania Dutch Days. A festival of food, crafts and culture in Hershey, PA, America's chocolate capital.

Goschenhoppen Folk Festival. An-other Pennsylvania Dutch festival, this one in East Greenville, PA.

September

Pepsi Penn's Landing Jazz Fest. Four days of live performances featuring some of the metropolitan area's and the country's most exciting jazz stars.

Penn's Landing In-Water Boat Show. Hundreds of sailing vessels, yachts and motorboats tie up at the Penn's Landing marina for a four-day exhibition.

Germantown Hospital Equestrian Festival. An international grand prix jumping competition held at the Devon Fairground on the Main Line in Devon.

Dressage at Devon. A world-class equestrian competition featuring the country's finest horses and riders in this very beautiful, very English event; Devon Fairground.

Von Steuben Day Parade. A tribute to the German general who whipped the Continental Army into fighting shape at Valley Forge and a salute to the city's rich German heritage. The procession runs down the Benjamin Franklin Parkway and then heads to Independence Mall.

Puerto Rican Day Parade. A celebration of Philly's Puerto Rican community. This parade starts on the Parkway, too.

Philadelphia Distance Run. A half-marathon through center city and Fairmount Park drawing a field of some 7,500 runners. The finish line is next to City Hall at JFK Plaza.

Harvest Show. A flower and garden show at the Horticultural Center in Fairmount Park, with entertainment, food and children's activities.

Fairmount Park Festival. A series of events including sports competitions, special tours, exhibitions and other recreational activities; through November.

Pennsbury Manor Fair. A recreated 17th-century country fair on the grounds of William Penn's Bucks County estate with costumed players, crafts demonstrations, puppeteers, musicians, food and dancers.

Battle of Brandywine. Re-enactment of the historic clash between rebels and redcoats south of Philadelphia at Brandywine Battlefield State Park.

October

Columbus Day. The city celebrates Columbus's voyage of discovery with a parade followed by a festival at Penn's Landing.

Pulaski Day Parade. A parade honoring the Polish patriot who rallied with American rebels during the Revolutionary War and the city's substantial Polish-American community.

Super Sunday. Sponsored by the cultural institutions along the Benjamin Franklin Parkway, this is a daylong party featuring games, rides, food stalls, entertainment, special exhibits, a flea market and more on the Parkway between Logan Circle and the Museum of Art.

Thomas Eakins Regatta. Collegiate crew teams across the country come out for a row down the Schuylkill River in honor of the city's famed artist, who immortalized rowers and the river in many of his finest works.

William Penn's Birthday. The Founder's birth is celebrated in period costume with a special party at Pennsbury Manor (Penn's country estate in Bucks County) as well as at various events in the city.

Battle of Germantown. Washington's heroic but failed attempt to dislodge the British from Germantown in 1777 is commemorated with a historic re-enactment and country fair at Cliveden.

November

Thanksgiving Day Parade. The oldest of its kind, the parade files down Market Street and west on the Parkway with giant balloons, colorful floats, brass bands, clowns and a cast of thousands.

Books, Toys and Tinkertoys. Both children and adults will get a kick out of the Giant Tinkertoy Extravaganza at the Franklin Institute.

Old Fort Mifflin. The siege of this historic fort in 1777 is re-enacted by soldiers in period costume. Scores of Americans died during the battle in order to protect Washington's army from a British attack on Valley Forge. The fort is located near the airport in South Philadelphia.

Philadelphia Crafts Show. A four-day juried crafts fair held at the Civic Center featuring the work of 100 artists from around the country.

December

First Friday. An ongoing art fest held at Old City galleries on the first Friday of every month between December and June.

Second Saturday. Exhibit openings, wine and cheese, and lots of artsy chitchat on the second Saturday of the month at galleries around Rittenhouse Square; through June.

Army-Navy Football Classic. West Point and the Naval Academy face off in Philly for their annual gridiron grudge match.

One City, One Song. Community caroling at the Museum of Art precedes the lighting of the city's enormous Christmas tree at City Hall.

Christmas Tours of Historic Houses. The mansions of Fairmount Park are decked with Christmas cheer for special tours. Holiday tours of Germantown's historic houses, and a Christmas party at the Ebenezer Maxwell Mansion, are offered, too. Contact the staff at Cliveden or at the Maxwell Mansion for details.

Lucia Fest. A traditional Swedish winter festival with folk music, crafts, food, a candlelight procession and a Christmas fair at the American Swedish Historical Museum in South Philadelphia and Old Swede's Church in Queen Village.

Kwanzaa. The African-American winter holiday is celebrated with a parade, special exhibits and other events. Contact the Afro-American Historical and Cultural Museum.

A Charles Dickens Christmas Past. Dickens and the cast from *A Christmas Carol* and other works are brought to life at the Mount Hope Estate and Winery by the people who present the Pennsylvania Renaissance Faire.

Washington's Crossing of the Delaware. Washington's bold river crossing in 1776 is re-enacted on Christmas Day at Washington Crossing State Park in Bucks County.

New Year's Eve Celebration. Ring in the new year with fireworks, music and hundreds of fellow revelers at Penn's Landing. Dress warmly.

Shopping

Shopping Areas

Center City Area

The largest shopping district in the city is on Market Street east of Broad Street. Here you'll find **Hecht's**, formerly John Wanamaker, (13th and Market. Tel: 331-5500. Monday–Saturday 10am–9.30pm, Sunday 11am–6pm), the grandad of Philadelphia department stores housed in a landmark building across from City Hall. Hecht's has five floors of retail space with a grand central court where shoppers can grab a bite at the gourmet counter, take in the daily organ concerts (performed on the world's largest organ) or enjoy the magnificent Christmas light show.

Farther east on Market Street, past discount shops, sporting goods, electronics, shoes and clothing stores, is **The Gallery**, a modern shopping mall which occupies three square blocks and four levels between 11th and 8th streets. There are over 200 shops and restaurants around the airy, skylit atrium including three department stores (Stern's, J.C. Penney and Strawbridge & Clothier) and a surprisingly interesting food court that's convenient for quick and inexpensive meals or snacks. The Gallery (Tel: 625-4962) is open Monday–Saturday 10am–7pm, Wednesday until 8pm and Sunday noon–5pm.

Market Place East is next to The Gallery at 8th and Market streets. Housed in a magnificent cast-iron structure once occupied by Lit Brothers Department Store, this block-long mixed-use complex is now divided between offices and about 25 stores and restaurants.

Also in the area, facing the Liberty Bell near Independence Mall, is the **Bourse**, a 19th-century commercial exchange with a glorious six-story central hall now occupied by stores, restaurants and offices. The location is perfect for a shopping or dining break close to Independence Hall.

A short walk away, **Jewelers' Row** – Sansom Street between 7th and 8th streets – is devoted exclusively to precious gems and metals. If you're looking for a gift, or thinking about getting hitched, the selection and prices can't be beat in Philadelphia.

Running parallel to Market Street, the **Chestnut Street Transitway** is closed to all traffic except buses between 6th and 18th streets. Most of the retailers on this strip are discount stores or specialty shops. The snazzy **Liberty Place** (Tel: 851-9055) complex is between 16th and 17th streets. The 70 shops and restaurants – including Sfuzzi, a smart Italian bar and restaurant, and Rand McNally Travel Bookstore – are set around a two-story glass rotunda. The shops are open 9.30am–7pm Monday–Saturday, until 8pm Wednesday, noon–6pm Sunday. The complex also includes the Ritz-Carlton Hotel.

For even fancier pickings, try the **Shops at the Bellevue**, a posh marketplace beneath the Hotel Atop the Bellevue at Broad and Walnut streets, where retailers like Ralph Lauren's Polo, Gucci, Pierre Deux and Tiffany & Co. do business in beautifully appointed shops. Most shops are open 10am–6pm Monday–Saturday, until 8pm on Wednesday evening.

Walnut Street near Rittenhouse Square also has its share of fancy retailers, including Rodier of Paris and Burberry's, and nearby fashion stops, Urban Outfitters and Toby Lerner.

For more adventurous tastes, **South Street** is the place to go. The shops and eateries on or near South Street from 9th to Front streets include everything from punk shops and art galleries to rock bars and fine restaurants. This is the hip, edgy part of town, popular with, but certainly not limited to, young people. It tends to be a bit of a carnival on Friday and Saturday nights, but it's almost always interesting. At one time, South Street ran through a large Jewish neighborhood. A remnant of those days can still be found on **Fabric Row**, which runs along 4th Street south of South Street.

Beyond Center City

In the far northeastern corner of the city, near the Bucks County border, **Franklin Mills** is a sprawling discount mall – the city's largest – with more than 200 outlet stores, 30 fast-food counters and restaurants, and a 10-screen cinema. The complex occupies more than 40 acres and is surrounded by a Carrefour Hyper Market and a complex of shops known as the Philadelphia Home and Design Center. From center city, take I-95 north to the Woodhaven Road exit. Hours at Franklin Mills are Monday–Saturday 10am–9.30pm, Sunday 11am–6pm.

To the north of the city, **Plymouth Meeting Mall**, off I-76, with department stores Hess's and Strawbridge & Clothier, is probably best-known for **Ikea**, a popular Swedish furniture and housewares company. The mall's hours of business are Monday–Saturday 10am–9.30pm, Sunday noon–5pm. Ikea opens Monday–Friday 11am–9pm, Saturday 10am–9pm, Sunday 11am–6pm.

Nearby, the **King of Prussia Mall**, off Route 202 about 30 minutes north of center city, is a huge complex with more than 300 stores and restaurants, including Bloomingdale's and Strawbridge & Clothier; Monday–Saturday 10am–9.30pm, Sunday 11am–5pm. And across the Ben Franklin Bridge in Cherry Hill, New Jersey, the **Cherry Hill Mall** (Monday–Saturday 10am–9.30pm, Sunday noon–5pm) is anchored by Macy's, Strawbridge & Clothier and J.C. Penney.

In Bucks County, **Peddler's Village**, on Route 202 between Doylestown and New Hope, offers 70 specialty shops featuring crafts, antiques and handmade gifts as well as several restaurants in a pleasant country village setting. **New Hope**, on the Delaware River, is a center of art galleries, antique shops, gift shops, crafts and fashion stores as well as many fine restaurants.

Antiques

Philadelphia is big on antiques. Once a major center of American craftsmanship, collectors and dealers still scour swap meets, flea markets and salvage operations in search of ancient treasures. The best place to start looking for antiques is Pine Street between 13th and 8th streets, otherwise known as **Antique Row**. There are about 20 or so antique dealers along this strip as well as jewelers, craft shops and several interesting spots for a bite to eat. You might also want to try the nearby **Antiquarian's Delight** (615 S. 6th St), an indoor antique market just off South Street with some 30 antique dealers hawking their wares under a single roof. There are dozens of other shops elsewhere in town, large and small, with a variety of specialties. Check the telephone directory's *Yellow Pages* for a listing. If you're serious about antiques, you should also check the "Weekend" section of the *Philadelphia Inquirer* for listings of special antique markets in and around the city as well as the yearly **Philadelphia Antiques Show**, usually held in April at the 103rd Engineers Armory at 33rd and Market streets.

Books and Music

There are lots of good bookstores in Philadelphia, many specializing in rare volumes or special themes. For the widest selection, try one of the three largest stores, each with thousands of titles: **Barnes & Noble** (1424 Chestnut St), **Tower Books** (425 South St) and **Borders Book Shop** (1727 Walnut St), which also has a cappuccino bar and a popular series of author readings. **Robin's Book Stores** (1837 Chestnut St and 108 S. 13th St) also have a wide selection. There are chain stores, including **Waldenbooks**, **Doubleday** and **B. Dalton**, at The Gallery and the Bourse, and a local discount chain, **Encore Books**, has locations in and around center city (2005 Market St, 609 Chestnut St and 205 S. 38th St). Two independent shops with a good selection of art, photography, graphic arts and literature are **Hibberd's** (1310 Walnut St) and **Joseph Fox Bookstore** (1724 Sansom St).

Among the many specialty bookstores are: the **American Institute of Architecture Bookstore** (17th and Sansom Sts), **Academy of Fine Arts Museum Shop** (Broad and Cherry Sts), **Museum of Art Bookstore** (Benjamin Franklin Parkway) for books on art and architecture, **Meridian** (7902 German-own Ave) and **Garland of Letters** (527 South St) for New Age books, **Giovanni's Room** (345 S. 12th St) for gay and feminist subject matter, **Way to Go** (4228 Main St) and **Rand McNally** (1 Liberty Place) for travel guides and maps, the **Philadelphia Drama Bookshop** (2209 Walnut St) for plays and books on film and theater, the **How-to-do-it Bookshop** (1608 Sansom St) for how-to books, **Who-dunit** (1931 Chestnut St) for mystery books and thrillers, the **Cookbook Stall** (Reading Terminal Market) for cookbooks, the **Book Trader** (501 South St) for used books and **W. Graham Arader** (1308 Walnut St) and **Bauman Rare Books** (1215 Locust St) for antique and rare volumes.

The annual **Book and the Cook Fair** brings together cookbook authors, food critics and many of the city's finest chefs for a two-day celebration of good eating and good reading.

Music

You'll find the city's best selection of compact discs and tapes at **Tower Records** (610 South St) and **Tower Records Classical Annex** (539 South St), open 9am–midnight seven days a week. Chain stores like **Wee Three Records** and **Sam Goody** have several locations and a good selection of popular music. There are also a number of specialty shops, including **Third Street Jazz and Rock** (20 N. 3rd St) for jazz, **Nathan Muchnick** (1725 Chestnut St) for classical and the **Book Trader Record Annex** (501 South St) and **Philadelphia Record Exchange** (608 S. 5th St and 30 S. 2nd St) for used and rare records.

Food

There are two spots in Philadelphia that gourmets and gourmands should not miss: Reading Terminal Market and the Italian Market. Housed in a historic train shed, **Reading Terminal Market** (12th and Arch Sts) has been enveloped by the new Philadelphia Convention Center. No matter, this is still one of the most entertaining spots in the city, with stall after stall of fresh fish, vegetables, meats and baked goods as well as counter service and restaurants offering everything from sushi to spaghetti shoofly pie. Reading Terminal Market is open 8am–6pm Monday–Saturday.

The **Italian Market** is a bit grungier but equally enticing. The offerings at this mostly outdoor market, stretching along 9th Street between Catharine and Wharton streets, are fresh and inexpensive. And at least a dozen good Italian restaurants are within easy walking distance, not to mention South Philly's cheesesteak royalty, Pat's and Geno's. Check Fante's for the latest cookware, cookbooks and culinary gadgets. Most outdoor stalls are open Tuesday–Saturday around 8.30am–5pm. Most shops, bakeries, delis and butchers are open Monday, too.

Among the city's many gourmet shops, **The Chef's Market** (231 South St. Monday–Thursday 8.30am–9pm, Friday 8.30am–11pm, Saturday 8am–11pm, Sunday 8am–9pm) is the largest, with a huge choice of gourmet groceries, supplies and prepared foods.

CLOTHING CHART

This table compares American, Continental and British clothing sizes. It's always advisable to try clothes on before buying as sizes can vary.

Women's Dresses/Suits

American	Continental	British
6	38/34N	8/30
8	40/36N	10/32
10	42/38N	12/34
12	44/40N	14/36
14	46/42N	16/38
16	48/44N	18/40

Women's Shoes

American	Continental	British
4.5	36	3
5.5	37	4
6.5	38	5
7.5	40	6
8.5	41	7
9.5	42	8
10.5	43	9

Men's Suits

American	Continental	British
34	44	34
–	46	36
38	48	38
–	50	40
42	52	42
–	54	44
46	56	46

Men's Shirts

American	Continental	British
14	36	14
14.5	37	14.5
15	38	15.5
15.5	39	15.5
16	40	16
16.5	41	16.5
17	42	17

Men's Shoes

American	Continental	British
6.5	–	6
7.5	40	7
8.5	41	8
9.5	42	9
10.5	43	10
11.5	44	11

Sports and Leisure

Philadelphia has professional teams in all the major American sports. Most play at Veterans Stadium or the Corestates Spectrum in South Philadelphia, reached by SEPTA bus C south on Broad Street or the Broad Street subway south to Pattison Avenue.

Tickets for major sports events may be purchased from **Ticketmaster** (Tel: 336-2000). You can hear the latest scores of major games nationwide by calling the *Philadelphia Inquirer* Dial-A-Score (Tel: 854-2500).

Participant Sports

Health Clubs

Several hotels have fitness facilities or links with nearby clubs. If not, these clubs take visitors on a daily basis: **LifeSport**, 2112 Fairmount Ave. Tel: 236-0763. **Market West Athletic Club**, 1835 Market St, 2nd floor. Tel: 963-2700. **Nirvana Fitness Club**, 105 S. 18th St. Tel: 988-0656. **Rittenhouse Square Fitness Club**, 2002 Rittenhouse Street. Tel: 985-4095. **Gold's Gym**, 834 Chestnut St. Tel: 592-9644.

Sherwood's Fitness Club, 2020 Sansom St. Tel: 972-0927.

12th Street Gym, 204 S. 12th St. Tel: 985-4092.

Bicycling

For information on bike tours and other special events, call the **Bicycle Club of Philadelphia**. Tel: 735-2453.

Bicycles may be rented in Fairmount Park at **Plaisted Hall**, 1 Boathouse Row, Kelly Drive.

Boating

Join the many rowing clubs that compete on the Schuylkill River and comprise the so-called Schuylkill Navy.

Rowboats and canoes may be rented at the **East Park Canoe House**, Kelly Drive. Tel: 225-3560.

Public Golf Courses

John F. Byrnes Golf Course, 9500 Leon St. Tel: 632-8666. 18 holes.

Cobbs Creek Golf Course, 72 St and Landsowne Ave. Tel: 877-8707. Two 18-hole courses.

Juniata Golf Course, M and Cayuga Sts. Tel: 743-4060. 18 holes.

Walnut Lane Golf Course, Walnut Lane and Magdalena St. Tel: 482-3370. 18 holes.

Franklin D. Roosevelt Golf Course, 20th St and Pattison Ave. Tel: 462-8997. 18 holes.

Tennis

There are over 200 public courts in Philadelphia. For information on locations, reservations and special programs, contact Fairmount Park (Tel: 685-0051) or the Department of Recreation (Tel: 685-0150).

Skiing

Alpine Mountain, Route 447, Analomink, PA. Tel: 717-595-2150.

Big Boulder, Route 903, Lake Harmony, PA. Tel: 717-722-0100.

Camelback, Routes 611 and 715, Tannersville, PA. Tel: 717-629-1661.

Doe Mountain, RD 1, Macungie, PA. Tel: 682-7109.

Fernwood, Route 209, Bushkill, PA. Tel: 717-588-6661.

Jack Frost Mountain, Route 940, White Haven, PA. Tel: 717-443-8425.

Saw Creek, off Route 209, Bushkill, PA. Tel: 717-588-9266.

Shawnee Mountain, Shawnee-on-Delaware, PA. Tel: 717-421-7231.

Tamiment Resort, Tamiment, PA. Tel: 717-588-6652.

Tanglewood, off Route 390, Tafton, PA. Tel: 717-226-9500.

Spectator Sports

Baseball

Philadelphia Phillies, Veterans Stadium, Broad St and Pattison Ave. Tel: 463-1000.

Basketball

Philadelphia 76ers, Corestates Spectrum, Broad St and Pattison Ave. Tel: 336-3600.

Football

Philadelphia Eagles, Veterans Stadium, Broad St and Pattison Ave. Tel: 463-5500.

College Sports

Philadelphia is also a great town for college competition. The Big Five in Philadelphia are: **University of Pennsylvania**, **Temple**, **Villanova**, **LaSalle** and **St Joseph's**.

Ice Hockey

Philadelphia Flyers, Corestates Spectrum, Broad St and Pattison Ave. Tel: 336-3600.

Horse Racing

Philadelphia Park, Street Road, Bensalem, PA. Tel: 639-9000.

Garden State Park, Route 70, Cherry Hill, NJ. Tel: 609-488-8400.

Off-Track Betting, 7 Penn Center, 17th and Market Sts, lower level. Tel: 246-1556. The **Clubhouse Turf Club** serves lunch, dinner and Sunday brunch.

Outdoor Activities

Parks and Environment Centers

Fairmount Park Commission, Memorial Hall, N. Concourse Dr. Tel: 685-0000. The country's largest municipal park stretches across more than 8,000 acres on both sides of the Schuylkill River. The Fairmount Park Commission also administrates:

Franklin D. Roosevelt Park, District #2, Broad St and Pattison Ave. Tel: 685-1837. 365 acres, American Swedish Museum, Roosevelt Golf Course, Bellaire Mansion, tennis courts, baseball diamonds, Meadows

Lake and other recreational facilities.

Cobbs Creek Park, District #4, 63rd and Market Sts. Tel: 352-8644. 800 acres, baseball diamonds, tennis courts, golf course, playgrounds and other recreational facilities.

Pennypack Park, District #5, Winchester Ave and Roosevelt Blvd. Tel: 335-8797. 1,300 acres, hiking trails, picnic areas, bird sanctuary and other recreational facilities.

Pennypack Environmental Center, Verree Road. Tel: 671-0440. Daily 9am–5pm, call ahead to confirm hours. Exhibit space and nature programs in Pennypack Park.

Andorra Natural Area, Northwestern Ave. Tel: 685-9285. Exhibits and nature programs in the northernmost section of Fairmount Park.

Penn Treaty Park, E. Columbia Ave and Beach St. Six-acre site on the Delaware River where William Penn is said to have negotiated his treaty with the Lenape Indians.

Awbury Arboretum, 1 Awbury Road near Chew Ave and High St. Tel: 849-5561. 55-acre park in Germantown offering nature and bird-watching programs.

Schuylkill Center for Environmental Education, 8480 Hagy's Mill Road. Tel: 482-7300. Monday–Saturday 8.30am–5pm, Sunday 1–5pm. Admission charge. 500-acre natural site with guided walks and exhibits on local ecology, plant and animal life.

John Heinz National Wildlife Refuge at Tinicum, 86th St and Lindbergh Blvd. Tel: 365-3118. Daily 9am–4pm. 1,200 preserved acres in South Philadelphia's wetlands; exhibits and guided walks focus on local wildlife and ecology.

Morris Arboretum, 100 Northwestern Ave. Tel: 247-5777. Daily 10am–5pm April–October, 10am–4pm November–March. Admission charge. Formerly the summer estate of the Morris clan, this 175-acre site in Chestnut Hill is now administered by the University of Pennsylvania.

Further Reading

General

Natural Lives, Modern Times: People and Places of the Delaware River by Bruce Stutz. New York: Crown Publishers, 1992.

Oh! Dem Golden Slippers: The Story of the Philadelphia Mummers by Charles E. Welch. Philadelphia: Book Street Press, 1970.

Philadelphia Architecture: A Guide to the City by John Andrew Gallery, General Editor. Cambridge, MA: The MIT Press, 1984.

Philadelphia: Beyond the Liberty Bell by Ron Avery. Philadelphia: Broad Street Books, 1991.

Philadelphia Gentlemen by E. Digby Baltzell. Philadelphia: University of Pennsylvania Press, 1979.

Philadelphia's Outdoor Art by Roslyn F. Brenner. Philadelphia: Camino Books.

Philadelphia Scrapple by Anonymous. Richmond: Dietz Press, 1956.

The Architecture of Frank Furness, by James F. O'Gorman. Philadelphia: Philadelphia Museum of Art, 1973.

The Autobiography and Other Writings by Benjamin Franklin. New York: Bantam, 1982.

The Mercer Mile: The Story of Henry Chapman Mercer and His Three Concrete Buildings by Heien Hartman Gemmill. Doylestown, PA: The Bucks County Historical Society, 1987.

The Perennial Philadelphians by Nathaniel Burt. Boston: Little, Brown and Co., 1963.

The Puzzles of Amish Life by Donald B. Kraybill. Intercourse, PA: Good Books, 1990.

The Riddle of Amish Life by Donald B. Kraybill. Intercourse, PA: Good Books, 1990.

The WPA Guide to Philadelphia. Philadelphia: University of Pennsylvania Press, 1937/1988.

History

A Little Revenge: Benjamin Franklin and His Son by Willard Randall. Boston: Little, Brown & Co., 1984.

"Attention, MOVE! This is America!" by Margot Harry. Chicago: Banner Press, 1987.

Benjamin Franklin: His Life As He Wrote It by Esmond Wright, ed. Cambridge, MA: Harvard University Press, 1990.

Burning Down The House: MOVE and the Tragedy of Philadelphia by John Anderson and Hilary Hevenor. New York: W.W. Norton & Company, 1987.

By the Beautiful Sea: The Rise and High Times of That Great American Resort Atlantic City by Charles Funnell. New York: Knopf, 1975.

Decision in Philadelphia by Christopher Collier. New York: Random House, 1986.

Faces of Revolution: Personalities and Themes in the Struggle for American Independence by Bernard Bailyn. New York: Alfred A. Knopf, 1990.

Franklin of Philadelphia by Esmond Wright. Cambridge, MA: Harvard University Press, 1986.

Gladly Learn and Gladly Teach: Franklin and His Heirs at the University of Pennsylvania by Martin Meyerson. Philadelphia: University of Pennsylvania Press, 1978.

"Let It Burn!" The Philadelphia Tragedy by Michael Boyette. Chicago: Contemporary Books, 1989.

Pennsylvania: A Bicentennial History by Thomas C. Cochran. New York: W.W. Norton & Company, 1978.

Philadelphia: A 300-Year History by Russell F. Weigley, ed. New York: W.W. Norton & Company, 1982.

Philadelphia: Holy Experiment by Struthers Burt. New York: Doubleday, Doran & Company, 1945.

Philadelphia: Portrait of an American City by Edwin Wolf, ed. Harrisburg: Stackpole Books, 1975.

Philadelphia Stories: A Photographic History, 1920–1960 by Fredric et al Miller. Philadelphia: Temple University Press, 1988.

Rizzo by Fred Hamilton. New York: Viking Press, 1973.

Still Philadelphia: A Photographic History, 1890–1940 by Fredric et al Miller. Philadelphia: Temple University Press, 1983.

The Cop Who Would Be King: Mayor Frank Rizzo by Joseph R. Daughen and Peter Binzen. Boston: Little, Brown and Company, 1977.

William Penn and the Founding of Pennsylvania, 1680–1684 by Jean R. Soderlund, ed. Philadelphia: University of Pennsylvania Press, 1983.

Other Insight Guides

The 190 books in the *Insight Guides* series cover every continent and include 40 titles devoted to the United States, from Alaska to Florida, from Seattle to New Orleans. Destinations in this particular region include:

Insight Guide: New York City. A comprehensive and beautifully photographed guide to the city of drama and dreams.

Insight Guide: Boston. An expert team of local writers and photographers celebrates one of America's most intriguing cities.

Insight Guide: Washington. Essential reading that conveys the power and the story of America's capital.

Art/Photo Credit

Photography by
British Film Institute 70, 71
Cigna Museum and Art Collection 33
John Gattuso 184/185
Independence National Historical Park
28, 29, 37L, 37R, 38, 112L, 122, 163
Catherine Karnow 24, 66/67, 177,
196, 220
Library Company of Philadelphia 25,
26/27, 34
Library of Congress 40, 41
Robert Llewellyn 2, 9, 10/11, 12/13,
14/15, 16/17, 20, 38, 58/59, 60/61,
72, 73, 86, 89, 91, 92/93, 117, 118/
119, 121, 131, 135, 136/137, 138,
144/145, 146, 147, 149, 150, 151,
156, 158, 160, 162, 169, 170R, 176,
182/183, 197, 198, 199, 201, 202,
206/207, 208, 209, 211, 212L, 215,
216/217, 222, 232
Eugene Mopsick 191
NASA 52
Joseph Nettis 1, 18/19, 32, 36, 43,
44/45, 46, 53, 62, 64, 65, 68, 69,
74/75, 77, 78, 82, 85, 88, 94/95,
96/97, 98/99, 100, 104, 105, 106,
107, 108L, 108R, 110, 111L, 111R,
112R, 114, 120, 123, 127, 130, 134,
141, 143, 148, 152, 153, 154/155,
157, 159, 164/165, 166, 167, 168,
170L, 173, 174/175, 180, 181L,
181R, 186, 189, 190L, 190R, 192/
193, 200, 203, 205, 212R, 213, 214,
218, 221, 223, 224/225, 226, 228,
230, 231L, 231R
**Edgar Allan Poe National Historic Site,
National Park Service** 204
Ann F. Purcell 116
Carl Purcell 47, 80, 109, 113, 115,
124, 125, 161, 179, 188
Marcus Wilson Smith 22/23
Urban Archives, Temple University 48,
49, 50, 51L, 51R, 81, 84
Ken Yanoviak cover, 54/5, 56/57, 76,
79, 128/129, 132, 139, 140, 142,
194, 195, 229

Maps Berndtson & Berndtson

Visual Consultant V. Barl

Index

A

Adams, Charles Francis 63
Adams, John 21, 34–35, 36, 105, 122
  124, 171
African slaves 28, 113
airport 190
Algonquin Indians 26
Allen, Richard 126
Allentown 35
American Bandstand 50
Amish 25, 87–90, 209–214
Ammann, Jacob 87
Anabaptists 87
Andalusia 219
Anglicans 28
Antique Row 142
aristocracy 64, 69–72
Arnold, Benedict 36
arts 76–80
Arts Bank, the 76, 159
art galleries 80, 116, 148, 158, 178,
  198, 221
Art, Museum of 79, 167, 169–170
Asian immigrants 187
Astor, John Jacob 202
Athenaeum 139
Atlantic City 101, 227, 230
auctions 213
Avalon 228
Avalon, Frankie 50
Avenue of the Arts 76, 159

B

Bache, Benjamin Franklin 108
Barnegat Lighthouse 231
Barnes, Albert 81
Barnes Foundation 81
Barry, John 122
Barry, Philip 69
Barrymore, Ethel 140
beaches 227–231
Beissel, Conrad 209
Benjamin Franklin 114, 115, 126
Benjamin Franklin Parkway 167
Bernhardt, Sarah 140
Bird-in-Hand 211
Bishop, John B. 135
Bland, James M. 84
Bonaparte, Joseph 124, 141
bookstores 133, 148
Booth, Edwin 140
Boston 34, 63, 69
Boston Tea Party 34
Bouvier, Michel 122

Brandywine 209, 215
Brigantine 231
Britain 21, 33–36
British settlers 27, 84
Broad Street 76
Brown, Joseph 158
Bryn Mawr 43, 70, 71
Buchanan, James 210
Buck, Pearl S. 64, 221
Bucks County 28, 49, 64, 101, 219–223
Bull's Island State Park 223
Burt, Nathaniel 69, 109, 125, 219

C

Cadwalader 29, 69, 122, 149
Calder, Alexander 167
Calder, Alexander Milne 157, 163, 167
Calder, Alexander Stirling 167
Callowhill, Hannah 163
Camden 39, 65, 126
Cape May 227
Carlyle, Thomas 117
Carpenter, Samuel 28
casinos 230
Cassatt 69
Cathedral of Saints Peter and Paul 52,
  167
Centennial Exhibition 43
Chambers, William 39
character 63–65
Charles II, King 25, 163
Checker, Chubby 50
cheesesteak 133, 161, 187, 188, 191
Chesapeake Bay 25
Chester County 28, 49, 71
Chestnut Hill 64, 69, 195, 198
Chew, Benjamin 69, 197
Chinatown 101, 162
cinema 80
City Hall 157–158, 167
Civil War 41–42
Clark, Dick 50
Clark, Joseph S. 49, 50
Clemm, Virginia 203, 204
Cliveden 197
Cobbett, William 117
Columbia 213
Concord 34
Conley, Thomas 153
Constitution 21, 36–37, 105, 107, 110
Conwell, Tommy 50
Cornwallis 36, 112
Cret, Paul Philippe 167, 169
Curtis Center 112, 139
Curtis Institute of Music 148
Cushman, Charlotte 142

D

Decatur, Stephen 125
Declaration of Independence 21, 34–
  35, 105, 110, 113, 114, 117, 189
Delaware Canal 222
Delaware County 71
Delaware River 25, 26, 28, 35, 42,
  101, 114, 126, 131, 167, 204,
  219, 222

Delaware Valley 27, 219
Devon Horse Show 72
DeWolf, Rose 84–85
Dickens, Charles 63, 140, 168
Dickenson, Jonathan 28
Dickinson, John 33, 37
Dilworth, Richardson 49, 51, 139
Douglass, Frederick 126
downtown 158–161
Doylestown 220
Drexel family 69
Drexel University 43, 177, 182
Dutch settlers 27

E

Eakins, Thomas 39, 65, 79, 142, 158,
  170
East European immigrants 42
Edward VII, King 71
Engman, Robert 158
Ephrata 209
equestrianism 72
Ermilio, Edward 153
Erwinna 223
Eyre, Wilson 147, 149

F

Fabian 50
Fairmount Park 101, 170–172
Fallsington 219
Fields, W. C. 63, 65, 76
Finnish settlers 28
Fishtown 204
Ford, Harrison 90
Forrest, Edwin 76, 140, 201
Forrest Theater 76, 140
Fort Mifflin 189
Foster, Sir Augustus 64
Founding Fathers 21
Frame of Government 21, 25
Frankford 204
Franklin Institute 168
Franklin, Benjamin 21, 27, 29, 33,
  34–35, 37, 39, 65, 101, 105, 106,
  108, 109, 114, 115, 116, 117,
  121, 122, 124, 143, 147, 151,
  158, 168, 177, 215
Franklin, Deborah 33, 108, 114
French Creek State Park 214
Furness, Frank 43, 147, 149, 158,
  159, 179, 181, 227
Furness, William Henry 41

G

gardens 107, 121
George III, King 33, 107
George, Henry 143
German settlers 28, 40, 42, 47, 84,
  153, 187
German Society of Pennsylvania 204
Germantown 28, 42, 111, 195–198, 215
Gettysburg 41, 42
Gettysburg National Military Park 214
Gillespie, Dizzy 50
Gimbels 43

Girard College 201–202
Girard, Stephen 105, 202
Glanton, Richard 81
Glory Dei 134
Graff, Joseph 113
Graham, Bruce 77
Grant, Carry 69
Gratz, Rebecca 141
Greber, Jacques 167, 169
Greeley, Horace 117
Gregory, André 132

H

Hamilton, Alexander 37, 105
Hamilton, William 180
Hancock, John 35, 110
Haviland, John 140, 159
Hawthorne, Nathaniel 117
Helvetius, Madame 117
Henry, Patrick 34
Hepburn, Katharine 69
Hersheypark 212
Hessians 125
Hewitt, George 149
Hispanic district 204
Historical Society of Pennsylvania 142
history 25–52
    Civil War 40
    foundation 25
    Independence 34
Hooters, The 50
Hopewell Furnace National Historic
    Site 214
Houston, Henry Howard 179, 198
Howe, General Sir William 35, 195,
    196, 215
Hudson, Henry 27
"hunt country" 71
Huston, John 105
Hutterites 87

I

immigration 40, 42, 65, 113, 187
Independence, Declaration of 21, 34–
    35, 105, 110, 113, 115, 117, 189
Independence Hall 21, 29, 42, 49, 50,
    101, 110–111
Independence National Historical Park
    105
Independence Seaport Museum 126
Independence, War of 34–36, 107,
    110, 189–190, 215
Indiana, Robert 167
industries 39, 43, 49, 90, 204–205
Ingersoll 69
Intercourse 211
Irish Settlers 28, 40, 42, 187, 199
Irving, Washington 141
Island Beach State Park 231
Italian immigrants 42, 48, 84, 187, 199
Italian Market 187

J

Jackson, Andrew 109, 158
James, Henry 65, 69, 147
Jefferson, Thomas 21, 34–35, 36,
    105, 106, 109, 110, 113, 125,
    151, 163
Jewish history 114
Jewish immigrants 131, 187
John F. Kennedy Plaza 167
John Heinz National Wildlife Refuge 190

K

Kahn, Louis 180
Keats, John 117
Kelly, Grace 70
Kensington 39, 40
Kosciuszko, Thaddeus 125
Kuralt, Charles 64
Kutztown 213

L

LaBelle, Patti 50
Lafayette, Marquis de 112, 122, 158
Lambertville 222
Lancaster 27, 28, 35, 87, 210
Lancaster County 209
Lanza, Mario 50, 134
Latrobe, Benjamin 39
Lawrence, D. H. 109, 117
Le Brun, Napoleon 159, 167
Lea and Febiger 139
Lee, Peggy 50
Lee, Richard Henry 34
Lee, Robert E. 41, 42
Lenape Indians, see Lenni-Lenape
    Indians
Lenni-Lenape Indians 26
Levy, Nathan 141
Liberty Bell 21, 29, 35, 49, 101, 111–
    112, 141
Lincoln, Abraham 41, 42, 151, 159,
    205, 214
Lind, Jenny 140
Lipchitz, Jacques 158, 171
Lipincott, J. B. 139
Little Italy 187
Logan, James 28, 29, 39, 167, 196
Long Beach Island 227, 231
Longport 229
Lumberville 223
Lynch, David 65

M

Mackay, Alexander 64
Macpherson, John 171
Macready, William 140
Madison, Dolley 106, 107
Madison, James 36, 37, 107
Main Line 42, 64, 69, 70
Manayunk 39, 42, 52, 195, 198–199
Margate 229
Market Place East 113, 161
Marshall, John 112, 152
Martino, Al 50

Mastbaum, Jules 169
McArthur, John 157, 201
McHugh, H. Bart 83
McManes, James 47
Meade, General George G. 41
Melville, Herman 117
Mencken, H. L. 63
Mennonite Information Center 197, 212
Mennonites 25, 28, 87, 195, 209
Mercer, Henry Chapman 220–221
Mey, Cornelius Jacobson 227
Michaux, André 63
Michener, James A. 221
Mifflin, George 134
monopoly 231
Montgomery County 49
Moore, Mayor J. Hampton 48
Moravians 25
Morley, Christopher 69, 187
Morris 29, 69
Morris Aboretum 101, 198
Morris, Robert 37, 171
Morrisville 219
MOVE 51–52
Moyamensing 40, 42
Mummers 48, 65, 83–85, 188–189
Museum of Art, Philadelphia 79, 167,
    169–170
museums 79, 107, 112, 113, 114,
    116, 126, 150, 151, 153, 162,
    167–170, 178, 182, 189, 196,
    201, 205, 221, 210, 211
music 50, 78–79
Muti, Riccardo 78, 159
Mutter Museum 152

N

Native Americans 26, 28
Nero, Peter 78
New Amsterdam (New York) 27, 114
New Hope 222
New Jersey 101, 227–231
New York 27, 35, 43, 63, 69, 76, 114
Nicetown 39
Nockamixon, Lake 223
Noguchi, Isamu 114
Norris, Isaac 28
North Philadelphia 201–205
Northern Liberties 202
Notman, John 39, 147 148, 149, 167,
    169

O – P

Ocean City 227, 229
Old City 39, 40, 42, 49, 52, 76, 101,
    105–116
Old Swedes' Church 134
Oldenburg, Claes 158, 170, 179
Orchestra Hall 159
Ormandy, Eugene 78, 159
Paine, Thomas 34
Paradise 211
Pass, John 111
Pastorius, Francis Daniel 28, 195
Paxton Boys 26–27
Peace Valley 223

Peale, Charles Willson 39, 80, 109, 111, 125, 158, 170, 171
Peddlar's Village 221
Pei, I. M. 122, 123, 159
Pemberton, Joseph 107
Penn's Landing 126
Penn, Admiral Sir William 25, 163
Penn, Hannah 219
Penn, John 143
Penn, Thomas 26
Penn, Treaty Park 205
Penn, William 21, 25–29, 63, 65, 87, 101, 105, 114, 115, 121, 122, 134, 139, 143, 157, 163, 167, 172, 195, 203, 205, 219
Pennsbury 26
Pennsbury Manor 219
Pennsylvania Academy of the Fine Arts 79
Pennsylvania Convention Center 161
Pennsylvania Dutch Country 101, 209–214
Pennsylvania Hospital 143
Pennsylvania Railroad 42, 43, 48, 70, 177
Pennsylvania Dutch Tourist Bureau Visitors' Information Center 212
Pennypack Creek 205
Pennypack Park 205
Philadelphia Clef Club of the Performing Arts 76, 78
Philadelphia Orchestra 76
Philadelphia Stock Exchange 160
Philadelphia Story, The 69
Philadelphia Visitors' Center 167
Philly Sound 50
Physick, Philip Syng 29, 39, 114, 124, 143, 152
Pietists 25, 28
Poe, Edgar Allan 39, 65, 203–204
Point Pleasant 223
Polish immigration 42, 199
Polish-American Cultural Center 107
Pottsdown 214
Powel, Samuel 29, 122
Powelton 182
Pratt, Henry 171
Presbyterians 28
pretzels 153, 162
Princeton 35, 77
Prohibition 47–48

Q – R

Quakers 25, 28, 40, 48, 63, 64, 114, 115, 134, 163, 195
Queen Village 52, 133–135
Ralph Stover State Park 223
Ray, Man 65
Reading Terminal Market 161
restaurants 105, 106, 126, 132, 133, 135, 142, 149, 159, 161, 172, 178, 187, 188, 199, 212, 227, 229, 230
Richmond 204
Ringing Rocks County Park 223
Rittenhouse, David 29, 143, 147, 172, 182

Rittenhouse Square 42, 101, 121, 147–152
Rittenhouse Town 172
RiverBlues festival 79, 126
Rizzo, Frank 51–52, 159
Rockwell, Norman 112
Rodin 79, 169
Rodin Museum 79, 169
Roosevelt, Franklin D. 48, 151
Roosevelt Park 189
Rosenbach, A. S. W. 150
Rosenbach, Philip 150
Ross, Betsy 35, 115, 116
row houses 28, 42, 106, 178, 181, 187, 199, 204
Rush, Benjamin 39, 114, 143
Russell, Bertrand 64

S

Schuylkill River 25, 42, 43, 101, 131, 167, 170, 177, 180, 199
Schuylkill River Park 151
Scott, Sir Walter 141
Sea Isle City 228
Seaside Heights 231
Sesame Place 219
Shippen 122
Shoe Museum 162
Smith, Robert 107
Smith, Robert 125
Society Hill 49, 101, 121–126
Somers Point 229
South Philadelphia 47, 49, 50, 51, 52, 83, 101, 187–190
South Street 101, 131–135
Southwark 39, 40, 42, 133
Sparks Shot Tower 135
Spring Lake 231
Springett, Gulielma Maria 163
Stallone, Sylvester 65, 169, 187
Stetson, John B. 39
Steuben, Baron Friedrich 215
Stokowski, Leopold 78, 159
Stone Harbor 228
Stow, John 111
Strasburg 211
Strawbridge & Clothier 43
Strickland, William 39, 105, 109, 111, 123, 125, 140
Stuart, Gilbert 39
Sully, Thomas 39
Swarthmore 43
Swedish settlers 27, 28, 134, 189
Syng, Philip 29, 39, 115, 124, 143, 152
  see also Physick, Philip Syng

T

Tacony 204
Tammany 26
Tchaikovsky 159
Thackeray, William Makepeace 140
Thaw, Harry K. 150
theater 76–77
Tiffany, Louis Comfort 112
Tinicum 190

Tinicum County Park 223
Todd, John 106
Tohickon Valley County Park 223
Townsend, Charles 33
Trollope, Anthony 63
Trollope, Frances 63
Twain, Mark 63, 69, 109

U – V

Uhlerstown 223
University of Pennsylvania 29, 43, 81, 101, 177–182
Valley Forge 190, 195, 215
Vare brothers 47
Ventnor 230
Venturi, Robert 106, 108
vineyards 223

W – Z

Walnut Street Theater 76, 140
Walter, Thomas U. 121, 141, 157, 201, 219
Wanamaker, John 43, 160
Washington Crossing State Park 222
Washington Square West 101, 139–143
Washington, George 34, 35, 36, 37, 105, 106, 109, 110, 112, 115, 116, 117, 122, 125, 151, 158, 190, 195, 196, 197, 215, 222, 223
Welsh settlers 28
West Philadelphia 42, 52, 77
West Point 36
White, Bishop William 106
White, Stanford 150, 159
Whitman, Walt 39, 65, 157
Wiccaco 134
Wildwood 227, 228
Wilma Theater 76, 159
wineries 214, 223
Wissahickon Creek 167, 172, 195
Wistar, Caspar 29, 39, 122, 143
Wister, John 196
Wister, Owen 63
Woodward, George 198
Workman, John 135
Wyeth, Andrew 158
Wyeth, N. C. 142
York 35
Yorktown 36, 112
zoo 172

A
B
C
D
E
F
G
,
I
J
a
b
c
e
f
g
h
i
j
k
l

The Insight Approach

The book you are holding is part of the world's largest range of guidebooks. Its purpose is to help you have the most valuable travel experience possible, and we try to achieve this by providing not only information about countries, regions and cities but also genuine insight into their history, culture, institutions and people.

Since the first Insight Guide – to Bali – was published in 1970, the series has been dedicated to the proposition that, with insight into a country's people and culture, visitors can both enhance their own experience and be accepted more easily by their hosts. Now, in a world where ethnic hostilities and nationalist conflicts are all too common, such attempts to increase understanding between peoples are more important than ever.

Insight Guides:
Essentials for understanding

Because a nation's past holds the key to its present, each Insight Guide kicks off with lively history chapters. These are followed by magazine-style essays on culture and daily life. This essential background information gives readers the necessary context for using the main Places section, with its comprehensive run-down on things worth seeing and doing. Finally, a listings section contains all the information you'll need on travel, hotels, restaurants and opening times.

As far as possible, we rely on local writers and specialists to ensure that the information is authoritative. The pictures, for which Insight Guides have become so celebrated, are just as important. Our photojournalistic approach aims not only to illustrate a destination but also to communicate visually and directly to readers life as it is lived by the locals.

Compact Guides
The "great little guides"

As invaluable as such background information is, it isn't always fun to carry an Insight Guide through a crowded souk or up a church tower. Could we, readers asked, distil the key reference material into a slim volume for on-the-spot use?

Our response was to design Compact Guides as an entirely new series, with original text carefully cross-referenced to detailed maps and more than 200 photographs. In essence, they're miniature encyclopedias, concise and comprehensive, displaying reliable and up-to-date information in an accessible way.

Pocket Guides:
A local host in book form

However wide-ranging the information in a book, human beings still value the personal touch. Our editors are often asked the same questions. Where do *you* go to eat? What do *you* think is the best beach? What would you recommend if I have only three days? We invited our local correspondents to act as "substitute hosts" by revealing their preferred walks and trips, listing the restaurants they go to and structuring a visit into a series of timed itineraries.

The result is our Pocket Guides, complete with full-size fold-out maps. These 100-plus titles help readers plan a trip precisely, particularly if their time is short.

Exploring with Insight:
A valuable travel experience

In conjunction with co-publishers all over the world, we print in up to 10 languages, from German to Chinese, from Danish to Russian. But our aim remains simple: to enhance your travel experience by combining our expertise in guidebook publishing with the on-the-spot knowledge of our correspondents.